Governance, Security and Development

Series Editor
Trine Flockhart
School of Politics and International Relations
University of Kent
Kent, UK

The series addresses issues related to an international system that is increasingly dominated by changing and inter-linked processes of governance involving formal and informal institutions and multiple processes of change and continuity within security and development. In the area of security the processes involve traditional key actors in international society and new much less traditional actors engaging with new forms of security and including individuals, groups, and states. In the area of development, focus is increasingly on improvements in political and economic conditions for individuals and groups but from an understanding that development is dependent on good governance and security. Books published in the Series may engage with any one of the three topics on its own merits - or they may address the interplay and dynamics that occur when Governance, Security and Development interact (or collide) in an increasingly interconnected and constantly changing international system.

More information about this series at
http://www.springer.com/series/15022

Patrick W. Quirk

Great Powers, Weak States, and Insurgency

Explaining Internal Threat Alliances

Patrick W. Quirk
Georgetown University
Washington, District of Columbia, USA

Governance, Security and Development
ISBN 978-3-319-83732-1   ISBN 978-3-319-47419-9 (eBook)
DOI 10.1007/978-3-319-47419-9

© The Editor(s) (if applicable) and The Author(s) 2017
Softcover reprint of the hardcover 1st edition 2017
This book was advertised with a copyright holder in the name of the publisher in error, whereas the author holds the copyright.
This work is subject to copyright. All rights are solely and exclusively licensed by the Publisher, whether the whole or part of the material is concerned, specifically the rights of translation, reprinting, reuse of illustrations, recitation, broadcasting, reproduction on microfilms or in any other physical way, and transmission or information storage and retrieval, electronic adaptation, computer software, or by similar or dissimilar methodology now known or hereafter developed.
The use of general descriptive names, registered names, trademarks, service marks, etc. in this publication does not imply, even in the absence of a specific statement, that such names are exempt from the relevant protective laws and regulations and therefore free for general use.
The publisher, the authors and the editors are safe to assume that the advice and information in this book are believed to be true and accurate at the date of publication. Neither the publisher nor the authors or the editors give a warranty, express or implied, with respect to the material contained herein or for any errors or omissions that may have been made.

Cover illustration: © J Marshall - Tribaleye Images / Alamy Stock Photo

Printed on acid-free paper

This Palgrave Macmillan imprint is published by Springer Nature
The registered company is Springer International Publishing AG
The registered company address is: Gewerbestrasse 11, 6330 Cham, Switzerland

For Sidney and Lauren

Preface

This book would not have been possible without the contributions, guidance, and support from loved ones, friends, and colleagues. Dr. Steven David and Dr. Daniel Deudney provided irreplaceable feedback and guidance throughout the entire writing process and my time as a doctoral student at Johns Hopkins. Various people provided useful feedback on chapters and the entire manuscript. Dr. Miguel Carter, Dr. Rubrick Biegon, Dr. Jeff Meiser, and Chris Schunk provided feedback on chapter drafts as well as support throughout the writing process. In its early stages, the project benefited from conversations with Mike McCarthy and Alex Alden. Anonymous reviewers provided thoughtful suggestions that improved the overall quality of the book. Jessica Mortellaro provided excellent research assistance. Loved ones are essential to the completion of any project like this one. In particular, I thank my wife, Lauren, who supported me throughout the process. She made sure that I kept a good sense of humor and perspective. I would also like to thank my mother and father, whose hard work and support enabled me to get to this point. Mia provided companionship during early mornings and late nights of writing. Any flaws presented here are my own. The ideas presented here do not represent views of the US government or Georgetown University.

Patrick W. Quirk
Georgetown University
Washington, DC, USA

Contents

1 Internal Threat Alliances: A New Conceptual Framework 1

2 US–Colombia Internal Threat Alliance (1980–2010) 37

3 US–Afghanistan Internal Threat Alliance (2001–2012) 101

4 Russia–Syria Internal Threat Alliance (2010–2016) 179

5 Conclusions 215

Appendix 1: US–Colombia Internal Threat Alliance (1980–2010) 225

Appendix 2: US–Afghanistan Internal Threat Alliance (2001–2012) 233

Appendix 3: Russia–Syria Internal Threat Alliance (2009–2016) 241

Bibliography 243

Index 273

List of Tables

Table 1.1	Summary of Internal Threat Alliance Dynamics	20
Table 2.1	US–Colombia Alliance Formation: From External to Internal Threat Alliance	51
Table 3.1	US–Afghanistan Internal Threat Alliance Formation	116
Table 4.1	Russia–Syria Internal Threat Alliance Formation	185

CHAPTER 1

Internal Threat Alliances: A New Conceptual Framework

International relations (IR) theory on alliances traditionally focuses on how and why states balance (resist) or bandwagon with (appease) other states.[1] But most threats that states confront today are not from other states. Rather, they come from within weak states themselves in the form of civil war, rebellions, and insurgencies. This book offers an original and theoretically rich examination into the dynamics of alliances that great powers and the leaders of weak states form to defeat such threats (rebellion and insurgency) within the smaller state's borders.[2] Examples of these "internal threat alliances" include Russia's collaboration with Syria's Bashar al-Assad to defeat anti-government rebels and US cooperation with Afghanistan's ruling political elite to combat the Taliban. In each case, the weaker state's leadership wanted to remain in power, while the great power sought to safeguard its interests linked to the regime's stability. As a result, the two states formed an alliance and cooperated to defeat a threat internal to the weaker state's borders yet with implications for the national security of (and thus common to) both states.

Extant IR theory is ill-equipped to explain this form of statecraft because it focuses heavily on the dynamics of traditional military alliances formed to combat or deter aggression from *other states*. This blind spot in the IR literature persists despite the dramatic decline over the last 25 years in *inter*-state warfare and surge of *intra*-state violence such as rebellion, insurgency, and civil war—and the threat such violence poses to weak states and great powers alike. Policy- or operationally oriented literature on counterinsurgency (COIN), intervention, or civil war is also not perfectly suited to explain the dynamics of this type of alliance. What these works gain in richly examining micro-level phenomena (e.g., the mechanics of "clear, hold, and build" COIN doctrine), they lose in not being able to problematize the higher-level, inter-state politics involved in quelling intra-state threats.

To fill this policy-relevant gap in the literature, the book contributes new insights to IR theory on alliances by offering a distinct theoretical framework that explains why internal threat alliances form, why some are more cohesive than others, and why some are effective while others are not. To evidence this framework, the book examines three contemporary cases of internal threat alliances: US cooperation with the Colombian government to defeat leftist rebels and narco-traffickers (1980–2010), US collaboration with Afghanistan's government to quell threats from the Taliban and Al-Qaeda (2001–2012), and cooperation between Russia and Syria's President Bashar al-Assad to defeat anti-government rebels (2010–2016).

Theoretical and Policy Relevance

The changing nature of threats across the globe makes understanding internal threat alliances exceedingly relevant because states are increasingly confronted by new non-state menaces to their security. Through the end of the Cold War, conflict with other nations represented the core threat to sovereign polities. During this period, states formed military alliances to defeat or deter attacks from adversaries outside of their borders.[3] In response to this trend, international relations scholars developed theories to understand why states formed such alliances and why some alliances achieved their objectives and others did not.

In particular after the Berlin Wall's collapse, however, political violence and intra-state conflict (especially within weak states) have eclipsed their inter-state counterpart as the major form of mass organized violence in the international system.[4] In tandem with the "long peace" and decline in battlefield deaths during conflict between states, fatalities resulting from violence within states have been on the rise and taken more than 25 million lives.[5] From 1995 to 2010, nearly 97 percent of conflicts were intra-state and not inter-state in nature. While 61 intra-state wars occurred from 1990 to 2007, only eight incidents of inter-state conflict transpired in the same period.[6] At the time of this writing, 21 civil wars are ongoing.[7]

Insurgencies represent perhaps the most potent threat within weak states—and from 1990 to 2012, they erupted in 49 countries across the globe.[8]

Just as inter-state war endangers the interests of states across the globe, rebellion and insurgency do as well. Such insurrections can topple the leadership of weak states and imperil the interests of great powers such as France, Russia, and the USA by challenging the survival of allies, creating instability that terrorist organizations exploit to orchestrate attacks, jeopardizing access to natural resource reserves, and causing mass migration of refugees, among others. To counter these threats, and much like their responses to external enemies, great powers and the rulers of weak states have pooled resources, aligned strategies, and cooperated (formed internal threat alliances) to secure their respective interests. However, the IR literature has yet to catch up and offer a theory to explain this emerging form of statecraft.

Understanding internal threat alliances is made more important by the likelihood that insurgency, rebellion, and civil war will continue well into the future because the principal causes of these forms of violence show no signs of abating.[9] As a result, states will require ways to secure their interests in the face of these dangers and internal threat alliances will endure as a central aspect of international relations. As we continue into an age where a core threat to states will likely be high levels of political violence (and its consequences) within weak states—rather than only state-on-state violence—this book will provide policy-makers and scholars a framework to understand the dynamics of state responses to these threats. From the policy perspective in particular, this book will be useful to practitioners considering to form a new—or calibrate an existing—alliance, searching for new insights into why past (or existing) such alliances have or have not achieved their objectives, or reviewing the range of options for mitigating threats from insurgency and rebellion.

The Argument

To address the aforementioned gap in the IR literature, I build on alliance theory to provide a new theoretical framework that explains why internal threat alliances form, why some are more cohesive than others, and why some are effective while others are not. Rooted in neoclassical realist IR theory, the framework contains the following three elements and associated arguments.

First, internal threat alliances will form in response to a threat that *is domestic in origin* and imperils the survival of a weak state's

leadership regime. The weaker state's leadership will seek cooperation because it needs military or economic resources to thwart challenges to its existence, while the great power will become involved in order to safeguard interests linked to the regime's stability or survival. This is different than traditional alliances, where the threat is *external in origin* (another state or group of states) and the involved states align in order to secure their national interest and territorial survival. The implication for policy is that practitioners should expect leaders of weak states (e.g., Syria's Assad) to actively seek assistance from external patrons (e.g., Russia) when internal actors pose an existential threat to their existence. Similarly, they should expect great powers to provide assistance (align) if the internal threat also imminently threatens its own interests (e.g., Russian access to its naval facility in Tartus, Syria).

Second, balancing (resisting the target threat) and "bandwagoning" (appeasing the target threat) will occur *simultaneously* during internal threat alliances. This is in contrast to traditional military alliances, where countries will *either* balance *or* bandwagon when faced with an external enemy. Due to the weaker state's internal fragmentation and lower capacity, its central leadership is unable to control all of its component actors (e.g., subnational governors, the military, or police forces), each of whom will routinely pursue their own interests (e.g., financial gain, cementing patron-client ties) at the expense of alliance goals. As a result, the central leadership may work with the great power to implement alliance strategy and defeat (*balance*) the common threat, while elements of its police or military are *colluding (bandwagoning) with* actors fomenting violence. In the case of cooperation between the USA and Colombia, for example, some elements of the Colombian army fought against the anti-government Revolutionary Armed Forces of Colombia (FARC) rebels, while others actively colluded with them; similarly, various Colombian governors resisted rebel incursions, while others actively cooperated with the worst of the terrorist organization's leaders. The implication for policy is that great powers engaging in this type of alliance will need to manage relationships between cooperative central leaders on the one hand and bureaucratic actors colluding with the enemy on the other. Simply because the USA and Afghan President Hamid Karzai agreed to a specific strategy, for example, did not mean Afghan actors at various subnational areas would play along—instead, they often pursued their own interests at the expense of alliance objectives. Before entering into such an alliance, therefore, the great power should fully grasp the extent of these parallel power structures and calibrate strategies accordingly.

Third and finally, the effectiveness of internal threat alliances will depend on whether allies have military resources sufficient to weaken their common enemy *and* are able to control collusion by regime actors (subnational bandwagoning) with the rebels or insurgents. The principal determinant of internal threat alliance effectiveness will be allies' ability to bring together capabilities sufficient to weaken or defeat the threat. And only when the great power and regime are able to agree on goals, strategy, and tactics and to coordinate associated activities will they be able to collectively amass resources sufficient to weaken or defeat their common menace. However, alliances will not be effective if the weaker state's leadership is not willing and able to stop their bureaucratic actors from colluding with the enemy. This central leadership circle may have political priorities or patron-client relationships that alter its willingness to curb subnational bandwagoning. At precise junctures and in response to threats, then, the regime may decide that working to defeat specific actors or implement specific tactics (and collaborating with the great power to do so) is detrimental to regime political survival, power, and influence. In other instances, collusion may be so widespread that even a highly cooperative national level leader may simply be unable to stop it. Either scenario can decrease alliance effectiveness. This is a distinct feature of internal alliances and not found in their traditional military counterpart examined in the IR literature where states engage in capital-to-capital communication and either do or do not work together to balance a common enemy.

To demonstrate these elements of the framework and associated arguments, the chapter unfolds in three core sections. The first section describes three elements of traditional military alliances formed to combat external threats. The second section presents my new conceptual framework and associated arguments. The third section provides conclusions, an outline for the balance of the book, and briefly explains the research methodology.

TRADITIONAL MILITARY ALLIANCES

Cooperation to Balance External Threats

Military alliances have been a fundamental aspect of international relations since the time of Thucydides. Spurred by "common perceptions of threat and overlapping strategic interests," states have formed alliances in order to deter attacks from common external enemies or offensively seek revisions to the status quo.[10] Reflecting the prevalence of alliances as a form of statecraft, the IR literature on military alliances is vast. It has enriched our understanding of why and under what conditions states form alliances in order to achieve their mutual security goals. This section provides a stylized summary of the following three main elements of alliances formed to cope with external threats—what I refer to as "external threat alliances": (1) why states form external threat alliances, (2) why and when allies "bandwagon," and (3) why some alliances are more effective than others. The purpose of this section is twofold: first, to demonstrate the gap in IR literature this book fills and, second, to be able to juxtapose these elements to those of internal threat alliances later in the chapter.

Alliance Formation: *External Threat to the National Interest*

States form military alliances in response to a threat external to their borders as represented by a state or groups of states. For example, beginning in 1891 France and Russia aligned to balance the Triple Alliance of Germany, Austria-Hungary, and Great Britain.[11] Similarly, in the early 1940s, Britain, France, and Poland (joined later by the USA) aligned to balance a resurgent Germany and its Axis power allies (Italy and Japan).[12]

Given the nature of this threat, the core factor motivating states to form traditional military alliances is their need to preserve security and the national interest—defined in terms of power and territorial survival—and amass those capabilities necessary to do so. As an automatic response (in neorealist IR accounts) or due to a "perceived" increase in threat (in neoclassical realist IR treatments), states A and B align because they recognize that threat T (external to their borders) imperils their security and that they alone lack resources (military, economic, territorial control, or other) sufficient to defeat or deter that threat.[13]

Most IR theory focuses on alliances formed by Western states (mainly great powers) of comparable degrees of development and internal cohesiveness. While external threat alliances involve countries that have some internal fragmentation, they are essentially between two cohesive actors. As a result, IR theory largely conceptualizes alliance member states as "like units" which serve the same list of functions yet differ according to their capabilities. Internally, their political order is structured hierarchically, and as a result they act in a "rational" manner: preferences are ordered when making decisions and preserving national security and associated territorial survival trump other concerns.[14] Due to their internally cohesive manner, the actors considered relevant to alliance dynamics are national level security policy decision-makers. These actors communicate between capitals to agree to form the alliance and then devise strategies to deter or defeat their common enemy. The main point here is that IR theory assumes that other actors (e.g., the military) within each ally are under the control of central decision-makers and therefore rationally execute alliance strategy.[15]

Bandwagoning: *Either Balance* or *Bandwagon*

In response to external enemies, states may form alliances to defeat or deter (balance) the prevailing threat, but they can also "align *with* the source of danger."[16] Defined as "bandwagoning," this can take two forms that are distinguished by the bandwagoning state's motivation or purpose.[17] "Offensive" bandwagoning occurs when a state aligns with the dominant state in order to share in that state's "spoils of victory." "Defensive" bandwagoning is a "form of appeasement"—this occurs when a state aligns with an aggressor in order to avoid attack and therefore survive (Walt 1987).[18] Some argue that states will bandwagon even in the *absence* of a threat—states enter a conflict and align with the side they perceive to be stronger because they want to secure material benefit in the event that side wins. That is, states "bandwagon for profit" (Schweller 1994).[19] Regardless of motivation, bandwagoning and balancing is a binary phenomenon during traditional military alliances. As Walt's seminal work on this topic argues: "when confronted by a significant external threat, states may *either* balance *or* bandwagon."[20] Bandwagoning implies departing an alliance, so single states cannot do both simultaneously.

Alliance Effectiveness: *Sufficient Resources to Thwart a Common Enemy*

After forming an external threat alliance, states work together "to agree on goals, strategy, and tactics, and to coordinate activity directed toward those ends."[21] This is referred to as alliance "cohesion." Whether the alliance achieves its goal is defined as alliance effectiveness. The IR literature generally agrees that level of threat from an external state will determine an alliance's cohesion. As the level of threat from a shared enemy increases, so too will the need for the allies to agree on goals and strategy and amass resources in order to safeguard their respective states. Should the threat decrease or adversely affect one ally more than another, collaboration between allies will decline. Effectiveness, in turn, is largely determined by whether the alliance has sufficient resources to deter or defeat their enemy. In examining cohesion and effectiveness of traditional military alliances, the IR literature assumes that alliance-relevant actors within each state (e.g., the military) will follow instructions from central decision-makers and apply resources according to agreed alliance strategy.

Gap in the Literature

Over the last 20 years, there has been a considerable amount of scholarship on alliance politics which has examined the aforementioned three elements. However, all of these works analyze why and when alliances form in response to threats from other states. Accordingly, their definition of threat remains focused on *external* enemies and largely overlooks why threats emanating from within a given state (such as insurgency or rebellion and the consequences such violence can have for great powers and their allies alike) may also motivate states to align. By focusing on external threats as the predominant factor affecting alliance formation, the seminal works on alliance theory by Walt (1987, 1988), Schweller (1994, 2004, 2006), Snyder (1997), and Weitsman (2004) overlook why *internal* threats might also inform alignment decisions. Focused on the alignment behavior of states in the "Third World," David (1991) is one of the few scholars to recognize that the leadership of weaker states seek alliances with more powerful states to balance external *and* internal threats (coups) to their survival. At the same time, David does not directly recognize that the threat internal to the weaker state could *also* threaten and therefore motivate alignment decisions of a larger power. That is, he does not offer a theory that explains alliance formation between great powers and the leadership of weaker states where the internal threat is *common to* and therefore motivates *both* states to form an alliance. Further, he nor any other scholar examines other aspects of internal threat alliances—namely, how bandwagoning manifests and why some are more effective than others. This book represents the next step in the evolution of the IR theory alliance literature. The theory presented in the next section builds on insights of the aforementioned scholars to produce a distinct theoretical framework on internal threat alliances.

The Argument

Internal Threat Alliances: A New Conceptual Framework

This section presents the book's theoretical framework and associated arguments. It demonstrates how external and internal threat alliances are distinct in each area, describes how theory needs to be updated to account for these differences, and outlines how the presented framework does so. Before proceeding to these three elements, however, I first lay out the theoretical framework's core tenets and assumptions.

Any attempt to explain state behavior must be grounded in theoretical assumptions regarding how states perceive threats, rank-order priorities, and take associated actions. Much of the extant alliance literature is rooted in realist or neorealist IR theory. To account for the distinct features of internal threat alliances, especially the nature of the threat and characteristics of the weaker state, my theoretical framework is grounded in neoclassical realism and its following core assumptions. After outlining each, I explain how it is relevant to and applied in the framework presented later in this section.

First, neoclassical realism holds *that threats influencing state behavior can be international or domestic in nature.* As Lobell notes, "threats can emanate from other great powers and extra-regional actors, regional powers in the locale, or domestic opponents."[22] Challenges from other states and imbalances in the distribution of power within the international system remain the paramount threat to states, but other challenges (e.g., terrorism or non-state actors) can also influence state decision-making and actions. This framing enables the theoretical framework to explore why rebellion or insurgency—a threat *internal* to one of the alliance members and that is not a state—could lead the rulers of a weak state and a great power to form an internal threat alliance. Insurgency and rebellion threaten the survival of leaders ruling the fragile state and in so doing imperil the interests of a great power. This assumption is critical for understanding the formation of internal threat alliances.

Second, neoclassical realism holds that the *domestic structure of great powers serves as an intervening variable that conditions their foreign policy in general and alignment decisions in particular.* These intervening variables include domestic politics, decision-makers' perception of threats, and the dominant intellectual currents that inform those perceptions. Security-related decisions are made by a central group of national security leaders (the "Foreign Policy Executive") and informed by the way in which these actors perceive threats.[23] In combination with the first assumption, this tenet enables the framework to explain why the great power would decide to aid a weaker state's leadership in order to defeat a rebellion or insurgency—that is, in order to safeguard the interests perceived to be associated with that regime's survival (e.g., regional stability, preserving access to natural resources, preventing terrorists from being able to take advantage of a failed state). Considering domestic politics and available state power enables the framework to account for the amount of resources the great power decides to allocate. This particular assumption, therefore, is crucial to understanding the formation of internal threat alliances as well as their effectiveness.

Third and finally, neoclassical realism holds that *states (in particular those outside of the West) are frequently* not *cohesive but, rather, fragmented and in some cases prone to instability* because they lack a monopoly on the legitimate use of force within their borders.[24] As such, the internal composition of these fragmented states—and the factors motivating actors therein—will influence their foreign policy decision-making. Great powers or Western states have strong institutions that help decision-makers "rationally" rank-order priorities and render decisions to advance the "national interest." By contrast, weaker states like those across the African continent—but also the "periphery" more broadly—often lack such robust institutions.[25] As a result, the "state" is often a group of elites (the central regime) who control foreign policy and render decisions based on what is best for *their own interests* and survival, rather than the country as a whole. That is, the leaders "protect themselves at the expense of promoting the long-term security of the state and the general welfare of its inhabitants."[26] Due to the weaker ally's internal fragmentation, however, this central leadership does not necessarily control all of its alliance-relevant actors (e.g., military, police, subnational governors), each of whom will routinely pursue their own interests (e.g., financial gain, cementing patron-client ties) at the expense of alliance goals. The factors that inform the central regime's decisions and those of other actors in the country are often rooted in patron-client relations. Rather than prioritizing loyalty to the state or "national interest," the elite and broader society act out of loyalty to a given patron (or client) or other (e.g., tribal, ethnic, religous) allegiance.[27] This assumption is important for explaining why weak states might form an internal threat alliance, the behavior of the weak state's leadership after the alliance has formed, and the effects of the weak state's characteristics onto alliance dynamics (especially bandwagoning and effectiveness). Grounded in these three theoretical tenets, the following sections present the three-part framework for understanding internal threat alliances.

Alliance Formation

In today's world, we are threatened less by evil empires and more by failing states. US President Barack Obama, 2016

This part of the framework theorizes regarding why great powers and the leadership of weak states form internal threat alliances. In so doing, it explains the nature of the threat involved in these alliances and the factors motivating great powers and leaders of weak states to form them. I predict that the weaker state's leadership will seek cooperation because it needs military or economic resources to thwart challenges to its existence, while the great power will become involved in order to safeguard interests linked to the regime's stability or survival. "Internal threat" is defined as *high levels of political violence, including but not limited to insurgency and rebellion, which threaten the survival (physical and/or political) of a weak state's leadership and by extension imperils a great power's interests.*[28] The threat must be *common* to the weak state's leadership and the great power.

This part of the theoretical framework draws from and builds on existing IR theory that explores alignment decisions of leaders in the Third World and a separate literature that examines why consequences of political violence (e.g., instability) imperil great power interests (and therefore could spur them to form an alliances to safeguard these interests). Case examples are provided throughout the section to evidence the theory and illustrate its key points.

Why the Weak State's Leaders Align

Insights from existing IR theory can be employed to explain why threats associated with political violence (insurgency and rebellion) would motivate a weak state's leadership to form an internal threat alliance. According to David (1991a, b), elites and leaders in the "Third World" face domestic threats that could end their reign including coup attempts or secessionist movements, among others. Remaining in power is the primary factor that informs decisions made by this elite circle controlling the state. Accordingly, such leaders will seek external alignments (even with states they consider a secondary threat) in order to balance against the "more immediate and dangerous" domestic threat to their survival.[29] This same insight can be applied to explain why the leadership of a weaker state would seek to form an internal threat alliance with a great power. When confronted with rebellions or insurgencies, these leaders will seek assistance from stronger states in order to defeat the threat and survive because they lack resources (military and other) to defeat the belligerents on their own.

Various examples demonstrate that these factors motivate the leadership of weak states to form internal threat alliances. Beginning in 2010, for example, the Syrian regime of Bashar al-Assad faced a mounting insurgency attempting to overthrow his government. In order to ensure his regime's survival, the embattled Syrian president sought support from Russia, which provided munitions, weapons, and helicopters to thwart anti-government rebels.[30] In Colombia, President Andrés Pastrana faced rising threats from rebel groups and drug-trafficking organizations but lacked the military hardware required to defeat these groups. To ensure his regime's survival, Pastrana sought US assistance to defeat the "narco-terrorist" threat.[31] And in Afghanistan, President Hamid Karzai's leadership circle faced rising danger from the resurgent Taliban and other insurgent actors. Without sufficient resources of his own to defeat the anti-government rebels, Karzai sought cooperation with the USA to balance these menaces.[32] Leaders in each country needed resources and support in order to defeat or weaken actors contesting their rule. Aligning with the great power, therefore, made sense.

Why the Great Power Aligns

To explain why great powers would decide to form an internal threat alliance, I leverage strains within the security studies literature which demonstrate that high levels of political violence (including insurgency and rebellion) in weaker states can have manifold consequences for the interests of great powers.[33] In turn, this is used to explain why great powers would take action to salvage their interests in the face of such political violence—including by propping up the leaders of weak states to serve as a bulwark against such instability.

Instability resulting from insurgency, rebellion, or civil war in weak states has been proven to affect the interests of great powers in various ways. These include, among others, lost economic opportunities, decreased access to crucial natural resources, and cross-border flows of refugees. Insurgency and rebellion further debilitate already weak states, providing terrorist organizations with "safe havens" from which they may orchestrate attacks on the territory or foreign assets of great powers.[34] Insurgency and rebellion raise the cost of and inhibit access to natural resources that great powers rely on to keep their economies running.[35] Trade and investments abroad are the lifeblood of economic well-being at home. High levels of political violence can create market uncertainty and severe drops in stock prices and escalate a great power's budget deficit, among other implications.[36] Insurgency and rebellion also threaten the citizens of great powers—either directly, by endangering expatriate communities, or indirectly, by pushing massive flows of refugees across borders and affecting communities on the other side.[37] For all of these reasons, great powers may perceive the consequences of high levels of political violence as a threat to their interests and take necessary action (including aligning with an embattled regime) to defeat the internal threat and salvage their interests.[38]

Various examples demonstrate that these factors motivate great powers to get involved in internal threat alliances. After the Cold War ended, for example, France formed such alliances with Mobutu Sese Seko (Zaire) and Omar Bongo (Gabon) in order to preserve these regimes and French interests linked to them. In Zaire, France needed to maintain a strategic ally in the region and protect the sizable contingent of French expatriates there.[39] And in Gabon, France needed to maintain stability to preserve access to the state's oil deposits and other natural resources, while Bongo required military capabilities to balance internal opposition. To guarantee stability within Gabon and maintain access to such resources, France provided Bongo with approximately $1 million in annual military aid and placed French army officers in the regime's security forces.[40] As Gabon's President Bongo himself described the core motivation for the alliance: "Gabon without France is like a car with no driver. France without Gabon is like a car with no fuel."[41] Returning to the more recent example of Syria, Russia provided military capabilities to the embattled Assad regime to safeguard its single military base outside the former Soviet Union, preserve access to oil and gas fields, and protect other economic interests including investments by Russian companies in natural gas extraction (a sector valued at $20 billion).[42] Finally, in Afghanistan, the USA provided assistance to the ruling elite in order to prevent terrorists from again using that country as a staging ground to attack US interests. As President Barack Obama noted in 2009, "We will prevent the Taliban from turning Afghanistan back into a safe haven from which international terrorists can strike at us or our allies. This would pose a direct threat to the American homeland, and that is a threat that we cannot tolerate."[43]

To summarize, this portion of the theory argues that **internal threat alliances will form in response to a threat that *is domestic in origin* and imperils the survival of a weak state's leadership regime. The weaker state's leadership will seek cooperation because it needs military or economic resources to thwart challenges to its existence, while the great power will become involved in order to safeguard interests linked to the regime's stability or survival.** Insurgency and rebellion in weak states directly imperil the physical and political survival of that state's leadership. Such violence also threatens the interests of specific great powers by endangering the survival of an ally or creating instability that generates critical consequences. Regarding why states form internal threat alliances, then, it can be expected that if a great power and weak state's leadership perceive a moderate level of threat (emanating from within the weaker ally's borders) and are dependent[44] on each other to balance it, then they will form an alliance to do so.[45] The next two parts to the framework aim to explain the allies' behavior after they form the internal threat alliance.

Why and When Actors Bandwagon

The [weak] state is not the sum of its parts...but instead the interplay of its various actors who sometimes hamper, and other times help, stability in the country.[46] *– Former Colombian Minister*

This part of the framework theorizes regarding how bandwagoning will occur during internal threat alliances. "Subnational bandwagoning" is defined as an actor aligning with the source of threat rather than fighting (balancing) against it. This includes any act of collusion with insurgents or rebels rather than working to defeat (balance) these actors. Due to the characteristics of the weaker state and nature of the threat, I argue that bandwagoning during internal threat alliance will manifest in two distinct ways.

First, balancing will occur *simultaneously with* bandwagoning. In combatting insurgencies or rebellions, the allies largely rely on the weak state's security forces (e.g., police, military, and other agencies) to defeat these internal menaces. Due to the weaker state's internal fragmentation and lower capacity, however, the central leadership is sometimes unable to control all of these alliance-relevant actors. As a result, such agencies or security forces involved in executing alliance strategy may decide to collude (bandwagon) with insurgents or rebels even as the central leadership is actively cooperating with the great power to defeat the belligerents. For example, army units in a remote state may feel increasingly threatened by the insurgency and therefore decide to collude (bandwagon) with the insurgents in order to survive (e.g., by defecting to the rebels or helping them in other ways). Similarly, police units or governors may decide to bandwagon because they feel the rebellion is likely to win and therefore want to share in that group's spoils of victory. If you can't beat them, join them. For internal threat alliances, then, we will expect to see key actors within the weak state (parts of its police, military, or other subnational officials) *bandwagoning (colluding) with* actors fomenting violence even as the central leadership works feverishly with its great power ally to combat (*balance*) the insurgents or rebels.

Two case examples help illustrate this aspect of bandwagoning during internal threat alliances. In the case of cooperation between the USA and Colombia, some elements of the Colombian Army fought against the anti-government FARC rebels, while others actively colluded with them; similarly, various Colombian governors resisted rebel incursions, while others actively cooperated with the worst of the terrorist organization's leaders. The same occurred during the alliance between the USA and Afghanistan. In 2005, as there appeared to be "momentum behind the insurgency" and victory looked probable, various actors within the Afghan Police and Army proceeded to "join the anti-government forces" and actively aid (bandwagon with) the Taliban because they had hedged their bets, decided the insurgents were the most likely winning coalition, and wanted to share in the spoils of its (at that point) likely victory.[47] As an additional example from the same case, in 2008 substantial "collusion took place" between two Afghan regime actors (a national police chief and governor) and the insurgents which enabled the belligerents to carry out a deadly surprise attack against alliance forces.[48] For internal threat alliances, therefore, it is simplistic to ask whether states balance *or* bandwagon, as in traditional military alliances. Instead, parts of the weaker state will do both *at the same time*.

Second, actors will bandwagon in pursuit of three aims, which include wanting to (1) survive, (2) benefit from the winning side's victory, and (3) advance patron-client relations. The third motivation, often a fundamental element of a weak state's social fabric, is distinct to internal threat alliances. What many actors in weak states prioritize first (and over any sense of loyalty to the state as a whole or national interest) is their patron-client relations rooted in illicit financial gain, tribal affiliation, and ethnic allegiance, among other motives. Recognizing this, I predict that elements of the weak state's government (e.g., a specific police unit) will collude with insurgents or rebels if and when they have patron-client links with such groups. And they will do so even in the absence of some high level of threat (in order to survive) or desire to benefit, should the insurgents win. Including patron-client linkages as a motivating factor for bandwagoning is important for theory because it will help explain why weak state actors (e.g., a military commander) will bandwagon in the absence of high threat levels.

Two examples demonstrate the three motivations driving bandwagoning. In the early 2000s, the USA had formed an internal threat alliance with Iraq's President Jalal Talabani to defeat anti-government insurgents and stabilize the country. Throughout this alliance, various elements of the Iraqi Army repeatedly colluded with (rather than fought against) insurgents because of the shared (Sunni) ethnicity between the army actors and the belligerents. As one assessment of this component to the US-Iraqi alliance noted: "In effect, we were equipping them (the Iraqi army) for *contributing to*…warfare rather than stopping it, because the units…often supported militias and criminals rather than oppos[ed] them."[49] This phenomenon plagued the alliance and undercut US-Iraqi strategy for several years. The same occurred during the US–Afghanistan alliance. Afghan governors in various states colluded with (rather than directed their forces to combat) the Taliban due to their shared Pashtun ethnicity or desire to advance personal financial interests.[50] And in Syria, the heavily Alawite al-Assad regime was confronted with Sunni army officers and rank and file defecting to join the largely Sunni opposition rebel forces to safeguard (or at minimum not be involved in killing) their fellow Sunnis.

To summarize, this portion of the theory argues that **balancing (resisting the target threat) and "bandwagoning" (appeasing the target threat) will occur *simultaneously* during internal threat alliances. Further, actors within the weak state will bandwagon to survive, share in the victor's spoils, or advance patron-client relationships.** Given that bandwagoning for internal threat alliances is not binary—that is, regime actors bandwagon, while the allies are together—it will have implications for alliance effectiveness, as addressed below.

Alliance Effectiveness: *Sufficient Resources and Ability to Curb Subnational Bandwagoning*

This third and final part of the framework aims to help explain why some internal threat alliances are effective and others are not. Effectiveness is defined as whether the allies weaken the insurgency or rebellion to the point that it no longer represents an imminent threat to the regime's survival. In the case study chapters that follow, specific metrics are used to determine degrees of effectiveness.[51] Much like traditional alliances, the amount of military resources the allies bring together will determine whether the great power and regime are able to achieve their goal. Unlike traditional alliances, however, distinct aspects of the weaker state will also influence effectiveness. The argument below modifies existing theory to account for this factor.

The core argument here is that effectiveness will depend on whether allies have military resources sufficient to weaken their common enemy *and* are able to control subnational bandwagoning. After forming an internal threat alliance, the great power and regime will work together to agree on a strategy and tactics and then implement associated activities (military and otherwise) to defeat their common enemy. Leveraging existing IR theory, the extent to which allies can effectively work together in these areas is defined as the alliance's "cohesion"—the more allies are able to cooperate, the more "cohesive" the alliance.[52] In keeping with existing alliance theory, two variables will influence cohesion: level of internal threat and the allies dependence on each other to balance it—as the threat to the regime increases, along with their continued dependence on each other to defeat it, so too will the need for the allies to work together to balance it. And only when the allies are able to consistently agree on strategy and tactics (enjoy high cohesion) will they be able to amass resources sufficient to weaken or defeat their common menace.

Due to the weak state's fragmented character, however, we cannot assume that the regime's security forces will follow alliance strategy and apply resources (e.g., military hardware, munitions, etc.) against the rebels or insurgents. As outlined above, elements of the weaker state's army, police, or other actors may decide to collude (bandwagon) with insurgents. During the alliance between Russia and Syria's President Bashar al-Assad, for example, alliance effectiveness initially decreased as a result of collusion by elements of the Syrian Army with the anti-government rebels. This included high-level generals (Army and Air

Force) as well as an estimated 50,000 soldiers (of 280,000) defecting to join the anti-government rebels in order to guarantee their own survival or prioritizing loyalty to fellow Sunnis.[53] For internal threat alliances, then, amassing resources sufficient to weaken the internal threat will be *necessary* to ensure effectiveness but not *sufficient*. Consequently, effectiveness will be further determined by the regime's willingness and ability to stop their bureaucratic actors from colluding with the enemy. However, the regime's willingness and ability to do so cannot be assumed. This central leadership circle (or specific individuals therein) may have political priorities or patron-client ties that alter its willingness to reign in actors colluding with the enemy (bandwagoning). These same interests may also complicate the allies' ability to work together to define a strategy and associate tactics and thus decrease cohesion. At precise junctures and in response to threats, then, the regime may decide that working to defeat *specific* actors or implement *specific* tactics (and collaborating with the great power to do so) is detrimental to regime political survival, power, and influence. And in turn, this can decrease alliance effectiveness.

Examples from two cases help illustrate that a regime's ability and willingness to stop bandwagoning will influence effectiveness. During the internal threat alliance between the USA and Colombia, various elements of the police were colluding with the enemy by providing the "narco-insurgents" with tips on US–Colombia military operations.[54] Components of the Colombian police and military were colluding with the narco-insurgents, while the central government and USA were *simultaneously* seeking to balance them. As a result, alliance effectiveness declined because insurgents were able to evade US–Colombian operations. It was not until Colombian presidents, beginning with Cesar Gaviria, took steps to curb this bandwagoning that alliance effectiveness increased. In order to curb collusion, Gaviria formed a new police unit comprised of officers loyal to the president's office (and therefore who would not collude with the narco-insurgents). Gaviria's Defense Minister called this unit an "island of integrity in a sea of corruption."[55] By dramatically decreasing the amount of secrete information flowing to the insurgents, Gaviria's efforts to curb bandwagoning increased the effectiveness of operations. Gaviria's successors as president, first Andrés Pastrana and then Alvaro Uribe, continued efforts to eradicate collusion by firing and prosecuting army or police leaders (and members of their units) proven to be colluding with the enemy. It was only because the central regime was willing and able to curb this bandwagoning and received an influx of arms via *Plan Colombia* that alliance effectiveness increased.

Nearly the opposite occurred during the latter half of the internal threat alliance between the US and Afghan President Karzai. In the run-up to Afghanistan's 2004 elections, a surge in threat from insurgents drove the allies together, pushed them to agree to a new strategy, and maintained cohesion through much of President George W. Bush's two terms in office. However, two regime-specific motivations also drove them together during this period: Karzai recognized that US influence could (1) help him win the 2004 presidential elections and (2) install an electoral system that would consolidate and reduce checks against Executive authority and thereby enhance his power/influence. Following Afghanistan's elections, insurgent violence kept alliance cohesion relatively high. But, signs began to emerge that Karzai was becoming less willing to cooperate across all alliance areas—in particular, to stop elements of his regime from bandwagoning. Given that Karzai's central regime relied on the alliance to combat insurgents seeking his overthrow, it remained in its interests to work with the USA (militarily) and *balance*. At the same time, Karzai had attained most items required to consolidate power and influence and therefore began making decisions that would help guarantee re-election in 2009 but also violated non-military aspects of the alliance and were contrary to the Afghan national interest. This included diverting (and using as patronage) alliance resources and appointing corrupt officials to bolster patron-client links' key to re-election. Karzai also refused to sack governors with proven links to insurgents and who were therefore essentially facilitating the death of hundreds of US troops in these areas. As a result, the alliance's ability to defeat insurgents in specific areas suffered—and along with it US interests.[56]

To summarize, this portion of the theory argues that **the effectiveness of internal threat alliances will depend on whether allies have military resources sufficient to weaken their common enemy *and* are able to control subnational bandwagoning.** The principal determinant of internal threat alliance effectiveness will be allies' ability to bring together capabilities sufficient to weaken or defeat the threat. And only when the great power and regime are able to agree on goals, strategy, and tactics and to coordinate activities directed toward those ends will they be able to collectively amass resources sufficient to weaken or defeat their common menace. However, alliances will not be effective if the weaker state's leadership is not willing and able to stop their bureaucratic actors from colluding with the enemy. This is a distinct feature of internal alliances and not found in their traditional military counterpart examined in the IR literature where states engage in capital-to-capital communication and either do or do not work together to balance a common enemy.

The table below summarizes the framework's three components and associated independent and dependent variables (Table 1.1).

LESSONS FOR POLICY

This book has several potential insights that could be useful for policy-makers, of great powers or weak states, who are grappling with how to secure their interests in the face or insurgency and rebellion, whether to form an internal threat alliance, and how best to navigate one in which they are already engaged.

First and foremost, great power policy-makers entering into such an alliance should assume that all actors within the weaker ally will not necessarily follow alliance strategy; that is, work together in a unified manner to

Table 1.1 Summary of Internal Threat Alliance Dynamics

Internal Threat Alliances: A New Conceptual Framework

Summary of Independent and Dependent Variables

	Formation	Bandwagoning	Effectiveness
Independent variable	IV 1. Perceived threat Violence from insurgency or rebellion IV 2. Allies' interests *Regime*: stay in power *Great power*: preserve interests associated with regime survival/stability	IV 1. Survive IV 2. Advance patron-client relations IV 3. Share in spoils of victory	IV 1. Sufficient capabilities to balance threat IV 2. Regime ability/willingness to curb bandwagoning
Dependent variable	Great power/regime align security policies	Regime actors support source of threat (insurgents/rebels)	Variance in level of perceived threat from insurgents/rebels

defeat the rebellion or insurgency. As a result, these policy-makers must carefully calibrate expectations about what their partners will and will not do. Simply because leaders in the capital agree to cooperate does not mean all of their bureaucratic actors (e.g., the police or military) or components therein will fall in line and proceed accordingly. Orders from the capital do not always trickle down to subnational districts and in some cases are never made from the center to begin with. In contrast to alliances formed to defeat other states, the major internal fragmentation of the weaker state and the clientelistic relationships that undergird power dynamics (financial and political) therein mean that the unified balancing commonplace with traditional alliances cannot be assumed. Instead, the great power should assume that some element within their weaker ally will endeavor to defeat the rebellion or insurgency, while others will actively collude with it. Simply because the USA and Afghan President Hamid Karzai agreed to a specific strategy, for example, did not mean Afghan actors at various subnational areas would play along—instead, they often pursued their own interests at the expense of alliance objectives.

Second, great powers engaging in this type of alliance should plan to manage relationships between cooperative central leaders on the one hand and (national and subnational) bureaucratic actors colluding with the enemy on the other. To account for this, policy-makers should carefully analyze the political, economic, and traditional relationships between key regime players in order to identify leverage points great powers can exploit to push these actors toward complying with alliance strategy and away from colluding with the enemy. Policy-makers would be well suited to perform in-depth analysis and intelligence gathering on their potential ally's internal make-up—particularly, whether its core bureaucratic agencies have intra-fragmentation that could lead to factions colluding with the target threat rather than working to defeat it.

Third, in cases where the weaker state's internal fragmentation is so deep to suggest no possible way to curb substantial collusion with the enemy, the great power should question the utility of forming such an alliance to begin with. Careful consideration should be given to the range of alternatives available (e.g., targeted special operations raids and counterterrorism operations) to secure their interests. Long-term, resource heavy engagements are not always the answer.

Fourth, great powers should be wary of leaders in weak states inflating the severity of the internal threat. Before agreeing to align, independent estimations of threat level—to that regime and associated great power interests—should be made.

Finally, policy-makers in the developing world or capitals of Western great powers should understand that capabilities alone will not be sufficient to achieve alliance objectives. This is contrary to a core assumption underlying traditional military alliances that states will be victorious provided they amass sufficient resources to defeat their enemy. In other words, capabilities are the recipe for a highly effective traditional alliance. With internal threat alliances, this assumption does not necessarily hold. In the cases of Colombia, Afghanistan, and Syria, we see that the regime's actors may—or may not—apply alliances resources against the target threat. As a result, to be effective an internal threat alliance must couple sufficient military resources as well as a host government taking action to prevent collusion with the enemy. To address this issue, great power policy-makers would be well served to devote more attention to using diplomacy and associated incentives to push actors to balance (or to prevent collusion) in addition to making sure that the alliance has sufficient resources to guarantee military victory.

Conclusions

In this chapter I drew from and modified aspects of existing IR theory to demonstrate the why internal threat alliances form, why some are more cohesive than others, and why some are effective while others are not. Collectively, the chapter's three core arguments provide a framework for understanding and explaining the more common type of alliance today. The three arguments are as follows.

First, internal threat alliances will form in response to a threat that *is domestic in origin* and imperils the survival of a weak state's leadership regime. The weaker state's leadership will seek cooperation because it needs military or economic resources to thwart challenges to its existence, while the great power will become involved in order to safeguard interests linked to the regime's stability or survival. This is different than traditional alliances, where the threat is *external in origin* (another state or group of states) and the involved states align in order to secure their national interest and territorial survival.

Second, balancing (resisting the target threat) and "bandwagoning" (appeasing the target threat) will occur *simultaneously* during internal threat alliances. This is in contrast to traditional military alliances, where countries will *either* balance *or* bandwagon when faced with an external enemy. Due to the weaker state's internal fragmentation and lower capacity, its central leadership is unable to control all of its component actors (e.g., subnational governors, the military, or police forces), each of whom will routinely pursue their own interests (e.g., financial gain, cementing patron-client ties) at the expense of alliance goals. As a result, the central leadership may work with the great power to implement alliance strategy and defeat (*balance*) the common threat, while elements of its police or military are *colluding (bandwagoning) with* actors fomenting violence.

Third and finally, the effectiveness of internal threat alliances will depend on whether allies have military resources sufficient to weaken their common enemy *and* are able to control subnational bandwagoning. The principal determinant of internal threat alliance effectiveness will be allies' ability to bring together capabilities sufficient to weaken or defeat the threat. And only when the great power and regime are able to agree on goals, strategy, and tactics and to coordinate associated activities will they be able to collectively amass resources sufficient to weaken or defeat their common menace. However, alliances will not be effective if the weaker state's leadership is not willing and able to stop their bureaucratic actors from colluding with the enemy. This central leadership circle (or specific individuals therein) may have political priorities (or patron-client ties to actors responsible for political violence) that alter its willingness to curb subnational bandwagoning. At precise junctures and in response to threats, then, the regime may decide that working to defeat specific actors or implement specific tactics (and collaborating with the great power to do so) is detrimental to regime political survival, power, and influence. And in turn, this can decrease alliance effectiveness.

Roadmap for the Remainder of the Book

The balance of the book aims to evidence the three core arguments presented in this chapter. Chapter 2 applies the theoretical framework to the US–Colombia internal threat alliance. It traces US–Colombia cooperation over the course of 30 years to defeat Marxist rebels and secure associated US interests. It shows that the Colombian government sought US assistance to thwart rising threats from rebel groups and drug-trafficking organizations, while the USA aligned in order to safeguard interests linked to the regime's stability including curbing drug flows onto American streets, maintaining access to oil reserves, and preserving stability in its "backyard." The chapter demonstrates that in internal threat alliances, it is simplistic to ask whether states balance or bandwagon. Instead, they do both at the same time. While some elements of the Colombian National Police fought against drug traffickers (balanced), others actively cooperated with them (bandwagoned). While some mayors resisted guerrilla incursions, others supported the belligerents. Finally, it demonstrates that alliance effectiveness was higher during the administrations of Colombian Presidents Andrés Pastrana and Alvaro Uribe due to the alliance's ability to amass sufficient resources (via *Plan Colombia*) and the Colombian leadership's consistent efforts to purge civilian and security agencies of actors bandwagoning with the "narco-guerrilla" threat.

Chapter 3 applies the theory to the US–Afghanistan internal threat alliance. It traces US–Afghanistan cooperation to defeat Taliban insurgents and secure associated US interests. It shows that the Afghan government of President Hamid Karzai sought US assistance to thwart rising threats to his survival from Taliban militants, while the USA aligned in order to ensure terrorists could not again use Afghanistan as a base to plan and launch attacks (as they did on September 11, 2001) and ensure access to natural resources in the region. Regarding bandwagoning, the chapter shows that some elements of the Afghan Army fought against the Taliban (balanced), while others actively cooperated with them (bandwagoned). Similarly, while some governors and elements of the national police resisted Taliban incursions, others aligned with the worst of the terrorist organization. Finally, the chapter shows that the alliance was less effective due to insufficient resources and Karzai's inadequate efforts to stop elements of his regime from colluding (bandwagoning) with the belligerents.

Chapter 4 is the final case study and applies the framework onto the Russia–Syria internal threat alliance. It traces Russia's cooperation with the Bashar al-Assad regime in Syria to defeat anti-government rebels. It shows that the Assad regime sought Russian assistance in order to thwart anti-government rebels seeking to overthrow his government, while Russia provided military capabilities to the embattled regime in order to safeguard its single military base outside the former Soviet Union as well as preserve access to oil and gas fields and other economic interests. Concerning bandwagoning, the chapter shows that some elements of Syria's military colluded (bandwagoned) with rebels, but the majority followed central orders and worked to defeat (balance) them. Finally, the chapter demonstrates that the Russia–Syria alliance has been effective due to its accumulation of sufficient resources to weaken rebels as well as the al-Assad government's ability to prevent its various bureaucratic actors from colluding with the belligerents.

In order to evidence the framework's core arguments across the three aforementioned cases, the book employs the case study research method of "structured, focused comparison."[57] This approach involved three principal steps. First, the three core arguments and associated hypotheses presented in this chapter were developed. Second, the individual cases were constructed using the methods of process-tracing and semi-structured interviews. Interviews were conducted in Washington, DC, as well as Afghanistan and Colombia. Development of the cases was "focused" in two ways—first, as delimited by the specified period of time and, second, in that analysis centered on evidencing the three arguments and not *all* aspects of the alliance writ large. Accordingly, each case begins with a historical overview of the alliance period, the purpose of which is to give the reader background on major events therein. Thereafter, the cases are structured by the three parts of the framework. The third and final step was to compare across cases in a structured, focused manner. This step was critical for confirming that identified mid-range, contingent theoretical generalizations were not only inherent to each alliance studied but, rather, generalizable to cases beyond those examined here. During this step, focus was given to similarities and variation across the cases for each of the four elements examined.

Chapter 5 is a relatively brief concluding chapter that completes various tasks. It summarizes the book's main arguments and contributions to IR theory, reinforcing its distinct addition to the field. It then outlines the book's main lessons for policy. And finally, it lays out an agenda for future areas of research.

Notes

1. In spite of the immensity of alliance theory, there is no one commonly accepted definition for the term. I do not attempt to contribute to this particular conceptual debate and instead use "alliance" and "alignment" interchangeably and to reflect the following: when a state brings its policies into cooperation with another state in order to pursue mutual goals related to security.

2. The debate surrounding conceptualizations of and definitions for those states outside what has been termed the "international liberal system" is often hotly contested, with some arguing that "periphery" should replace previously employed "Third" or "Second World." One useful conceptualization is offered by Goldgeier and McFaul (1992), who divide the post-Cold War era into "core" and "periphery" states (or "spaces") according to factors related to economy and power. The "core" is comprised of the industrialized states of Western Europe, North America, and Japan. By "periphery" they refer to "the agriculturally based, industrializing states of the developing world." Concerning measure of "power," the peripheral space is occupied by "states which are 'weak' relative to the core of great powers." Steven David (1992) makes a persuasive case that despite the decline in utility of the term "Third World," many states who were formerly associated within this name indeed often share the same characteristics. James M. Goldgeier and Michael McFaul, "A Tale of Two Worlds: Core and Periphery in the Post-Cold War Era," *International Organization*, Vol. 46 (Spring 1992), 467. Steven R. David, "Explaining Alignment in the Third World", *World Politics*, Vol. 43 (January 1991)." Steven David, "Why the Third World Still Matters." *International Security* 17, No. 3 (Winter, 1992), 127. Great Power: International power" and "great power" are used interchangeably throughout and refers to those countries considered, broadly within the IR literature, as great powers following the end of World War (WW) II, given the book's focus on alliances formed during this period. Scholars employ different measures for and definitions of what constitutes a great power. The book recognizes that the list of great powers evolved from WWI as well as through inter-war period and during and after WWII. While recognizing this as well as the debate within IR theory on thresholds of power and definitions for great power, the book does not aim to make a theoretical contribution here. Rather, it accepts and employs the following conceptualization of state power and how a given state's "rank" of great power should be determined: "States are placed in the top rank because they excel in one way or another. Their rank depends on how they score on *all* of the following items: size of population and territory, resource endowment, economic capability, military strength, political stability, and compe-

tence. Kenneth N. Waltz, *Theory of International Politics* (New York: McGraw-Hill, 1979), 131. Based on this criteria as well as status in international organizations such as the UN Security Council, the following states can be considered great powers: the USA, China, the U.K., France, Japan, and Russia. For an overview of the evolution of great powers in the international system, see Paul M. Kennedy, *The Rise and Fall of the Great Powers: Economic Change and Military Conflict from 1500 to 2000*, 1st ed. (New York, NY: Random House, 1987).

3. In keeping with prior work on alliance theory, capabilities are defined as any military or economic resource aggregated between the great power and weak state's regime, the purpose of which is to shift the balance of power in favor of the alliance and against the target threat. This book recognizes the contested nature of the term "national interest" and does not seek to contribute to this debate. Rather, it uses the term interchangeably with "national security" and employs the definition provided by Morgenthau: "national security must be defined as integrity of the national territory and its institutions." In other words, and as applied to alliances, states form traditional alliances so as to aggregate sufficient power to safeguard the integrity of their national territory and associated domestic apparatus. Morgenthau, *Politics Among Nations (New York: Knopf Publishing, 1959)*, 586.

4. In this book "civil war," "intra-state war," and "internal war" are used interchangeably. Although many agree that civil wars have negative consequences, the definition for what actually constitutes a "civil war" is itself disputed. This debate essentially revolves around the number of battlefield deaths that must occur initially and for each year of the conflict thereafter. I use the essential elements of the CoW definition as set forth by Small and Singer, that a civil war comprises the following elements: (1) military action internal to borders of the state, (2) active military action taken by the national government, and (3) effective resistance from the national government and opposition group or groups. Melvin Small and David Singer, *Resort to Arms: International and Civil War, 1816–1980* (Beverly Hills, CA: Sage Publishing, 1982). I find the 1000 battlefield death threshold somewhat arbitrary and do not include it here; however, nor do I offer a different threshold.

5. Stephen M. Saideman, *The Ties That Divide: Ethnic Politics, Foreign Policy, and International Conflict* (New York: Columbia University Press, 2001).
6. Correlates of War (COW) project, Inter-State War Data Set (4.0) and Intra-State War Data Set (4.0). Available for download here: http://www.correlatesofwar.org/COW2%20Data/WarData_NEW/WarList_NEW.html#Intra-State War Data.
7. *Human Security Report 2009/2010: The Causes of Peace and the Shrinking Costs of War*; second figure according to the Uppsala Conflict Data Program (UCDP), which collects information on various aspects of armed violence that have occurred since 1946. For a review of the methodology underlying this estimate, see the UCDP website. http://www.pcr.uu.se/research/ucdp/program_overview/
8. Statistics presented in Max Boot's "Invisible Armies Insurgency Tracker – A Visual History of Guerrilla Warfare from 1775 to 2012."
9. For an excellent analysis of why civil wars will continue and persist as the principal form of mass organized violence, see Steven R. David, *Catastrophic Consequences: Civil Wars and American Interests* (Baltimore, MD: Johns Hopkins University Press, 2008). See also Ann Hironaka, *Never-ending Wars: The International Community, Weak States, and the Perpetuation of Civil War* (Cambridge, MA: Harvard University Press, 2005).
10. K.J. Holsti, "Diplomatic Coalitions and Military Alliances," in *Alliance in International Politics*, Julian R. Friedman, Christopher Bladen, Steven Rosen, eds. (Boston, MA: Allyn and Bacon Inc., 1970), 102.
11. The alliance was formalized in 1894 in what is referred to as the Franco-Russian Alliance. William L. Langer, *The Franco-Russian Alliance, 1890–1894* (New York, NY: Octagon Books, 1967).
12. Martin Gilbert, *The Second World War: A Complete History* (New York, NY: Holt, 2004).
13. Nonstructural treatments of military alliance dynamics as reviewed in next chapter hold that alignment decisions are based on the "perception" of these threats. Prominent examples of neoclassical realism include Michael E. Brown et al., eds. *The Perils of Anarchy: Contemporary Realism and International Security* (Cambridge: MIT Press, 1995); Randall L. Schweller. *Deadly Imbalances:*

Tripolarity and Hitler's Strategy of World Conquest (New York: Columbia University Press, 1998); William Curti Wohlforth, The Elusive Balance: Power and Perceptions during the Cold War (Ithaca, N.Y.: Cornell University Press, 1993); Fareed Zakaria, *From Wealth to Power: The Unusual Origins of America's World Role* (Princeton, N.J.: Princeton University Press, 1998); Gideon Rose, "Neoclassical Realism and Theories of Foreign Policy," *World Politics* 51, No. 1 (1998), 144–172; and Steven E. Lobell, Norrin M. Ripsman, and Jeffrey W. Taliaferro, *Neoclassical Realism, the State, and Foreign Policy* (Cambridge, UK: Cambridge University Press, 2009).

14. Kenneth N. Waltz, "Political Structures" in Keohane, ed., *Neorealism and its Critics* (New York: Columbia University Press, 1986), 90.
15. Though other bureaucratic agencies (in particular the armed forces of each partner) are also involved in devising strategy and applying aggregated resources to balance a common threat, alliance theory, as reviewed in the next chapter, largely does not theorize explicitly regarding effectiveness—and those select few scholars who do problematize effectiveness tend to conceptualize partner regimes as unitary.
16. Stephen M. Walt, *The Origins of Alliances* (Ithaca: Cornell University Press, 1987), 17.
17. Stephen M. Walt, *The Origins of Alliances* (Ithaca: Cornell University Press, 1987), 17.
18. Walt, *The Origins of Alliances* (1987), 21.
19. Walt, *The Origins of Alliances* (1987), x and 21–26. See also Stephen M. Walt, "Testing Theories of Alliance Formation: The Case of Southeast Asia," *International Organization* 42, No. 2 (1988), 277. Randall L. Schweller, "Bandwagoning for Profit: Bringing the Revisionist State Back in," *International Security* 19, No. 1 (Summer, 1994), 72–107; Schweller, *Deadly Imbalances: Tripolarity and Hitler's Strategy of World Conquest* (New York: Columbia University Press, 1998).
20. Walt, *The Origins of Alliances* (1987), 17.
21. Cohesion as outlined in Ole R. Holsti, P. Terrence Hopmann, and John D. Sullivan, *Unity and Disintegration in International Alliances: Comparative Studies* (New York: John Wiley & Sons Publishing, 1973), 94–95 and 100–102.

22. Steven E. Lobell, "Threat assessment, the state, and foreign policy: a neoclassical realist model," in Norrin M. Ripsman and Jeffrey W. Taliaferro, *Neoclassical Realism, the State, and Foreign Policy* (Cambridge, UK: Cambridge University Press, 2009), 51.
23. Steven E. Lobell, "Threat assessment, the state, and foreign policy: a neoclassical realist model," in Norrin M. Ripsman and Jeffrey W. Taliaferro, *Neoclassical Realism, the State, and Foreign Policy* (Cambridge, UK: Cambridge University Press, 2009), 43. Definition quoted in Steven E. Lobell, "Power Disparities and Strategic Trade: Domestic Consequences of U.S.-Jordan Trade Concessions," in Kristen P. Williams, Steven E. Lobell, and Neal G. Jesse, Eds. *Beyond Great Powers: Why Secondary States Support, Follow, or Challenge* (Stanford: Stanford University Press, 2012, 82). Work that examines the role of the FPE in devising foreign policy is within the strain of literature that examines the influence onto foreign policy outcomes of "small group dynamics" in general and "societal elites" in particular. On small group dynamics, see Jeffrey W. Taliaferro, *Balancing Risks: Great Power Intervention in the Periphery* (Ithaca, NY: Cornell University Press, 2004). See also Steven E. Lobell, "The International Realm, Framing Effects, and Security Strategies: Britain in Peace and War," *International Interactions* Vol. 32, No. 1 (2006), 27–48.
24. Steven David makes this point in (1991) "Explaining Alignment in the Third World," 239. See also David (1992) "Why the Third World Still Matters."
25. For three excellent analyses of the "non-modal" patterns of state-building and what this process differed from that of Western states, see Miguel Angel Centeno, *Blood and Debt: War and the Nation-State in Latin America* (University Park, PA: University of Pennsylvania Press, 2002); Jeffrey Herbst, *States and Power in Africa* (Princeton University Press: Princeton, 2000); and Catherine Boone, *Political Topographies of the African State: Territorial Authority and Institutional Choice* (Cambridge University Press: Cambridge, 2003).
26. David (1991), *Choosing Sides*, 7.
27. Patron-client relations, also referred to as "clientelism," is a form of relationship widely examined in the political science literature at both the micro- and macro-levels—examples of the former include studies of village level politics, where macro-level studies might, for

example, demonstrate why an entire political system could be characterized as "clientelistic" in nature. Robert R. Kaufman, "The Patron-Client Concept and Macro-Politics: Prospects and Problems," *Comparative Studies in Society and History* 16, No. 3 (1974), 285.

28. Where referenced, insurgency is defined as "a struggle to control a contested political space, between a state (or group of states or occupying powers), and one or more popularly based, non-state challengers." David Kilcullen, "Counter-Insurgency *Redux*," *Survival* 48, No. 4 (2004), 112. A recent useful study differentiates between rebellions and insurgencies that seek to replace the government (replacement) or alter the relationship between government and society (legitimacy). David Sobek and Caroline Payne, "A Tale of Two Types: Rebel Goals and the Onset of Civil Wars," *International Studies Quarterly* 54, No. 1 (March 2010), 213–40.
29. David, (1991), "Explaining Alignment in the Third World," 236.
30. There are conflicting reports as to the precise level and type of assistance Russia provided to Syria. However, reports indicate this assistance included guns, helicopters, and a missile defense system. See, for example, Chris McGreal, "US says Russian-made weapons are killing Syrians on 'an hourly basis'," *The Guardian*, June 13, 2012. Syria also sought similar military assistance from China.
31. Further details regarding this case as well as evidence for the regime's motivations are presented in Chap. 3.
32. Further details regarding this case as well as evidence for the regime's motivations are presented in Chap. 4.
33. For the most comprehensive analysis of why internal war affects the interests of states in general and the USA as great power in particular, see Steven R. David, "On Civil War," *The American Interest* (March/April 2007), and David (2008), *Catastrophic Consequences*.
34. Various scholars demonstrate that weak states and "ungoverned territory" therein may provide the space in which non-state actors including terrorist organizations may plan and launch attacks against states in general and great powers (as well as their assets) in particular. See, for example, Stewart Patrick, "Weak States and Global Threats: Fact or Fiction?" *The Washington Quarterly* (Spring 2006), 30. Patrick elaborates on this initial version of the framework in Stewart Patrick, *Weak Links – Fragile States, Global*

Threats, and International Security (Oxford: Oxford University Press, 2011), pp. 18–60. See also Angel Basa, Steven Boraz, Peter Chalk, Kim Cragin, Theodore W. Karasik, Jennifer D.P. Moroney, Kevin A. O'Brien, and John E. Peters. "Ungoverned Territories: Understanding and Reducing Terrorism Risks" (Santa Monica, CA: RAND Corporation, 2007.). Steven R. David, *Catastrophic Consequences: Civil Wars and American Interests* (Baltimore, MD: Johns Hopkins University Press 2008).

35. David (2008), *Catastrophic Consequences*.
36. David (2008) makes this argument with regard to China, which holds a large amount of US Treasury bonds. Sustained civil conflict in China, then, could have negative implications for the US budget deficit.
37. David (2008) makes this argument with regard to Mexico, which borders the USA and hosts a large expat community.
38. Overall argument made by David (2008) *Catastrophic Consequences*.
39. The rebels contesting Mobutu's rule were led by Laurent Kabila, a Katangan soldier who served under Patrice Lumumba in the early 1960s. He led the rebellion under the name of the Alliance of Democratic Forces for the Liberation of Zaire-Congo (ADFL) and, at the outset of the fighting, quickly made significant gains in eastern Congo. Raymond Bonner, "France Linked to Defense of Mobutu," *New York Times*, May 2, 1997.
40. James Brooke, "Gabon Keeps Strong Links with France," *New York Times*, February 23, 1988.
41. "Obituary: The corrupt nepotist who ruled Gabon for 40 years," *The Independent (UK)*, June 9, 2009.
42. Various articles and analyses have examined Russia's interests in Syria and therefore why the great power might align with the Assad regime. For a review of these factors, see "Why Russia Protects Assad," CNN, January 26, 2012. Analysis provided by Oxford Analytica and reposted by CNN. Available here: http://globalpublicsquare.blogs.cnn.com/2012/01/26/why-russia-protects-assad/.
43. The White House, "Remarks by the President on a New Strategy for Afghanistan and Pakistan," March 27, 2009. Available here: http://www.whitehouse.gov/the_press_office/Remarks-by-the-President-on-a-New-Strategy-for-Afghanistan-and-Pakistan/.

Second portion of quote as stated in Woodward, *Obama's Wars*, (2010), 113.
44. The presence of threat will be necessary but not sufficient for states to bring their security policy into close cooperation to balance it—for an alliance to form, the two states must perceive the threat as sufficiently high and thus imperiling their security *and* dependent on each other to balance it. States pursue alliances to balance internal threats because they cannot balance this threat alone—they are dependent, for a range of reasons, on another state to do so. Considering this factor helps explain why, for example, a great power will choose to work with and through the peripheral regime, as opposed to employing unilateral intervention, and why the peripheral regime will seek assistance from the great power to quell a rebellion. To conceptualize military dependence, I use Glenn Snyder's (1997) definition of the term. Although Snyder's alliance "management" framework examines external threat alliances, its military dependence concept comprised of the following three core factors is applicable for examining dynamics of internal threat alliances: (1) *a state's need for military assistance* [as informed by the threat it faces and whether it has sufficient capabilities to balance that threat], (2) *the degree to which the ally fills that need*, and (3) *alternative ways of meeting the need*. As the great power and peripheral regime are more dependent on each other, they will be more likely to form an alliance (to meet the need they cannot fill alone) as well as remain within it and work with their ally to agree on goals and strategy associated with aggregating capabilities. As these three factors increase for both alliance partners, their need for each other will also increase. A state's need for military assistance is a reflection of its existing capacity (military and economic) and therefore intimately linked to the level of threat perceived by the peripheral regime and great power. As applied to internal threat alliances, these factors are applicable to the great power and peripheral regime in the following ways. For the peripheral regime, the need for assistance derives from lacking capabilities (military and economic) needed to balance the internal threat to its survival. If the peripheral regime has an alternate way to obtain these capabilities—through increasing its own spending or finding another ally to offset the need—its dependence in general and on the great power in particular will decrease. For the great power, the need for

assistance derives from requiring cooperation from the peripheral regime to combat their common threat—either tacit or direct—to address the threat within the regime's borders. This specific attribute of internal threat alliances, therefore, increases the great power's dependence on its ally. As the great power perceives the threat to its interests increasing, it will be increasingly dependent on the peripheral regime to balance that threat—and without other options to do so (such as adding a different or additional ally) aside from aggregating more resources.

45. The *formation* of an internal threat alliance is defined as when two states bring their security policies into close cooperation. An internal threat alliance has formed when the two states have aligned their security policies as well as agreed to aggregate military and other capabilities in order to balance their commonly perceived threat internal to the weak state.
46. Anonymous former Colombian government official, interview with author, citing his own scholarly work, Bogota, Colombia, October 2012.
47. "Countering Afghanistan's Insurgency: No Quick Fixes," Crisis Group Asia Report N°123 (Brussels/Kabul: International Crisis Group, November 2, 2006), 11.
48. "Report Says Afghan Police Chief, Governor Aided Insurgents Attack," *Fox News*, November 4, 2008.
49. On government actors in Iraq colluding with Sunni insurgents, see, for example, Michael Eisenstadt and Jeffrey White, "Assessing Iraq's Sunni-Arab Insurgency," *Military Review* (May/June 2006). As outlined in O'Hanlon and Sherjan (2010), referring to the Iraqi security forces and US efforts to train them: "In effect, we were equipping them for *contributing to* sectarian warfare rather than stopping it, because the units were heavily infiltrated by extremists who often supported militias and criminals rather than opposing them." Michael E. O'Hanlon and Hassina Sherjan, *Toughing it out in Afghanistan* (Washington, DC: Brookings Institution Press, 2010), 92.
50. On government actors in Afghanistan colluding with insurgents due to ethnic ties, see. This and other examples of collusion between the Afghan regime's agencies with sources of threat are outlined in "The Insurgency in Afghanistan's Heartland," *International Crisis Group* (Brussels, Belgium: June 2011). On

government actors prioritizing illicit business ties, see, for example, Dexter Filkins, "Convoy Guards in Afghanistan Face an Inquiry," *New York Times*, June 6, 2010.

51. *Effectiveness* of internal threat alliances is demonstrated by indicators that reflect the capability of the internal threat and will range from low to high—low when the threat continues to imperil the security of both allies and high when the threat is no longer a core threat to partners' security. To conceptualize variation *in alliance effectiveness* and therefore measure whether the internal threat has been debilitated as a result of the alliance, the following measures related to the opposition are used: (1) total number of opposition personnel relative to the government's military personnel, (2) amount of territory controlled by the opposition, and (3) number of attacks employed by the opposition (and where possible, frequency and intensity of those attacks). A decrease in these factors is considered an increase in ally government ability to balance against an internal threat to its sovereignty. The first data factor provides a measure of the size of the opposition (threat) vis-à-vis the peripheral regime, while the second provides an indication of the opposition's ability to organize and leverage their personnel to obtain territory. This second factor is also a useful measure to track changes in strength of the threat opposition strength throughout the intervention and identify relationships between these factors. For example, should amount of opposition-held territory decrease following formation of the alliance and continue to decline, this may be an indication of alliance effectiveness. The third and final data factor also provides an indication of the opposition's ability to organize and leverage their personnel, yet in this case to plan and implement kinetic actions. This third factor is also a useful measure to track changes in intensity of the threat over the course of the alliance. For example, if the number of opposition-employed attacks decreases following initial alliance formation and continues to decline, this may be an indication of alliance effectiveness. By tracing variation on these factors, I seek to demonstrate potential effect of the alliance onto the targeted internal threat.

52. The "strategy, tactics, and activities" are those items on which the alliance partners agree to achieve this purpose and are related to aggregating capabilities perceived as necessary to balance the internal threat. Ole R. Holsti, P. Terrence Hopmann, and John

D. Sullivan, *Unity and Disintegration in International Alliances: Comparative Studies* (New York: John Wiley & Sons Publishing, 1973), 94–95 and 100–102.
53. Due to the fluid situation in Syria and inability of journalists to access areas and interview individuals as well as verify reports, it is difficult to corroborate statistics regarding bandwagoning (defections) as well as their impact onto alliance effectiveness. For a running estimate of "high-level" defections, see "Interactive: Tracking Syria's defections," *Al-Jazeera*. Available here: http://www.aljazeera.com/indepth/interactive/syriadefections. Various news reports since the beginning of the internal conflict evidence that army officers, cabinet officials, and others have defected. For example, see Suleiman Al-Khalidi, "Syrian army defectors say Assad regime crumbling," *Reuters*, July 18, 2012.
54. Interview with author, Rafael Pardo, former Minister of Defense of Colombia, Bogota, Colombia, October 2012.
55. Following Escobar's escape, the USA and Colombia worked closely to track him down and kill him, demonstrating the ability of the USA and Colombia to closely cooperate and coordinate their policies and activities. The effort involved collaboration by the CIA, DEA, and their counterparts in Colombia. Interview with author, Rafael Pardo, former Minister of Defense of Colombia, Bogota, Colombia, October 2012.
56. Astri Sukre, "Reconstruction as Modernization (2007), 1299–1300.
57. For a detailed overview of "structured, focused comparison," see Alexander and George and Bennett, *Case Studies and Theory Development* (2005), 67–73.

CHAPTER 2

US–Colombia Internal Threat Alliance (1980–2010)

This chapter applies the theoretical framework presented in Chap. 1 to the US–Colombia internal threat alliance. It traces US–Colombia cooperation over the course of 30 years to defeat Marxist rebels and secure associated US interests. It shows that the Colombian government sought US assistance to thwart rising threats from rebel groups and drug-trafficking organizations, while the USA aligned in order to safeguard interests linked to the regime's stability including curbing drug flows onto American streets, maintaining access to oil reserves, and preserving stability in its "backyard." The chapter demonstrates that in internal threat alliances, it is simplistic to ask whether states balance or bandwagon. Instead, they do both at the same time. While some elements of the Colombian National Police fought against drug traffickers (balanced), others actively colluded with them (bandwagoned). While some mayors resisted guerrilla incursions, others supported the belligerents. Finally, it demonstrates that alliance effectiveness was higher during the administrations of Colombian Presidents Andrés Pastrana and Alvaro Uribe because the alliance amassed resources (via *Plan Colombia*) sufficient to reduce the internal threat and because Pastrana and Uribe's increased (compared to prior presidential administrations) efforts to identify and eliminate actors (within civilian or security agencies) who were colluding with the "narco-guerrilla" threat.

The chapter begins with a brief historical overview of the alliance and discussion of the characteristics of the Colombian state. It then examines the formation, bandwagoning within, and effectiveness of the alliance in order to evidence the theoretical framework's core arguments.

US–Colombia Internal Threat Alliance (1980–2010):
Historical Overview

From the "Brink of Collapse" to "Turning the Tide"

The USA and Colombia began to bring their security policies into close cooperation in the 1960s in response to threats each state perceived from a surge in Colombia's internal violence. This political violence is rooted in a civil war (*La Violencia*)[1] between supporters of the Liberal and Conservative Parties that, since its inception, has claimed between 50,000 and 200,000 lives and internally displaced 3 million.[2] Two main actors emerged through this conflict that threatened the Colombian state and associated US interests: (1) leftist guerrilla groups that aimed to topple various Colombian presidential administrations, principally the *Fuerzas Armadas Revolucionarias de Colombia—Ejército del Pueblo* (Revolutionary Armed Forces of Colombia or FARC) and the *Ejército de Liberación Nacional* (National Liberation Army or ELN), and (2) narco-trafficking "cartels" who regularly attacked Colombian officials, sowed fear, and produced/transported narcotics that took American lives and provided funding to the guerrillas.[3]

Initially, the USA sought to cooperate militarily with Colombia as part of Plan LASO (Latin American Security Operation) that aimed to eliminate the "leftist" guerilla movements in order to balance Soviet influence in the Hemisphere.[4] As the Soviet Union waned, though, and guerrilla forces, drug traffickers, and associated political violence they wrought began to surge, the threat to the great power and the regime (and thus dynamics of the alliance) began to change.

Facing a narcotics "epidemic" in the 1970s and with drug traffickers exploiting Colombia as a transshipment point for cocaine,[5] the USA decided to balance this threat by attacking drugs "at their source." The Andean nation became ground zero for the great power's "war on drugs"[6] and the regime (and therefore its survival) vital to balancing this threat. As a result, the USA and Colombia further aligned their security policies and agreed that the USA would provide military and other resources for Colombia to balance the threat from narcotics and actors involved in the trade: "The combination of leftist guerrilla activity with the narcotics industry...added a major dimension to what was already viewed as a security threat...officials treated the guerrilla movement as a threat to Colombia, the U.S., and the region."[7]

Through the administration of US President Ronald Reagan (1981–1989), US threat perception and associated decisions vis-à-vis Colombia were informed by the need to balance the Soviet Union's influence in America's "backyard" and curb the flow of drugs onto US streets. And in the administration of Colombian President César Turbay (1978–1982), the USA found a like-minded ally whose hardline approach to the guerrillas made "him consistent with the views and policies of the Reagan administration."[8] Closely consulting the USA, Turbay gave the army "carte blanche to crack down on communist guerillas and other lawless elements"[9] and signed into law a treaty allowing the extradition of narco-traffickers to the USA for prosecution.[10]

As the Reagan administration gave way to the presidency of George H.W. Bush (1989–1993), the alliance changed in full to an internal threat alliance. As the Berlin Wall fell, the basis for the alliance officially morphed. What began as an alliance based on the great power's need for Colombia as a means to balance the Soviet Union and preserve territorial security (and rooted in Colombian regimes' need for military capabilities to thwart groups attempting to topple the government and weakening its economy) changed to one motivated primarily by high levels of political violence (and its consequences) common to both allies.

If the states were only motivated to combat an external enemy, security cooperation between the USA and Colombia should have stopped with the Soviet Union's demise. But instead, it escalated: "Despite the end of the Cold War, U.S. military aid has not only continued but towards the end of the 1990s it radically increased and made Colombia the third largest recipient of U.S. military aid in the world."[11] Building from prior engagement, the two states continued to work together to devise strategies to weaken and defeat insurgent forces and narco-traffickers and, by the late 1980s, were engaged in an internal as opposed to external threat alliance. As Randall argues, "The combination of guerrilla activity with the narcotics industry...was viewed as a major national security threat," leading the USA to "assist Colombia in containing armed insurrection."[12] The USA viewed political violence in Colombia as a threat to its ally's survival, and this threat perception drove the USA to form (and maintain) an alliance whose core motivation was to preserve the regime and thereby safeguard American interests associated with it.

Despite work to quell violence and dismantle burgeoning drug-trafficking outfits, the Medellin and Cali drug cartels increased in influence and operational capability. This brought renewed concern from the USA that its ally may fall. Echoing the US Ambassador to Colombia's cable noting that increased violence was "threatening to topple the state,"[13] domestic US policy-makers began calling for further US action to shore up its ally and curb this challenge to national security. Representative of such demands are remarks by US Congressman Charles Rangel, who said: "If Colombia falls, we could find ourselves an island of democracy in a sea of narco-political rule."[14]

This escalation in "narco-terrorist" violence during the Virgilio Barco (1986–1990) presidency pushed the USA and Colombia closer together and into an "*abrazo de oro*" [golden embrace], where "Bogotá needed Washington's cooperation" and the USA needed the Barco administration's cooperation to pursue what had become a "top national security priority" of curbing drug flows into the USA[15] As part of this enhanced alignment, the USA provided funding and training to better equip the Colombian military and police to offensively combat the FARC as well as dismantle the Medellin and Cali drug cartels.[16] In accordance with the Bush administration's regional strategy (the "Andean Initiative") to quell narco-trafficking, the USA augmented assistance to Colombia including $65 million in emergency military aid to help Colombian security forces regain control territory held by the FARC and drug traffickers.[17] Though official US policy-stated funds were only for use against narcotics trafficking, "a significant amount of U.S. assistance" was "employed to combat the guerrillas."[18]

Political priorities and regime-specific interests hindered cooperation somewhat during the Barco and then Cesar Gaviria (1990–1994) administrations. Nonetheless, the USA and Colombia were still able to devise alliance strategy and tactics and carry out associated activities because these Colombian administrations needed to demonstrate progress to key political supporters and the citizenry against the guerrillas *and* narcos to ensure political survival. The USA continued to cooperate because it needed a stable regime in place to curb drug flows.[19] As a result, by the end of Gaviria's term, the "foundations of a good working relationship" had been established and associated enhanced cohesion yielded alliance victories, including the capture and killing of Medellin drug cartel boss Pablo Escobar.

In spite of such advancements, however, alliance effectiveness remained low. Insufficient military resources and collusion (bandwagoning) by elements of the Colombian government (notably the police and components of the Judiciary) with insurgents and narco-traffickers hindered the alliance's ability to weaken or defeat the insurgents and narco-traffickers. By the time Colombian President Gaviria left office, FARC attacks were at levels not seen under prior presidents.[20] Even though the infamous Pablo Escobar was dead, other drug-running outfits filled his void and continued to sow fear and violence. US and Colombian interests were far from secure.

Relations between the allies deteriorated with the election of Ernesto Samper (1994–1998) due to suspicion among core US policy-makers that Samper colluded with drug cartels. This was confirmed when evidence surfaced that Samper had accepted $6.1 million from a cartel for his presidential campaign. This so-called "Processor 8000"[21] case/scandal[22] sent US–Colombia relations into a tailspin: "The country went through four years of relative international isolation, as an historic alliance...was interrupted by constant and public confrontations between Washington and Bogota."[23] The USA needed a central Colombian government committed to defeating the narco-insurgents and began publicly recriminating Samper in an attempt (according to some) to discredit the president domestically and internationally so that he would resign or be impeached and be replaced with a more reliable president prone to balancing (rather than colluding with) their common enemy.[24]

The USA deemed Colombia not sufficiently cooperative in counter-narcotics efforts and "decertified" it. As a result, Colombia was in 1996 and 1997 ineligible to receive US assistance for anti-narcotics efforts fight in this area.[25] Partly as a result of the nearly complete stoppage of resource flows to Colombia and tense relations between the allies, which hindered their operations, the guerrillas were given a window in which to expand their reach throughout the country: "By placing Colombia in the decertification doghouse and regularly bashing Samper, [U.S. President William] Clinton created a schism in Bogota that ruptured the credibility of the government and allowed the armed groups in the civil conflict to multiply their presence inside the borders of the nation...the bullying of Bogota aided the guerrillas."[26] As Samper stepped down, Colombia had reached a near "failed state" scenario with the "FARC at its zenith and the Colombian military at its all-time low."[27]

It was in this state of hyper-violence that Andrés Pastrana (1998–2002) campaigned for president and won on a "strong peace platform" and promises to end decades of conflict. As he took office in 1998, Colombia faced a surge in political violence arguably not witnessed since the early days of the nation's civil war.[28] Unless Colombia's Army was "drastically restructured" and strengthened, it faced an "absolute defeat within five years" from "drug-financed Marxist guerrillas," according to a leaked US Intelligence Report.[29] A US military official who in 1997 assessed the "strength of the Colombian state" echoed this by telling me that Colombia "was on the brink of failure" and needed "increased assistance from the U.S. to prevent its full collapse."[30]

Pastrana's administration had a clear view on why prior presidents failed to weaken the "narco-terrorist" threat. Informed by this position, his administration assumed a different approach and policy agenda to do so: negotiate from a position of power and, if that fails, have the military means to wipe out the belligerents.[31] Further diverging from prior presidential administrations, Pastrana openly recognized the link between the insurgents and narco-traffickers, and that to defeat the former, his regime needed to curb cocaine-linked financing. As he said, "To achieve peace in Colombia...we needed to strengthen all the programs related to the fight against narcotics, because they were the main financial sources of the illegal armed groups." Accordingly, Pastrana's advisors began developing a strategy to balance the "narco-insurgent" threat (later developed into *Plan Colombia*). A prerequisite for implementing the plan, however, was amassing the financing and resources necessary to expand Colombia's security forces. And in the administration of US President Bill Clinton (1993–2001), Pastrana found a great power ready to assist, secure its interests tied to the regime, and sharing Pastrana's view on the conflict: "Growing U.S. recognition of the insurgent threat turned Colombia into a top national security priority" and (through 1998/1999) "support among U.S. policy makers for a more direct role in the Colombia counterinsurgency effort grew considerably."[32] Colombian and US threat perception at this point was closely aligned. As Clinton said in a press conference with Pastrana: "The narcotics trade and the civil conflict have fed off each other as rebels" do business "with violent drug traffickers" making the "fight" against them "our joint responsibility."[33] Noting why US assistance was justified to balance this threat, Jesse Helms, Chairman of the Senate Foreign Relations Committee, said that "well-armed narco-terrorists" posed such a threat that "without U.S. help," Colombia could "lose this war."[34] Early in Pastrana's term, a common refrain among core US policy-makers was: "This is our war as much as Colombia's."[35] And Pastrana clearly shared the US assessment, stating that "narco-terrorism" was the main threat to Colombia and a "common enemy" he and USA had to "unite our efforts to fight."[36]

In 1998, as peace negotiations between Colombia and the guerrillas were ongoing but appearing likely to break down, the USA and Colombia formed a bilateral working group "to facilitate increased U.S. training, sharing of aerial and satellite intelligence data" and to generate strategies for "the modernization of the Colombian military."[37] Building from task force recommendations,[38] the USA provided $289 million in military capabilities to Colombia for their security forces' campaigns against the "Unholy Alliance" of guerrillas and narco-traffickers.[39] After this military aid proved inadequate to stifle political violence, the USA and Pastrana agreed that further military resources were required and began discussing a strategy that would eventually become *Plan Colombia*. Following high-level meetings between US and Colombian delegations,[40] and after US officials publicly called for a new strategy (and escalation in military aid) to balance the narco-terrorist threat, Pastrana released the broad contours of his regime's "Marshal Plan for Colombia": a $7.5 billion initiative to lessen violence by increasing military capacity to defeat drug traffickers/guerrillas and addressing sources of violence through economic development.[41]

Informed by prior discussions with Pastrana and his plan, in 2000 Clinton announced a proposed $1.6 billion aid package for Colombia, asserting to Congress that the majority of resources therein would enhance the capacity of Colombia's military through training and new equipment (mainly helicopters) for two new specialized army battalions. After being decreased, the US Congress approved the $1.3 billion *Plan Colombia* aid package.[42] By the end of Pastrana's term, cohesion was high and the allies had weakened the belligerents, but not to the point they no longer threatened regime survival and US interests. Nonetheless, US-Pastrana relations "laid the foundation" for "an even closer, more effective alliance" between the successor to Pastrana (Alvaro Uribe) and US President George W. Bush (2001–2009).[43]

When Uribe (2002–2010) took office, Colombia remained under a consistent and formidable threat from opposition forces. Though Pastrana and the USA had developed and began pooling military resources according to their *Plan Colombia* strategy, insurgent attacks reached all-time highs in

2002.⁴⁴ Colombia's security forces were still not up to the task of weakening the narco-insurgents. This rising threat affected alliance dynamics by making it more urgent for the USA and Colombia to find a solution to dampen political violence and pushed Uribe and Bush together to do so. Increased threat level certainly increased alliance cohesion. However, it also escalated because Uribe strongly desired a second term, needed to bolster domestic support to pass the required constitutional amendment to allow presidential re-election, and therefore urgently needed to strengthen his military to be able to secure immediate results vis-à-vis the insurgency. This pushed Uribe closer to the USA and to strategically agree (as Pastrana had already begun to do) to cast the narco-*belligerents* as narco-*terrorists* to ensure the USA would augment its flow of military aid. And in the Bush administration, he found a great power ready to assist and secure its interests tied to the regime. As Bush said, "we stand with the Colombian people in their fight against narco-terrorists who threaten their democratic way of life."⁴⁵

Following the 9/11 attacks, the USA viewed "ungoverned spaces" in general and those proximate to the American homeland particularly as a national security threat because terrorists could exploit them (as in Afghanistan) to launch attacks onto US interests. As reflected by Ann Patterson, US Ambassador to Colombia: "*Plan Colombia* continues to be the most effective anti-terrorist strategy we could ever have designed," as the 9/11 attacks turned US "attention to linkages with international violence; that includes terrorism, drug trafficking, money laundering and organized crime."⁴⁶ Linked to this, the USA classified the FARC as a national security threat and "the most dangerous international terrorist group based in this hemisphere."⁴⁷ As per the 2002 US National Security Strategy, insurgents threatening regime survival were terrorists, drug-trafficking their key source of financing, and the USA needed to shore up its ally to defeat both.⁴⁸

Recognizing the increase in threat from instability in Colombia, and within the post-9/11 context, US domestic policy-makers augmented the "state power" available to the alliance by authorizing all capabilities to be applied as a "unified campaign" against "narco-trafficking and against activities by organizations designated as terrorist organizations."⁴⁹ This "expanded authority" enabled Bush and Uribe to openly use capabilities against the guerrillas ("narco-terrorists").⁵⁰ To be sure, since the 1980s the allies had used alliance resources against both actors; however, the change enabled the USA "to be more transparent with regard to the enemies it defined" and "present a more overt strategy for dealing with them."[51]

As part of the ongoing *Plan Colombia*, the USA and Uribe devised a strategy and associated tactics to weaken the "narco-terrorist" FARC that eventually took the form of Uribe's new national security strategy, the Democratic Security and Defense Policy (DSDP). The core of the DSDP strategy, which drew criticism from domestic and foreign human rights groups,[52] was to crush the guerrillas and "consolidate" state control throughout Colombia's territory.[53] As part of the DSDP, Colombia launched an extensive military offensive (*Plan Patriota*), developed with the USA and supported by 800 American advisors, to dislodge the FARC from urban areas and subnational strongholds.[54] US SOUTHCOM assisted the Defense Ministry in "operational and logistical support" and "security planning" and trained Colombian military units.[55] Further, the USA trained approximately 2000 Colombian troops in skills specific to weakening the narco-terrorist threat, and[56] ally agencies devised (and Uribe implemented) a restructuring of Colombia's Army.[57]

In 2002, in part to increase the effectiveness of Colombia's military operations, Bush signed US Presidential Directive 18, which expanded intelligence sharing with Colombia from only "drug-related targets" (as allowed under Clinton) to all US-gathered intelligence including "tactical information such as insurgent groups' movements and locations."[58] Uribe needed to generate immediate results to advance his re-election prospects and leveraged this "flood" of intelligence and new military hardware to conduct "an unprecedented effort to identify and kill those individuals orchestrating the violence for the narco-terrorists."[59] Uribe also increased extraditions.[60] During this same period, the USA and Colombia devised and began implementing *Plan Colombia's* non-military component, the National Consolidation Plan (NCP), which aimed to decrease threats to the regime by distributing social/economic assistance in cleared areas to prevent a recurrence of violence.[61] In 2005 *Plan Colombia's* mandate ended, but the threat remained; accordingly, the USA funded a three-year extension [Plan Colombia Consolidation Plan (PCCP)] to enable the regime to continue balancing the "narco-terrorists."

As Uribe prepared to leave office (having won a second term), alliance effectiveness was high. Though minor disagreements occurred,[62] the allies had weakened the narco-terrorist threat and accomplished "goals thought impossible in 1998."[63] The guerrillas and narco-traffickers no longer posed a threat to regime survival, Uribe had secured the amendment to allow and won a 2006 presidential election, and the USA had stabilized its Andean ally, removed terrorist safe havens, and secured increasingly significant oil stores.[64]

Characteristics of the Colombian State: Internal Fragmentation, Multiple Actors, and Competing Interests

Before proceeding to examine the dynamics of this alliance, it is first necessary to explore the characteristics of the weaker state. As noted in Chap. 1, neoclassical realism holds that *states (in particular those outside of the West) are frequently* not *cohesive but, rather, fragmented and in some cases prone to instability* because they lack a monopoly on the legitimate use of force within their borders.[65] As such, the internal composition of these fragmented states—and the factors motivating actors therein—will influence their foreign policy decision-making.

In line with the characteristics of weak states involved in internal threat alliances, Colombia lacked strong state institutions, firm control over those agencies that exist, or a writ that extends throughout its complex topography. This weakness stems partly from a history devoid of centuries of state-building, where a lack of external threats meant government actors were not compelled to create institutions to protect the nation and by extension command loyalty from the populace.[66] Over time, Colombia would develop central agencies charged with maintaining a monopoly on the use of force; however, this "consolidation of a central state" was a "slow and difficult accomplishment" given the nation's "daunting geography" and "weak, outwardly oriented economy," among other factors.[67] The products of Colombia's state formation relevant to alliance dynamics would be twofold: first, bureaucratic agencies that were weak, corrupt, and did not always act to advance the central regime's interests and a central regime that could not wholly control their actions, and, second, a fragmented nation characterized by subnational systems of political and economic power, the state actors in which prioritized *their* interests (e.g., patron-client ties, survival, or a share in the spoils of victory) over the central regime (and eventually alliance strategy). As Bejarano and Pizarro (2004) argue, where the "central state has severely contracted" at the subnational level, there are "unparalleled opportunities for accumulation of group and personal power and wealth" where actors "invest heavily in controlling or overcoming their competitors in order to enjoy the advantages of power within a secure and expanding territory."[68]

For the period examined, Colombia's *central regime* was comprised of the president and his cabinet.[69] These actors worked with the USA to align security policies and agree to alliance strategy and tactics. The Executive has authority to formulate (and quickly alter) foreign and defense policy, enabling these alliance-relevant policies to change quickly from one presidential administration to the next.[70] The implication for alliance dynamics, and combined with (until 2004) single-term limits on the presidency, was that the USA faced an ally whose policies, political priorities, and preferred strategies turned over rapidly.

The *core bureaucratic agencies* involved in devising alliance strategy and carrying out agreed tactics were the Ministries of National Defense and Interior and the National Army and Police.[71] Technically, Colombia's Ministry of Defense controls the Army. However, Colombia's lower level of development and political history combined to grant them greater autonomy in terms of policy planning and activities, especially in subnational areas.[72] This is rooted in reforms in the 1940s/1950s aimed to "depoliticize" the armed forces which had the unintended consequence of providing a degree of autonomy more "than would be desirable within a democratic regime."[73] As Bejarano (2011) argues, over time "Colombia's civilian elite openly abdicated their responsibility in terms of formulating and implementing defense and security policy, therefore granting the military key reserved domains in these policy-making areas."[74] The military's autonomy "consistently expanded" and includes "capturing and preserving" key "domains in the areas of internal security and public order."[75] Through the period examined, the military continued "to have a powerful veto on matters of internal security."[76] Leveraging this autonomy from the central regime and to maximize resources flowing into their coffers, the military and police (and components therein) would take actions (including violating central regime guidance) to jockey for a greater share of the defense budget.

Colombia's fragmented character is aptly encapsulated by Geddes (1994), who argues that analysis of the state in Latin America generally, and Colombia particularly, assumes that states "behave as unitary actors," whereas "in reality, they often do not." The issue is not that the level of development is so low that there is *no* state or, as she says, "that there is 'no there there,'" but instead that there are "*too many theres there*"—the fragmented state is comprised of component parts not necessarily under the control of a central government, "each having different capacities, intentions, and preferences."[77]

In sum, the state's fragmented character meant that agencies leveraged their autonomy and made decisions (and used government resources) to advance their interests rather than alliance goals. What is more, the further *intra*-fragmentation of ministries and security forces meant that specific components therein (e.g., "Police unit A") may be balancing the threat, but others ("Police unit B") could simultaneously be colluding with that same enemy.

Various scholars of Latin American politics and history have documented the root causes and presence of patron-client relations (clientelism) in Colombia as well as its effect onto the Andean nation's politics, governance, and economic development.[78] A full review of these texts is beyond the scope of this chapter and marginal to its central analysis; however, a brief outline of the causes and main manifestations of clientelism (relevant to driving actions by regime elements) in Colombia is necessary to demonstrate its influence onto alliance dynamics.

Lacking a strong central state apparatus and faced with a vast and mountainous topography, Colombia was unable (and for years made few attempts) to extend its writ throughout its territory; individuals therefore forged loyalty to powerful actors in their given region as opposed to the national interest. Though state weakness in some ways enabled clientelism to emerge, the contours of these relations—the identity of the patron and forms of patronage—and their affect onto politics and decisions made by regime actors evolved over time. Initially, patron-client relations were rooted in "*caciquismo*" or loyalty to an individual strongman, generally a large land-holding elite.[79] For these regional elites and their clients, "local power was more important than the abstract concept of a nation-state."[80] The effect was to firmly embed a sense of loyalty—and thereby influence onto decision-making—to regional powerbrokers over a central state or national interest/identity. As the country's main political parties emerged and their reach into subnational areas grew, party leaders largely supplanted regional strongmen as primary patron. Relations in these areas evolved into a clientelistic system based on party patronage. Regional and local leaders received patronage (money, regime posts) in exchange for mobilizing votes for party leaders in Bogotá, while individuals and the state institutions they ran prioritized fealties to party over the national interest or other considerations.[81] The effect was that "when Colombian leaders had to choose between their need for political survival [clientelism] and longer-term interests in regime stability [building the state], they chose the former."[82]

As Colombia modernized the basis of clientelism morphed again. The state became patron: "Rather than the dominant party," the state "would provide services in the best clientelistic tradition, with support presumably flowing throughout the formal hierarchical structure."[83] Drug-trafficking's rise further consolidated (including among government actors) prioritizing patron-client relations over the national interest: "Along with the new resources these actors [drug traffickers] injected…they also helped create new regional alliances, linking sectors of the security forces, traditional party cadres, drug traffickers, and local elites behind private violence."[84] These regime actors favored relationships that would enhance their personal wealth and power as opposed to loyalty to the state, and drug-trafficking revenues enhanced the incentive to do so.

Political and economic "decentralization" reforms (1988–1991) changed the contours of clientelism further.[85] By increasing the amount of public funding going to local governments and the control subnational officials had over these monies, the reforms swelled the pool of resources guerrillas could attempt to extort from subnational officials. This also further incentivized attempts to press regime representatives to bandwagon (for survival or clientelism). As a result, "the same patronage practices that used to bolster the traditional parties alone now benefit the FARC."[86]

The detailed trajectory of Colombia's variant of clientelism aside, this process yielded two products that continued to make regime actors choose their interests and patron-client relations over loyalty to the national interest (and thus colluding with narco-belligerents, rather than working to defeat them) during the period examined and are directly relevant to examining alliance dynamics. First, it firmly entrenched and incentivized prioritizing increasing power/influence over the national interest and therefore colluding with non-state actors over working to defeat them: "the allegiance…to patron was more basic than identification with an amorphous national identity known as Colombia."[87] And second, regionally based power structures emerged where maximizing personal power/influence via fealty to patron/client trumped loyalty to the central government (and alliance) or national interest. Referred to as "political archipelagoes," mini "mafia" states, or regional "control systems," these subsystems based on maximizing personal power/influence over alliance goals motivate regime agencies to contravene orders from the central regime: "It is at the regional and local level that the political archipelagoes are most evident with politicians from those areas with different power bases than the national president, hence at times likely to oppose (either overtly or covertly) what the chief executive is trying to do."[88]

In sum, Colombia was a fragmented nation characterized by subnational systems of political and economic power; relationships therein incentivized actors involved in the alliance to go against orders of the central presidential administration.

Having provided an overview of the alliance period and characteristics of the Colombian state, the following sections apply the theoretical framework to the case. In so doing, they evidence the three main parts of the framework related to alliance formation, bandwagoning, and alliance effectiveness.

ALLIANCE FORMATION

In Washington's eyes, the Colombian government was fighting for its survival.[89]

The purpose of this section is to evidence the theoretical framework's first core argument: that internal threat alliances will form in response to a threat that *is domestic in origin* and imperils the survival of a weak state's leadership regime. The weaker state's leadership will seek cooperation because it needs military or economic resources to thwart challenges to its existence, while the great power will become involved in order to safeguard interests linked to the regime's stability or survival. To address each part of this argument, the section first demonstrates that the USA and Colombia formed an alliance in response to a threat consisting of high level of political violence generated by insurgents and narco-traffickers. It then demonstrates that the core motivation underlying US/Colombia alignment was to ensure the regime's survival and the great power's interests associated with it. In so doing, the discussion below demonstrates that by 1991 the USA and Colombia had shifted from an alliance motivated principally by the need to balance an external threat (the further spread of Communism via formation of another Soviet satellite state) to one based on a *common* threat from *within* the weaker state. Table 2.1 illustrates this shift from external to internal threat alliance.

Table 2.1 US–Colombia Alliance Formation: From External to Internal Threat Alliance

	Threat / Motivation for USA	Threat / Motivation for Colombia	Type of Alliance
1960s to early 1970s	(Threat): Soviet Union disrupting balance of power (Motivation): Ensure regime survival to balance Soviet influence	(Threat): Political violence from guerrillas (Motivation): Obtain capabilities to ensure physical/political survival	External threat alliance
Late 1970s to 1980s	(Threat): Political violence from guerrillas and narco-trafficking; Soviet Union disrupting balance of power (Motivation): Ensure regime survival to ensure regional stability, stem flow of drugs, and maintain access to oil	(Threat): Political violence from guerrillas (Motivation): Obtain capabilities to ensure physical/political survival	Internal threat alliance
1991 to 2010	(Threat): Political violence from guerrillas and narco-trafficking (Motivation): Ensure regime survival to ensure regional stability, stem flow of drugs, and maintain access to oil	(Threat): Political violence from guerrillas (Motivation): Obtain capabilities to ensure physical/political survival	Internal threat alliance

Profile of the Internal Threat: *Insurgents and Narco-traffickers Imperiling Regime Survival and US Interests*

The threat that spurred the USA and Colombia to bring their security policies into close cooperation (form an alliance) consisted of political violence from insurgents and narco-traffickers that endangered regime survival (physical and political) and the consequences such instability posed to US interests.

This political violence is rooted in a civil war ("*La Violencia*")[90] between supporters of the Liberal and Conservative Parties.[91] Referred to as the "unholy trinity" of "generators of violence," three actors emerged from this conflict that threatened the Colombian regime and associated US interests: (1) the leftist guerrilla groups FARC and ELN that aimed to topple the Colombian regime, (2) narco-trafficking cartels who employed violence that threatened regime survival and produced/transported narcotics that took American lives and provided funding to the guerrillas, and (3) paramilitary organizations that citizens formed for protection against the guerrillas.[92] Though the paramilitaries have their roots in and contributed to Colombia's internal violence, sufficient evidence exists to suggest that the allies largely did not view these actors as a core threat to regime survival. On the contrary, Colombia's military in many cases colluded with them to combat the guerrillas.[93] The paramilitaries' human rights abuses notwithstanding, then, the threat is viewed as principally comprised of guerrilla organizations and narco-traffickers.[94]

Evolution of the "Narco-Guerrilla" Threat

To protect against Conservative Party supporters and their paramilitary "death squads," members of the Liberal and Communist Parties established guerilla units in the Colombian country-side.[95] Though most guerilla groups were demobilized before or killed/captured in a 1964 military offensive, others established five "Independent Republics" in southern Colombia and continued to contest the regime's authority and monopoly on the legitimate use of violence.[96] The ELN was established in 1963 and concentrated in the northeast, while the more formidable FARC was established in 1964 and centered in the southern and eastern regions.[97] Broadly speaking, their goals remained relatively constant: to topple the central Colombian government in order to represent the interests of the rural poor.[98]

A confluence of factors led by demand from US consumers contributed to a boom in cocaine production in Colombia in the 1970s[99] and the emergence of three principal cartels through the late 1990s[100]: Medellin, Cali, and Norte del Valle.[101] This expansion of Colombia's cocaine "industry" posed threats to the regime and associated US interests in three ways that contributed to the formation and maintenance of the alliance between Colombia and the USA

First, the flow of cocaine onto American streets killed US citizens and sucked tax payer dollars to crack down on dealing as well as associated crime and healthcare costs. Second, the cartels targeted and killed representatives of the Colombian regime (national and subnational) and threatened the state's control over the country. The "narco-terrorist"[102] Pablo Escobar and his associates intimidated, kidnapped, tortured, or assassinated rivals and uncooperative government officials who posed obstacles to their enterprise. As an official in the Colombian Ministry of Defense in the 1980s told me in an interview: "The narco-traffickers shook the country to its core and threatened the government's very survival."[103] Cartels exploited a political system rooted in patron-client relations and used bribes to ensure government officials would turn a blind eye to (or actively assist) their operations.

Third and finally, narco-trafficking endangered regime survival by providing an additional source of financing to the guerrillas. As US "Drug Czar" Barry McCaffrey said in the mid-1990s: "It is undeniable that the FARC and ELN are funded with millions of dollars in drug money."[104] Following the influx of drug production into southern Colombia, the FARC generated revenue from cocaine by "taxing" coca farmers and traffickers operating in guerrilla-held territory, leading then US Ambassador to Colombia Lewis Tambs to dub them "narco-guerrillas."[105] In the late 1980s, the relationship between the FARC and narco-traffickers became more symbiotic: "The drug traffickers struck a deal with the guerrillas: lay off the business, and we'll pay the taxes. The rebels charged for everything."[106] By the early 1990s, the USA and Colombian policy-makers essentially viewed the FARC as a "drug cartel" using revenues to grow its military capacity.[107]

In sum, brazen attacks, assassination attempts, and other forms of violence and illicit activity carried out by guerillas and narco-traffickers threatened the physical and political survival of various Colombian presidential administrations (central regimes). These Colombian administrations, lacking the military/economic capabilities necessary to maintain their hold on power, aligned with the USA to obtain resources necessary to do so.

Why the USA and Colombia Aligned: *To Safeguard the Regime and US Interests Associated With It*

Responding to the threat outlined above, the USA and Colombia decided to cooperate in order to weaken the non-state actors threatening their respective interests. For Colombia's presidential administrations, guerillas and traffickers indirectly and directly generated violence that threatened their physical survival and hold on political power. For the USA, Colombia's internal violence threatened their ally's survival as well as sowed instability that enabled narco-traffickers to operate. Colombia has consistently been one of the top sources of narcotics consumed in the USA and in the 1990s was responsible for 90 percent of cocaine on American streets. The flow of narcotics produced in or trafficked through Colombia had real costs for the USA in money and lives: from 1989 to 1999, 100,000 Americans (14,000 annually) suffered cocaine-related deaths; 70 percent attributed to cocaine from Colombia.[108]

In addition to being a core source of cocaine, Colombia was strategically important to the USA for various reasons. In addition to the size of its population, location, and proximity to the Panama Canal, which make Colombia of geostrategic importance, it is consistently in the top ten suppliers of oil to the USA[109] The Andean nation is also a prime trading partner with the USA and major destination for US investment, with annual bilateral commerce averaging $11 billion through 2009.[110] US ability to extract oil and investors' confidence and ability to reap financial rewards depend on political stability there. Further, political violence in Colombia threatens US expatriates and can push individuals to seek refuge and economic opportunities elsewhere. The needs these individuals require upon arrival can strain the resources of the destination state; by 1999 Colombians were the second largest group of illegal aliens in the USA after those from Mexico.[111] Due to these strategic considerations, the USA had an interest in aligning with Colombia to weaken the insurgents and narco-traffickers and ensure regime survival.

The discussion below analyzes policy documents and statements by policy-makers to demonstrate that why the great power/regime aligned was clear and in line with the core motivations for forming an internal threat alliance.

External and Internal Threats (1981–1989): Reagan [USA] and Turbay, Betancur [Colombia]

Through the Reagan administration, US threat perception and associated decisions vis-à-vis Colombia were informed by the need to balance the Soviet Union's influence in America's "backyard" and curb the flow of drugs onto America's streets. Threats from Marxism's potential expansion and the drug trade in the Western Hemisphere were perceived as intimately linked: the USA believed that Communist ally governments in Latin America collaborated with guerrillas in South America to facilitate the drug trade and used financing from these illicit operations to "support insurgencies and subversion."[112] In Colombia, Reagan saw a regime that might fall to the increasingly strong FARC and ELN and become "another Nicaragua or Cuba."[113] Facing skyrocketing consumption of drugs at home, though, Reagan also needed to stem the flow of narcotics onto US soil. In 1982, he declared the "war on drugs."[114] The Reagan administration saw Colombia as a core producer of and transshipment point for narcotics. He also viewed the drug trade as an increasingly important source of financing for the insurgents that threatened to topple the "friendly" Colombian ally. The narco-traffickers and guerrillas were perceived to be collaborating (and in some cases one in the same). If unchecked, these groups had the potential to topple the fragile regime.[115] Safeguarding US national security and interests, therefore, required stopping the flow of drugs into the USA and weakening the non-state actors threatening Colombia's central government. That the USA viewed these elements as a threat to its national security is evidenced in Reagan's April 6, 1986, National Security Decision Directive 221 (NSDD-221):

> The national security threat posed by the drug trade is particularly serious outside U.S. borders...Of primary concern are those nations with a flourishing narcotics industry, where a combination of international criminal trafficking organizations, rural insurgents, and urban terrorists can undermine the stability of the local government...The narcotics trade threatens the integrity of democratic governments by corrupting political and judicial institutions. The effect on U.S. interests from such a situation can range from a regime unwilling or unable to cooperate with counter-narcotics programs to a government that is unable to control key areas of its territory and elements of its own judiciary, military, or economy... The international drug trade threatens the national security of the USA by potentially destabilizing democratic allies. It is therefore the policy of the USA...to halt the production and flow of illicit narcotics, reduce the ability of insurgent and terrorist groups to use drug trafficking to support their activities, and strengthen the ability of individual governments to confront and defeat this threat.[116]

During the same period, the administration of Colombian President Turbay was confronted with burgeoning violence from guerrillas and narco-traffickers. In addition to violence, the narco-trafficking industry was bringing "distortions into the Colombian economy and increasing the drug problem among Colombians."[117] To quell violence and address these issues (among others) necessary to remain in power, Turbay worked with Reagan to "establish a drug control agreement" involving "additional security measures" in subnational areas.[118] That Bogota and Washington were in agreement on the threats they faced, and therefore needed to remain aligned, is further echoed by Randall: "Turbay's perception of the insurgency...made him consistent with the views and policies of the Reagan administration."[119]

When Belisario Betancur became president, his administration shifted Colombia's priorities and associated view on the alliance. However, he still needed capabilities to balance the internal threat and therefore continued to collaborate with the USA "Despite Betancur's goal of non-alignment in foreign policy," Kline (1995) demonstrates, "extradition of Colombian drug dealers to the United State continued."[120] Late in Reagan's term, Colombia further realized that narcotics trafficking, alone and through financing the guerrillas, "affect[ed] both internal stability and the democratic prospective of the country."[121] Different presidential administrations had varying degrees of willingness to work closely with the USA to balance these threats, but all continued to do so because the capabilities provided by the USA were vital to fulfilling political mandates and preserving their hold on power. The USA and Colombian government agreed on the "narco-guerilla link" and to bring security policies into close cooperation and pool resources to balance both non-state actors.[122]

The Shift to Internal Threat Alliance (1989–1993): Bush [US] and Barco [Colombia]

The period when US President H.W. Bush and Colombian President Barco were in office includes the juncture at which the alliance morphed from an alliance driven by the need to balance an external enemy to one centered on defeating an internal threat. Like Reagan, the Bush administration began its term perceiving a dual set of threats from Colombia: its potential to serve as grounds for further Soviet influence in the region and the threat to US national security posed by narco-trafficking, belligerent forces, and political violence that endangered Colombia's stability. Such continuities from Reagan to Bush notwithstanding, the latter administration represents a change in the primary threat the USA perceived from Colombia and therefore basis for alignment. As of 1982 and summarized in NSDD 71, Reagan's "highest priority" vis-à-vis Colombia was *external* and described as "the reduction—and eventual elimination—of the influence and presence of the Soviet Union on its client states in our immediate environs."[123] Similarly, through 1991 the Soviet Union remained a threat to US national security under Bush; however, not in the context of "containing" Soviet influence in the region—an objective associated with territorial survival declared "complete" in a 1989 National Security Decision Directive.[124] By 1989, then, the principal threat from Colombia to US national security had evolved: from Colombia's importance to balancing an external enemy, to perceiving political violence, instability, and narco-trafficking as the *principal* threat to the USA. The August 1989 NSDD 18 demonstrates that instability in Colombia generated by guerrillas/narco-traffickers was the core threat to US national security.[125] The directive made clear that these sources of political violence were a threat because they destabilized and endangered ally regimes in the Hemisphere and killed American citizens addicted to drugs:

> One of the principal foreign policy objectives of this Administration is to reduce, and if possible, eliminate, the flow of illegal narcotics to the United States. The impact of illegal narcotics use on our society has been and continues to be devastating…the violence and corruption of the drug traffickers and their alliance with insurgent groups has had a destabilizing effect on friendly governments. It is thus imperative…that this problem be dealt with aggressively…Colombia…will be the primary focus of our effort … [to assist them to] regain control of their country from an insidious combination of insurgents and drug traffickers.[126]

Despite another change in administration, Colombia under Barco continued to require capabilities to balance internal threats. The regime initially pursued an "ideologically neutral" foreign policy in order to focus on its top priority of growing the (faltering) Colombian economy.[127] As part of this stance, Barco at first distanced himself from the USA for political purposes and refused American requests to extradite Colombian nationals. This reticence soon gave way to close collaboration, however, after the Medellin cartel assassinated presidential candidate Luis Galan.[128] A more hardline stance was required to respond to calls from politically influential actors. Consequently, and recognizing the "key U.S. support being provided to the police to defeat the traffickers," Barco agreed to a strategy in line with US recommendations and ordered an "all-out offensive" against the narco-traffickers: "The death of Galan prompted the Barco government to declare (with support of the Bush Administration) a 'War on Drugs'."[129] Following consultations with the USA, Barco reinstated extradition by executive order.[130]

As the Berlin Wall fell, then, the basis for the US–Colombia alliance officially morphed. What began as an alliance based on the great power's need for Colombia as a means to balance the Soviet Union and preserve territorial security (and rooted in Colombian regimes' need for military capabilities to thwart groups attempting to topple the government and weakening its economy) changed to one motivated primarily by high levels of political violence (and its consequences) common to both countries. As of 1991 the USA and Colombia were engaged in an internal threat alliance. The following section examines one aspect of alliance dynamics after they form—bandwagoning.

BANDWAGONING

The Colombian state is not the sum of its parts but, instead, the interplay of these actors and their competing interests...which would go on to sometimes hamper, and other times help, efforts to bring peace and stability to the country.[131]

It is now clear that the USA and Colombia were engaged in an internal threat alliance. But, how did elements of the Colombian regime act after the alliance formed? Did all of these entities adhere to alliance strategy and seek to defeat (balance) the narco-insurgent threat or did some elements of the Colombian state collude (bandwagon) with the rebels and traffickers? Through examining these questions, this subsection evidences the portion of the theory which argues that balancing (resisting the target threat) and "bandwagoning" (appeasing the target threat) will occur *simultaneously* during internal threat alliances. Actors within the weak state will bandwagon to survive, share in the victor's spoils, or advance patron-client relationships.

The discussion below will demonstrate that elements of the Colombian regime in the capital or subnational areas including police, military, and governors violated alliance strategy and colluded with the non-state actors fomenting violence (narco-traffickers and insurgents) in order to survive, "for profit" (share in the spoils of victory), or to maximize their own power/influence (as rooted in patron-client relations). Even as the USA and various Colombian presidential administrations collaborated to defeat insurgents and narco-traffickers, various Colombian agencies (and components parts therein) were *simultaneously* colluding with these actors.

Bandwagoning to Survive: *Defections and Diverting Alliance Resources*

As part of their repertoire of action aimed at toppling the regime, guerrillas entered subnational areas and threatened civilian (e.g., mayors) and security sector (national police, in many cases) actors to the point they agreed to collude with the insurgents in order to survive. As of 1998, for example, more than 70 percent of mayors in one province indicated that they had to "hand over 10 % of their budgets to finance the narco-FARC" or be "killed or kidnapped."[132] To ensure their survival, representatives of the Colombian state handed over money or agreed to appoint FARC-preferred candidates to positions with control over government coffers. The guerrillas "would tell us to either agree to our terms, resign, or die," one official holding office in the late 1980s said.[133]

Following the decentralization reforms, FARC attempts to force government actors to collude with the belligerents increased. Through 1998, with the aim of obtaining funding for operations, the FARC had become increasingly "involved in the armed oversight of municipal budget administration, which has involved kidnapping and threatening mayors."[134] According to estimates from the Colombian Army, 13 percent of Colombia's mayors through the late 1990s had "direct links" with the FARC or ELN, with a further 44 percent "collaborat[ing] in some form with the insurgency" including by "implement[ing] policies that are favorable to the insurgency" as well as "divert[ing] government funds to the guerrillas."[135] In the Department of Valle de Cauca, for example, by 1998 the threat level from guerrillas pushed the governor, in a move "independent of the national government" (and contrary to alliance strategy), to seek a "peace" deal for his department with the guerrillas. He went so far as to travel abroad to garner international support for the deal.[136] As these mainly subnational elements of the Colombian state were colluding with insurgents in order to survive, central Colombian presidential administrations and other agencies were actively working to defeat the same insurgents.

Narco-traffickers also used violence to push elements of the Colombian state to collude with the cartels in exchange for survival. Escobar's Medellin outfit notoriously harassed, intimidated, and threatened to kill regime actors and their families until they agreed to turn a blind eye to trafficking and production or actively aid in the enterprise. Throughout the "halcyon days of the 1980s and early 1990s," the Medellin cartel "intimidated and murdered scores of Colombian government officials at all levels to protect its drug operations."[137] In a clear example of regime actors colluding with narco-traffickers to preserve their own survival, in 1987 a "thoroughly intimidated Colombian Supreme Court" ruled that that extradition treaty between the USA and Colombia was unconstitutional.[138] As these judges and other regime representatives *colluded with* drug lords to save their own lives, the central regime and components of the police force were simultaneously devising and implementing strategies to *defeat* the narco-traffickers.

Bandwagoning for Power and Patron: *Self-Interest Over National Interest*

Distinct to internal threat alliances, fear for survival or a share in the spoils of victory cannot account for all instances of regime bandwagoning during this period. Interviews and secondary sources indicate that central and subnational regime actors also colluded with narco-traffickers and guerrillas in order to maximize their power or influence (mainly financial).[139] Similar to the examples cited above of bandwagoning to survive, these forms of collusion occurred at the same time as other regime actors were actively attempting to balance the guerrillas and drug traffickers.

In deciding whether to implement alliance strategy and tactics, actors in the capital or subnational areas decided to prioritize augmenting their power and influence and to take action that benefited the patron-client links necessary to do so. This manifested principally in Colombian government representatives accepting financial payment in exchange for passively or actively assisting the armed actors. As Mauceri argues with regard to insurgents and narco-traffickers and their clientelistic ties to the regime at all levels: "The ability of these groups to corrupt state officials and challenge the state's monopoly on violence has...in many ways co-opted the state itself. Either through support, bribery, or intimidation, violent groups have gained influence over mayors, judges, bureaucrats, and other state officials, thus reducing and restricting the policy autonomy of state institutions."[140] The narco-traffickers in particular, one analyst of the conflict noted, "enjoyed enough money, power, resources, and flexibility to efficiently neutralize the government's countermeasures."[141]

Through payoffs to government actors, the narco-traffickers and in some cases the FARC "developed a very effective counter-intelligence network that neutralized most state action against them."[142] By 1980 narco-traffickers had "put dozens of strategic middle-level government bureaucrats on their payroll in order to know the regime's "every move.""[143] Through the 1990s no agency or level of government was immune from these influences. The narcos had "infiltrated politics in all its electoral and non-electoral forms to the point of jeopardizing the stability of the regime" and through pay-offs and other actions "undermined the key state institutions such as the judiciary, the army, and the police."[144] Thereafter and through the 1990s, "traffickers increasingly fueled corruption in the justice, police, and political structures of the country."[145]

According to a former US official involved in the alliance, the influence of patron-client ties "reached the highest levels of government" and made it "easy to bribe government, police, and military officials in exchange for turning a blind-eye to their activities."[146] Indicative of the degree to which regime actors were bandwagoning through the late 1980s, a cartel was able to "hire" a military unit to break into an apartment building in Bogota and kill a rival.[147] Collusion by government actors had by 1998 "penetrated all branches of government, from the national to the local level: dozens of congressmen have accepted drug money in return for providing political protection for the mafias...countless judges have released traffickers because of bribery or intimidation...military officers [have] not been exempt from such temptations."[148] Ambassador to Colombia Curtis Kamman said years later that, in his view, 70 percent of Colombia's Congress was by 1997 "bent": corrupt and influenced by the drug trade.[149]

Colombian state actors continued to collude with insurgents and narco-traffickers during the Pastrana and Uribe presidencies. According to a May 1999 report, police and army elements would allow the FARC to transport trucks filled with military arms for a bribe of $365.[150] Like decisions by regime actors from 1980 to 1997, these police and military actions often went against central regime guidance and made the USA and central Colombian government less able to weaken the internal threat.[151]

Circumventing Bandwagoning Regime Actors

Three specific examples from the Colombian presidential administrations of Barco, Gaviria, and Samper further demonstrate that balancing and bandwagoning occur simultaneously with internal threat alliances and that such bandwagoning generates actions by the allies not found in traditional alliances.

During the Barco regime, he and US President Reagan worked closely together, particularly on devising strategy and tactics to crush the narco-traffickers in general and the Medellin cartel particularly. Although the *central* regime and the great power were able to work closely to defeat their common threat, the Colombian Judiciary hindered alliance efforts to implement an anti-cartel strategy because it was "in the pocket" of and colluding with influential drug lords.[152] The cartels recognized that Barco was committed to extradition and dismantling their operations. The cartels pushed the Judiciary and Supreme Court to not prosecute cartel members out of fear (death threats were levied onto family/friends) or patron-client incentives (cartels paid judges large sums in exchange for favorable court decisions). Bribes, "violence," and "threats thereof" were used "with the goal of paralyzing the justice system."[153] At least partly due to this campaign, Colombia's Supreme Court deemed the extradition treaty unconstitutional.[154] It had become increasingly "clear that the Colombian judiciary" had become "corrupted."[155] Following consultations with Washington, Barco sidestepped the Judiciary and reinstated extradition through an executive order.[156]

Similar bandwagoning occurred during Gaviria's tenure. Despite close collaboration between Gaviria and US President H.W. Bush on strategy and tactics, Colombian police (and some military) elements continued to collude with the narco-traffickers either due to death threats (to survive) or in exchange for bribes (patron-client motivations).[157] This hindered the allies' ability to weaken the internal threat. In order to circumvent these bandwagoning elements, the USA and Colombia formed a police unit of vetted (non-bandwagoning) staff to destroy the cartels. As Gaviria's Defense Minister recounted to me in an interview: "The unit can be viewed as an "island of integrity in a sea of corruption" where the police and the military had links with the drug-traffickers; by creating this special unit, we were able to crush the larger cartels."[158] The implication for allies' ability to achieve their objectives, as Gaviria's Minister of Interior told me during an interview, was that "by creating this unit to get around those actors working with the cartels, we killed Escobar."[159]

Developments during the Samper presidency demonstrate that a *central* regime may bandwagon in order to advance its own interests and generate additional actions not found in (nor applicable to understanding) traditional alliances: a great power bypassing the central leadership to work directly with a (balancing-prone) regime agency.

The USA in 1994 faced another situation not found in traditional alliances: determining how to secure its interests vis-à-vis an alliance, within a country, when faced with a bandwagoning *central* regime. As outlined above, Samper was implicated in colluding with the narco-traffickers, a core target of the alliances. The USA view that Samper's regime was bandwagoning is reflected in testimony on decertification:

> We work with some extremely dedicated Colombian officials who...have continued to attack drug syndicates...these efforts have been undercut at every turn, however, by a government... plagued by corruption [and] fostering corruption to protect themselves.[160]

The testimony also indicates that in order to secure its interests, the USA bypassed Samper and worked with specific (balancing-prone) regime actors ("extremely dedicated Colombian officials") *outside* the central regime, as does the following from a policy-maker who said decertification had "cut the life line of our allies."[161] And indeed, to secure its interests, the USA sidestepped the (bandwagoning-prone) central regime to work directly with regime agencies more prone to balancing (primarily the police but also the Prosecutor General) to weaken the narco-traffickers. While juggling its relations with the central regime, the USA played into the agencies' desire for resources to push the police to balance. As Myles Frechette, US Ambassador to Colombia during Samper's tenure, told me in an interview: "We worked closely with [Police Chief] Serrano and simply bypassed Samper. This is why all was not lost during this period." This US confidence in the police was echoed by Thomas McNamara, former US Ambassador to Colombia, who told me that Colombia was "able to hold up their end of the bargain because of the Police chief."[162] Officials within the Ministry of Interior during Samper's regime echoed this position: "the U.S. trusted Serrano, continued to collaborate as a result of this relationship, and despite strains in the relationship with Samper."[163] Though US relations with Samper's *central* regime were "difficult," its relationship with the police was "excellent," and US assistance "continued to find its way into Colombia" and "almost entirely to support the police."[164]

The above section demonstrated that elements of the Colombian state colluded with the alliance's primary threat (insurgents and narco-traffickers) rather than working to defeat these actors. The following section explains how this influenced the alliance's effectiveness.

ALLIANCE EFFECTIVENESS

The influx of military resources, further alignment of political priorities between Bogota and Washington, and Colombia's culling of crooked actors all combined to turn the tide.

It is now clear that the USA and Colombia were engaged in an internal threat alliance and that components of the Colombian state were actively colluding with the enemy, rather than implementing alliance strategy and seeking to defeat it. But, did the alliance achieve its objectives? Why, or why not, were the USA and Colombia able to weaken the insurgents and narco-traffickers? How did the interests of the various Colombian presidents (e.g., patron-client ties and political priorities) influence their willingness to work with the USA and therefore alliance cohesion and effectiveness?

Through examining these questions, this subsection evidences the portion of the theory which argues that effectiveness of internal threat alliances will depend on whether allies have military resources sufficient to weaken their common enemy *and* are able to control subnational bandwagoning. The principal determinant of internal threat alliance effectiveness will be allies' ability to bring together capabilities sufficient to weaken or defeat the threat. And only when the great power and regime are able to agree on goals, strategy, and tactics and to coordinate activities directed toward those ends (enjoy high alliance cohesion) will they be able to collectively amass resources sufficient to weaken or defeat their common menace. However, alliances will not be effective if the weaker state's leadership is not willing and able to stop their bureaucratic actors from colluding with the enemy. Capabilities *and* curbing bandwagoning must be the recipe for success. In evidencing this argument, the section demonstrates that political priorities or patron-client ties may complicate a central leadership circle's willingness ability to work with their great power ally to define a strategy and associate tactics, and thus decrease cohesion.

To evidence this argument, the section cites examples from 1980 to 2010 and during the following presidential administrations: *Colombia*—Turbay [1978–1982], Betancur [1982–1986], Barco [1986–1990], Gaviria [1990–1994], Samper [1994–1998], Pastrana [1998–2002], and Uribe [2002–2010] and the *USA*—Reagan [1981–1989], H.W. Bush [1989–1993], Clinton [1993–2001], and W. Bush [2001–2009]. The section is divided into two periods demarcated by the different levels of alliance effectiveness. The first period ("to the brink of collapse") runs from the Turbay to Samper administrations (1980–1998), when the threat level remained high and alliance effectiveness was low. The second period ("turning the tide") spans the Pastrana and Uribe administrations (1998–2010), when increased capabilities and more concerted efforts to curb government collusion enabled the USA and Colombia to vanquish the internal threat.

"To the Brink of Collapse": Low Alliance Effectiveness (1980–1998)

During the Turbay presidency (1980–1982), three factors increased cohesion and the allies ability to work together—a surging threat, dependence on each other to balance it, and the Colombian president's need to get a win against the narco-traffickers in order to sidestep a scandal. A report aired on the CBS "60 Minutes" television program alleged that Colombian politicians (including Turbay) had links to the drug-trafficking industry.[165] Turbay needed to "clear his name" and take a hardline stance on drugs in order to salvage his political mandate and avoid speculation that regime was "crooked," could have jeopardized access to export markets for Colombian produce.[166] As a result of this domestic political pressure, Turbay "play[ed] an active role in negotiating the extradition treaty" and controlling the drug trade; this "proactive stance" "inspired" the USA to give the regime "funding and equipment" needed to balance insurgents/narco-traffickers.[167] Though high threat levels certainly drove Turbay closer to Washington, he cooperated mainly because doing so was an asset (not a liability) to his political survival.

Betancur (1982–1986): *Close Alignment Morphs from Political Liability to Asset*
After Betancur's election in 1982, a continued threat kept the allies working together, but their ability to agree on alliance goals, strategy, and tactics deteriorated because the new Colombian president perceived close collaboration as a political liability. As Thomas Boyatt, former US Ambassador to Colombia, said in an interview: "Betancur was more nationalistic than Turbay," and "this put a damper on our relationship."[168] To win and remain in office, Betancur pursued a foreign policy "independent" from the USA, which[169] informed how his administration worked with the USA against the insurgents and narco-traffickers. Diverging from

Turbay's approach (military strategy to defeat the guerrillas),[170] Betancur established negotiations with the guerrillas[171] and agreed to a ceasefire with the FARC.[172] While Turbay had worked closely with Reagan because doing so was a political necessity, Betancur jettisoned anti-communist rhetoric and cooperation on anti-belligerent military efforts because pursuing these avenues would have been a political liability.[173]

Regime political priorities also initially hindered cooperation against narco-trafficking because working closely with the USA on this issue was at odds with Betancur's campaign platform calling for relying on Colombian domestic assets to solve its own problems. Due to this stance, Betancur initially avoided close collaboration with the USA on counter-narcotics initiatives and instead attempted to address the issue with domestic means.[174] He also rejected USA several extradition requests. Linked to the regime's nationalist stance, it viewed Colombia as less militarily dependent on the USA and instead sought support from other countries in the region.

Toward the end of Betancur's tenure, however, the president's calculus changed. Rising violence morphed collaboration with the USA to defeat guerrillas and narcos from a *liability* to regime political survival to an *asset* to salvaging it. A combination of failed negotiations and reports that Betancur was considering reintroducing extradition made internal violence surge: belligerents seized Colombia's Palace of Justice (leaving hundreds dead) and the Medellin cartel assassinated Justice Minister Rodrigo Lara. Responding to this dramatic increase in threat and calls for greater action, Betancur's administration adopted a "militarist" and "overtly repressive strategy against the insurgency,"[175] ended talks with the guerrillas, and agreed to extradite narco-traffickers.[176] The regime needed to curb surging violence to avoid being pushed out of office; this "moved Betancur to bend toward the U.S. pressure" in order to "obtain resources for the war."[177] The 1985 debt crisis and the regime's need for US help to address it also increased cohesion by pushing Betancur "closer towards the USA inasmuch as Washington was crucial for obtaining the $1 billion dollar "jumbo" loan in 1985."[178] In exchange for US backing with the banks, the embattled Betancur cooperated with US counter-narcotics efforts.[179]

Barco (1986–1990): *Political Interests Push Regime/USA into "Golden Embrace"*
Described as a "pragmatic turn" in Colombian foreign policy, Barco's top priority was to grow the faltering economy by maximizing markets for

Colombian exports and access to IMF financing. Barco was initially hesitant to work closely (or overtly) with the USA on military actions against the insurgents because he perceived that doing so would endanger ties important to bolstering Colombia's economy. The USA remained in a Cold War paradigm, and Barco needed to "decontaminate" the internal conflict from external actors.[180] Accordingly, it pursued a negotiated solution (with some military actions) to guerrilla violence, while US President Reagan continued to push a military-oriented approach.[181]

Even as the USA and Barco did not see eye to eye on combatting the insurgents, they closely cooperated on anti-narco-trafficker operations. Narco-trafficking produced violence and commodity distortions that hurt the economy, which was Barco's main political priority; as a result, the Colombian leader was more willing to work with the USA on anti-trafficker operations. As Barco said, the "threat" drug-trafficking posed to Colombia was "a matter of survival of democratic institutions and public liberty."[182] Similarly, for Reagan, the "twin evils" of "narcotics trafficking and terrorism" were the most "dangerous threat to the hemisphere today."[183] As a result of this increased alignment, the USA and Colombia worked closely to eradicate crops and capture (albeit low-level) cartel leaders.

In the second half of Barco's tenure, rising violence from insurgents *and* narco-traffickers pushed Barco closer to the USA. The Medellin cartel assassinated a presidential candidate in 1989,[184] and violence from the FARC and ELN was on the rise,[185] with "the guerrilla groups...clearly hurting the economy."[186] Facing political pressure to mitigate this surge in violence,[187] Barco augmented his government's internal military action against insurgents and decided to work more closely with the US Close cooperation was also in Reagan's interests because quelling both the FARC and cartels was necessary to safeguard a core ally and help curb drug flows into the USA. As a result, the USA and Colombia began what has been described as a "golden embrace."[188] Reagan and Barco worked together to implement several actions that point to the allies' increased ability to devise and then implement strategy, including Barco ordering an "all-out offensive" against narco-traffickers (per US recommendations),[189] Barco issuing an executive order to increase military patrols and penalties for drug offenses,[190] and Barco accepting "more overt and covert military help" from the USA to do so.[191] The allies devised a strategy to dismantle the Medellin cartel[192] and (particularly after Bush assumed office) US funding/training for Colombia's military/police escalated.[193]

Barco recognized that some elements within his government were colluding with narco-traffickers. He fired the National Police Chief over connections with drug traffickers. The Chief's replacement sacked 2075 officers because of similar links.[194] Nonetheless, bandwagoning continued. Many "high-level" regime elements "were on the payroll of the drug groups" and continued to collude with the narco-traffickers.[195] This hindered the alliance's ability to defeat the internal threat.

Gaviria (1990–1994): *Cooperation Increases to Quash "Narco-Terrorism Plague"*

Gaviria inherited a country faced with surging violence and himself faced an assassination attempt from the Medellin cartel during the presidential campaign. As he took office, FARC attacks had increased threefold and the cartels continued to sow violence. Politically, Gaviria's administration needed to respond to this escalation in violence with firm action against the belligerents and cartels. For the USA, this surge in violence was perceived as a threat to its Andean ally. Per US National Security Policy at the time, the USA needed to safeguard Gaviria's administration in order to balance the "threat" from "instability itself" in Colombia.[196] This high level of threat and continued dependence on each other increased alliance cohesion. Yet, the USA and Gaviria were also more able to agree on a strategy that involved militarily confronting the guerrillas *and* narco-traffickers because doing so now aligned with the Colombian president's political interests.

Having attempted to negotiate peace (talks with the guerrillas broke down)[197] and in response to rising belligerent-initiated violence, Gaviria changed his administration's policy (and its political promise to Colombia's people) to a *military* victory over the guerrillas.[198] To do so, he changed the military's mandate from external defense to "internal security" and took domestic measures to accrue resources (a "war tax," among others) necessary to quell the insurgents. A rise in military spending did not yield "increased efficacy in the field of battle,"[199] however, and Gaviria needed supplementary military capabilities to augment security forces, weaken the belligerents, and, by extension, secure his political interests and priorities.[200]

To offset this shortcoming and fulfill his policy agenda, Gaviria turned to closer collaboration with the USA. An increase in cohesion during this period is demonstrated by Gaviria accepting US assistance to reorganize military intelligence gathering against "armed subversion,"[201] the USA allocating

$65 million in (emergency) military aid[202] to help the regime "regain control" of territory,[203] and the USA allowing its military assets to participate in (as opposed to only advise) counter-narcotics military operations including against the FARC [viewed as an extension of the traffickers].[204] Regime political imperatives also drove it to cooperate more fully with the USA to combat "narco-terrorism," which Gaviria described as "the principal threat to our democracy" that "we will confront it without concessions."[205]

Despite a clear escalation in narco-violence, though, the regime was initially reticent to fully adopt the US preferred approach to dismantle Cartels—extradition and robust military force. Gaviria was reluctant to accept this strategy due to formidable political pressure from elites important to the president's political interests who wanted him to strike a deal with the cartels—rather than confront them militarily—as a means to decrease narco-violence.[206] Gaviria relented to the political pressure—because these individuals were vital to remaining in power—and agreed (despite US opposition) not to extradite drug lords in exchange for their agreement to go to prison (including Escobar).[207]

The strategy soon unraveled. Escobar escaped from prison, and his commanders began to employ "violence as a means to money," which involved an uptick in assassinations.[208] After the cartels attacked a wealthy neighborhood of northern Bogota, the same political forces that had urged Gaviria to negotiate with (instead of militarily pursue) the cartels now pushed the president to use military force to vanquish the drug lords.[209] Accordingly, and in order to offset the potentially devastating political blow of Escobar's escape and shore up his political standing with these sectors, Gaviria flipped back to a hardline strategy to crush the cartels. To pursue this approach and salvage political standing, Gaviria sought cooperation with the USA, telling "the Americans as far as he was concerned the door was now open...and would welcome any and all help the Americans could give."[210] The USA was ready to assist. Narcotics trafficking remained a core national security threat in so far as drugs continued to "severely" damage the "social fabric" of US society.[211] In order to stop the flow of drugs onto American streets, the USA needed to crush the cartels and safeguard its ally and worked closely with the regime to do so.

Perhaps more so than his predecessors, the Gaviria administration took proactive steps to curb bandwagoning by, for example, attempting to curb collusion by members of the Judiciary through reforms including "anonymous judges" (so cartels could not target individuals) and creating the Office of the General Prosecutor. Even during this period, however, collusion between government actors, narco-traffickers, and belligerents was present. Armed actors used bribes and other payoffs to "seduce hundreds of important armed forces officers, police officials, judges and political actors."[212] The Commander of the police anti-drug unit and three Ministers of Defense, for example, accepted bribes from the Cali cartel purportedly in exchange for not deploying security forces to disrupt their operations.

Samper (1994–1998): *Central Regime Bandwagons, Sends Alliance into Tailspin*

US–Colombia relations deteriorated with Ernesto Samper's election due to evidence that he colluded with drug cartels. If Samper was acting in the national interest, he would have pursued a hard line against narco-trafficking and adhered to Colombian campaign finance regulations and eschewed any such monies flowing from illegal actors. Instead, he initially waffled on counter-narcotics efforts and accepted $US millions from the Cali cartel to bankroll his campaign.

After determining that Samper's administration was not sufficiently cooperating on counter-narcotics efforts, the USA "decertified" Colombia and in so doing rendered the country (in 1996 and 1997) ineligible to receive US support in this area.[213] Facing calls for his impeachment, Samper's political survival depended on looking "hard on drugs" and pushed him to accept US preferred strategies, which involved using force and extradition against the cartels. In order to secure American interests, the USA exploited Samper's political vulnerability and pushed him to take firmer action against narco-trafficking.[214] As a result of Samper's vulnerability and seemingly due to US pressure, his administration agreed to nominate the US-favored choice for National Police Chief (General Serrano), ordered agencies to execute an "all-out war" against drug traffickers, and passed legislation that reinstated extradition.[215] Further, he took action to curb collusion between government forces, insurgents, and narco-traffickers by issuing a decree to "cleanse" the police of individuals bandwagoning with criminal elements.[216] Samper also authorized the National Police Chief to fire police officers with such links.[217]

Alliance Effectiveness Remains Low as Samper Steps Down

By the end of Samper's presidency, the internal threat level remained high. Various metrics demonstrate this. The number of insurgent forces aiming to topple the regime swelled through 1998: the FARC from a few hundred adherents to 17,000 soldiers and the ELN from a few dozen to 4,500.[218] Insurgents leveraged their increased size to seize and take control of more territory, reflecting an increased threat to the regime. In the late 1970s, the FARC-controlled areas amounting to a few hundred hectares; by the late 1990s, it occupied 40–50 percent[219] of *all* Colombian territory.[220] Reflecting the proximity of threat to the regime, by 1998 the FARC was active in 70 percent of municipalities in the Department of Cundinamarca, which surrounds the capital.[221] Partly due to their increased territorial reach, the FARC increased drug-linked revenues to $551 million annually by 1998.[222] Intensity of the conflict reflected in total annual deaths is also indicative of the threat to the regime and US interests. From 1988 to 1999, annual fatalities never fell below 1200 and rose from 1236 (1989) to 1582 (1996) and then 2710 (1999).[223] By 1999 Colombia was in a state of "hyper-violence with 30,000 murders per year."[224]

The efficiency and brazen nature of insurgent attacks also demonstrate that the proximity and intensity of threat to the regime remained high through 1998: "most observers in Colombia and the United States considered the security situation grave."[225] This "grave" scenario and associated threat level is reflected in a FARC attack in *El Billar* in Caquetá Department (260 miles from Bogota) where 500 insurgents killed 62 soldiers from one of Colombia's most elite brigades.[226] In August 1998 alone, the FARC completed 55 raids onto key regime targets across 18 departments including a US-funded police outpost 250 miles from Bogota where 600 FARC destroyed the base. A few months later, more than 1,000 FARC soldiers crushed a contingent of 150 police and held a town (Mitú) for nearly three days.[227]

Combined, these statistics indicate that the alliance between the USA and Colombia was by 1998 largely unable to weaken the internal threat to the point it no longer represented a threat to the regime and US interests. Alliance effectiveness, therefore, remained low—for two reasons. First, as demonstrated through the above discussion, none of the Colombian presidents had taken actions sufficient to curb government collusion with narco-traffickers and insurgents. As a result, narco-traffickers continued to operate with impunity and, as a result of insider information, one step ahead of US–Colombia anti-drug efforts. Similarly, the FARC remained strong and continued to carry out attacks. Second, the alliance had not pooled resources sufficient to weaken these actors. By the end of the Samper administration, the military and police—the main agencies charged with defeating the narco-traffickers and insurgents—lacked the forces and resources to do so. "The irregular guerrilla war that the military was fighting" was "difficult to win" without creating "mobile ground forces" supported "by an effective air force and navy."[228] Neither of the allies "was willing to assume these costs."[229] Though Colombia's Army had 146,000 soldiers, it was, according to a former US Ambassador to Colombia, "basically a barracks military," not "organized to go after the guerrillas," and essentially "a reaction force, and not a very mobile one at that."[230] Colombia's Air Force was similarly ill-equipped, making it a "fair-weather, daytime" force."[231] The National Police was better equipped, with 87,000 members, 56 helicopters, and 17 fixed-wing aircraft but, even so, unable to deploy to the majority of Colombian municipalities.[232] As a Ministry of Defense official noted, "we simply didn't have the manpower," and this enabled "the FARC and other actors to expand their control of and activities in vast expanses of territory."[233] While the regime was "starved of revenues" due to the recession and "sharp reduction" of aid, belligerents "captured hundreds of millions of dollars in funding from drugs."[234] Combined, the insufficient resources and ongoing bandwagoning mean that the threat level remained high through the end of Samper's presidency (1998) and therefore that alliance effectiveness was low.

"Turning the Tide": Higher Alliance Effectiveness (1998–2010)

Toward the end of Samper's term, with violence levels remaining high, Andrés Pastrana campaigned on a "strong peace platform" that included demilitarizing part of the country for talks with the FARC.[235] Worn down by ever-escalating violence, the Colombian citizenry wanted a "messiah of peace" and elected Pastrana chiefly on his pledge to end the conflict with a combination of resuscitating failed negotiations with the belligerents and applying military pressure. "I assume the leadership to build peace," Pastrana said, "and call on all Colombians to follow and work within the agenda for peace that I am going to direct."[236] Pastrana's administration, recognizing why prior presidents failed to weaken the "narco-terrorist" threat, assumed a different approach (and policy agenda) to do so, fulfill his mandate, and secure its political interests: negotiate from a position of power and, if that fails, have the military means to wipe out the belligerents.[237] But, he first needed to obtain the resources to implement this plan.

In tandem with the aforementioned surge in violence, Colombia was experiencing the worst economic crisis in its history.[238] This pushed Pastrana to sign a $2.7 billion credit deal with the IMF. These and other crisis-related adjustments shrunk Pastrana's pool of resources available to implement his strategy for ending the internal conflict and, in so doing, to advance his political mandate. Pastrana had originally intended to unilaterally drum up resources required for *Plan Colombia* and was pushing this agenda forward to quell calls from politically important urban elite to dampen violence at their doorsteps. However, the fiscal austerity plan meant "Colombia was not in a financial position to pay for the escalation in the civil conflict...and would have to turn to the United States to secure additional military and economic assistance."[239] The recession pushed Pastrana's administration further toward the USA in so far as doing so would help him amass the capabilities needed to carry out *Plan Colombia* and fulfill his campaign promises.

Alliance cohesion increased during 1998 due to the ongoing surge in violence and the allies' dependence on each other to balance it. Yet, cohesion also increased because working with the USA to balance guerillas and narco-traffickers aligned with and would further the Pastrana regime's interests and political survival. For Pastrana, working closely with the USA was a formidable asset to his political prospects: the regime needed US resources to implement its counter-insurgent approach (negotiations plus military action) and therefore agreed to more close collaboration with the great power, specifically on counter-narcotics efforts. As for the USA, it needed Pastrana to dampen drug flows and therefore agreed to help grow Colombia's military and police.[240]

Diverging from prior presidents, Pastrana took more proactive and consistent efforts to curb bandwagoning rooted in patron-client relations. As part of this effort, Pastrana's central government consistently attempted to cull the police and army of elements colluding with either insurgents or the cartels. This included issuing a decree mandating that officers with these links be dismissed from service and subject to further sanction, which led to numerous such expulsions. To assure the army was run by personnel serious about restraining collusion with narco-traffickers and insurgents, Pastrana replaced its head with the more hardline Fernando Tapias, who fired dozens of officers and other high-level officials during his time in office. In addition, Pastrana fired three generals for purportedly colluding with non-state actors.[241] Pastrana's efforts to eradiate collusion, however, did not stop with the military or police: in 1999, for example, he prosecuted the National Drug Council's director due to links with actors threatening the regime and[242] in 2000 fired the intelligence service's director and director of counter-intelligence for bandwagoning with narco-traffickers.[243]

Representing a further shift from prior administrations, Pastrana established two mechanisms to identify and prosecute individuals who were corrupt and diverting alliance resources. First, he formed the Presidential Program to Fight Corruption (*Programa Presidencial de Lucha contra la Corrupcion*)[244] that established interagency coordination to better identify and prosecute individuals involved in the abuse of government resources, including those to be used against insurgents and narcos.[245] Additionally, Pastrana established Colombia's first agency to curb money laundering and continued the process started under prior administrations to further professionalize the police. Pastrana's string of high-profile sackings and decrees diverged from prior administrations, which had at most fired a handful of low-level officers and did not pass relevant reforms (aside from Gaviria's reforms to the Judiciary).

Uribe (2002–2010): *Regime Needs Resources to Secure (Unprecedented) Re-election*

In the wake of Pastrana's failed negotiations, the Colombian citizenry elected Alvaro Uribe largely based on the "appeal of a hardline candidate at a critical juncture in Colombia's internal conflict"[246] and his promise to take an "iron fist" approach to defeat the "narco-terrorist" guerrillas.[247] Unlike prior presidential administrations, Uribe had essentially written off a political solution to insurgent-initiated violence and turned fully to a military campaign to crush the belligerents. The Uribe administration's interests extended beyond fulfilling this political mandate, however, and to seeking an unprecedented (and not constitutionally allowed) second term. Given the single-term limit for Colombian presidents, doing so required amending the country's constitution. To that end, and with an eye toward a second term and associated spoils, Uribe began drumming up support for and pressing the Constitutional Court to allow re-election (approved in 2005).[248]

Fulfilling his political mandate to crush violence and obtain support sufficient to amend the constitution relied on having a military capable of weakening the narco-terrorists and demonstrating immediate results in crushing the insurgency. Political elites would not back amending the constitution to assure a second term for a president that failed to bring greater stability to the nation. Accordingly, Uribe moved closer to the USA and strategically agreed (as Pastrana had already begun to do) to cast the narco-*belligerents* as narco-*terrorists* to ensure the USA would augment the military resources flowing to the regime. And in the George W. Bush administration, he found a great power ready to assist in order to secure US interests tied to the regime.

The surge in violence and dependence on each other to balance it had driven the allies closer together. Cohesion was high, and the allies would devise and implement Uribe's new strategy for quelling violence, however, because working with the USA to balance "narco-terrorists" aligned with and would further the Uribe regime's interests (political survival). Working closely with the USA was an asset to the Uribe administration's political prospects: it needed US resources to implement its military campaign and secure re-election and therefore agreed to more close collaboration with the great power. This extended to publicly backing the US decision to invade Iraq,[249] which was followed by the regime receiving an additional $100 million in military aid for its "struggle against terrorism."[250]

Effectiveness increased during Uribe's administration at least in part because he took actions not seen in prior regimes to eliminate government actors colluding with the enemy. Within his first two weeks in office, Uribe declared a "State of Internal Unrest," which permitted the central government (in addition to levying a "war tax") to use executive decrees to defeat the insurgents, bypass agencies that may decide to refuse to implement alliance strategy, authorize the military (without Judiciary approval) to make arrests without warrants, and establish subnational areas under military (not civilian) rule.[251] The USA fully backed this move.[252] Some dubbed this an "authoritarian turn" and against Colombia's *national* interest; however, it was what Uribe needed to ensure unified balancing, crush the insurgents, and therefore secure *his regime's* interests.[253]

In addition to these new efforts, Uribe continued efforts started under Pastrana to remove bandwagoning regime elements. By 2007, for example, Uribe's Defense Minister had fired more than 100 officers and through 2009 purged the military of elements colluding with or supporting actors targeted by the alliance.[254] The Uribe regime convicted former police General Mauricio Santoyo over collusion with narco-traffickers[255] and prosecuted 23 individuals (including former Director of the Army's intelligence branch) for cooperating with narco-traffickers and other actors fomenting violence.[256] To prevent recurrence of bandwagoning,

Uribe passed legislation that prohibited individuals prosecuted for collusion with the enemy from re-entering the regime.[257]

Building from Pastrana's anti-corruption efforts, Uribe established "*Colombiemos*," a program that enabled citizens to share information on bandwagoning regime elements, and formed a nationwide "citizen informant network" whereby regime actors stationed in subnational areas could inform the central regime of collusion between local officials and guerrilla forces.[258] Pastrana and Uribe proactively purged bandwagoning government actors and established formalized mechanisms to curb such actions. In doing so, they made more concerted efforts to shift what had become widespread bandwagoning to a government whose component agencies and actors were unified in seeking to defeat the internal threat. Uribe's actions represented a marked shift from the willingness exhibited by prior presidents to curb bandwagoning and transform the weak state into a more unified and reliable ally.

Alliance Effectiveness Soars Under Pastrana, Uribe
By the end of Uribe's presidency (2010), the internal threat level was drastically lower. Various metrics demonstrate this. The FARC's size declined from an all-time high in 1998 to fewer than 8000 in 2009 due to deaths (by the military and police)[259] and defections (which increased by 2000 percent).[260] Coupled with this decline in force size, the FARC lost several high-level commanders to alliance operations including its second-in-command, Raul Reyes (2007),[261] and three members of its central committee (2008).[262] The ELN decreased in size by more than half through 2009.[263]

The number of opposition attacks also decreased consistently through 2009. FARC attacks declined by 86 percent from 2002 to 2009 and ELN-initiated attacks decreased by 90 percent during the same period.[264] Other forms of violence that belligerents used to fund operations also declined including acts of "terrorism" [from 1645 (2000) to 46 (2009)][265] and kidnappings [849 (2000) to less than 120 (2006)].[266] Protecting oil interests was a core factor motivating US alignment, and attacks onto oil pipelines decreased from 110 in 2000 to 17 in 2005.[267]

The opposition's control of territory also declined. By 2008 the government controlled 90 percent of territory, up from 70 percent (2007) and 50–60 percent (early 1990s).[268] Significantly, by 2009 the regime controlled the Department of Macarena, once the primary FARC stronghold.[269] FARC-controlled municipalities also decreased from 54 (1998) to 15 (2001) and then to two (2008) and nine (2009). Municipalities with some presence or under some threat (not under opposition control) decreased by more than half through 2009.[270] Reflecting a *decline in the proximity of threat* to the Colombian regime, by 2009 the FARC had no presence (aside from intermittent attacks) in urban areas and was operational mainly in remote border locations.[271] In 2003 the Colombian military "ended the threat to Bogota" in the "largest, most complex, and most successful operation conducted by Colombian forces."[272] The number of municipalities under ELN control declined as well: from 13 (1998) to 8 (2000) and then 2 (2009). FARC profits from cocaine also declined.[273] Combined, these statistics indicate that by the time Uribe stepped down, the alliance was largely able to weaken the threat to the point it no longer imperiled the regime and US interests.

Alliance effectiveness, therefore, was higher during the Pastrana and Uribe presidencies, for two reasons. First, the two administrations more actively, consistently, and effectively prevented or stopped actors within their respective governments from colluding with the insurgents or cartels. And second, the increase in capabilities aggregated by the allies—particularly though *Plan Colombia*—enabled Colombia to weaken the internal threat. Beginning with Pastrana's election, Colombia and the USA were able to consistently work together on all facets of the alliance. For the Pastrana and Uribe administrations, core interests fully aligned with balancing the narco-traffickers and belligerents, and doing so required obtaining capabilities from the USA. In contrast to the fragmented cohesion across prior presidential regimes, during this period cohesion was consistently high and enabled the allies to steadily work together to amass resources and implement strategy. In part due to these resources, higher than those amassed from 1980 to 1997, Colombia's military forces increased in size, effectiveness, and mobility: "the security forces that had been not up to the task of confronting and defeating the insurgents in 1998 dominated the country-side; attacked an enemy reduced in strength by combat actions, desertions, and government programs; and conducted successful hostage rescues and high-value target attacks that demonstrated skillful, professional planning and execution based on actionable intelligence, capable units, and rapid reaction."[274] In turn, these actors were able to weaken the sources of violence to the point they no longer posed a core threat to Colombia's survival and US interests. These capabilities seemed to have tipped the balance in favor of the alliance due to three factors.

First, alliance resources enabled the Colombian government to drastically increase the number of professional soldiers and mobile units trained in tactics specific to balancing the internal threat (the police and military doubled to a combined 500,000 members)[275] and, as a result, to augment the strength, frequency, and success rate of operations.[276] With such capabilities the regime was able to carry out *Plan Patriota* and, with more helicopters, deploy more forces with greater frequency and geographic spread to engage and defeat the guerrillas.

Second, military hardware and intelligence gathering technology transferred to Colombia enhanced the security forces' effectiveness. Military capabilities (and their impact) included transfer of logistics and communications equipment (army more able to coordinate activities and raids), provision of a real-time intelligence through an established satellite-enabled surveillance system (security forces more able to track and target the internal threat), transfer of radar systems to the military (army more able to track guerrilla force movements), and training and armaments for army units targeting guerrillas (skills enhanced battlefield effectiveness).[277]

Third and finally, alliance resources to the National Police enabled Colombia to increase state presence throughout the country. The aforementioned decline in guerrilla presence and increase in government control should be viewed in the context of increased capacity and presence of the National Police beginning in 2002 and then 2004, the first time the police had presence in *all* Colombian municipalities.[278]

In contrast to administrations in office from 1980 to 1997, Pastrana and Uribe increased the degree to which the weak state balanced the alliance's common threat in a unified manner. With the necessary capabilities to balance the threat, and with fewer elements of the regime bandwagoning as opposed to balancing, the alliance was able to weaken the threat to the point where it no longer jeopardized regime survival and associated US interests.

Case Conclusions

In this chapter I used the US–Colombia case to evidence the three main elements of the book's theoretical framework. The chapter traced US–Colombia cooperation over the course of 30 years to defeat Marxist rebels and secure associated US interests. It showed that the Colombian government sought US assistance to thwart rising threats from rebel groups and drug-trafficking organizations, while the USA aligned in order to safeguard interests linked to the regime's stability including curbing drug flows onto American streets, maintaining access to oil reserves, and preserving stability in its "backyard." The chapter demonstrated that in internal threat alliances, it is simplistic to ask whether states balance or bandwagon. Instead, they do both at the same time. While some elements of the Colombian National Police fought against drug traffickers (balanced), others actively colluded with them (bandwagoned). While some mayors resisted guerrilla incursions, others supported the belligerents. Finally, it demonstrated that alliance effectiveness was higher during the administrations of Colombian Presidents Andrés Pastrana and Alvaro Uribe because the alliance amassed resources (via *Plan Colombia*) sufficient to reduce the internal threat and because Pastrana and Uribe's increased (compared to prior presidential administrations) efforts to identify and eliminate actors (within civilian or security agencies) who were colluding with the "narco-guerrilla" threat.

Notes

1. Geoff Simons, *Colombia: A Brutal History* (London: Saqi Publishers, 2004).
2. The annual death toll from 1988 to 2008 ranged from 1330 to 4038. See Jorge Restrepo and Juan F. Vargas, "The Severity of the Colombian Conflict: Cross-Country Datasets versus New Micro Data," Seminar paper presented at the 8th ECAAR Conference on Economics and Security, Bristol, UK, July 2004. The elements and death toll of the war satisfy the definition of a civil war used in this dissertation. Meredith Reid Sarkees "The Correlates of War Data on War: An Update to 1997," *Conflict Management and Peace Science*, Vol. 18, No. 1 (2000), 123–144.
3. See Manuel Jose Bonett Locarno, *Estrategia General De Las Esfuerzas Militares Por La Seguridad de la poblacion y sus recursos*, December 1997. As quoted in Spracher in Zackrison, *Crisis? What Crisis?*
4. Julia Sweig, "What Kind of War for Colombia?" *Foreign Affairs*, Vol. 81, No. 5 (2002), 122.
5. According to data obtained by Marcy (2010, 13) as of 1976 the USA had traced 90 percent of cocaine destined for the USA as having passed through Colombia.

6. US foreign policy had become "narcoticized." Russell Crandall, *Driven by Drugs: U.S. Policy Toward Colombia* (Boulder: Lynne Rienner, 2002).
7. Randall, *Colombia and the United States* (1992), 248.
8. Randall, *Colombia and the United States* (1992), 251.
9. Drexler, *Colombia and the United States* (1997), 112.
10. Johnny Holloway, *Superiority and Subordination in US-Latin American Relations: A Discourse Analysis of Plan Colombia* (Ph.D. Dissertation, American University, School of International Service, 2012), 102.
11. Doug Stokes, *America's Other War—Terrorizing Colombia* (London, Zed Books: 2009), 79.
12. Stephen J. Randall, *Colombia and the United States: Hegemony and Interdependence* (Athens, GA: University of Georgia Press, 1992), 248–254.
13. Mark Bowden, *Killing Pablo—The Hunt for the World's Greatest Outlaw* (New York: Penguin Books, 2001), 55.
14. Charles Rangel, "Yes We Can Do Something for Colombia, *The Washington Post*, August 24, 1989.
15. Quote from Juan Gabriel Tokatlian, "The Drug Problem in US-Colombian Relations" (Washington, DC: CSIS Americas Program Report, August 15, 1994), citing Juan G. Tokatlian, "La política exterior de Colombia hacia Estados Unidos, 1978–1990: El asunto de las drogas y su lugar en las relaciones entre Bogotá y Washington," in Carlos G. Arrieta, Luis J. Orjela, Eduardo Sarmiento, and Juan G. Tokatlian, *Narcotráfico en Colombia* (Santafé de Bogotá: Ediciones Uniandes/Tercer Mundo Editores, 1990).
16. Military support was primarily in the form of arms transfer and training to units charged with attacking the cartels and FARC. US Special Forces provided training to the Colombian military as well as assisted with planning missions.
17. "Whereas from Harry Truman to Ronald Reagan, no US politician wished to be considered "soft" on Communism, at the end of the 1980s no one wanted to be seen as flexible on the issue of drugs." Juan Gabriel Tokatlian, "Latin American Reaction to US Policies on Drugs and Terrorism," in *Security, Democracy and Development in US-Latin American Relations*, edited by Lars Schoultz, William C. Smith, and Augusto Varas (Miami, FL: University of Miami North-South Center, 1994), 123.

18. David E. Spencer et al., *Colombia's Road to Recovery: Security and Governance 1982–2010* (Washington, DC: Center for Hemispheric Defense Studies, National Defense University, June 2011), 18.
19. In turn, this meant that whereas the US policy was to combat narcotics trafficking, "a significant amount of U.S. assistance... would be employed to combat the guerrillas." Spencer et al., *Colombia's Road to Recovery* (2011), 18.
20. To an average of 457 per year. For these statistics refer to table on level of threat in the Annex to this chapter at the end of the dissertation.
21. On the Processor 8000 Scandalm, see Thoumi, *Illegal Drugs* (2003), 200–251, and "¿Narcopolítoicos?: Colombia del circo a la política," *El Norte*, April 23, 1996.
22. Chepesiuk, *The Bullet or the Bribe* (2003), and Bowden, *Killing Pablo* (2001).
23. Borda, *The Internationalization of Domestic Conflicts* (2009), 60.
24. Interviews in Washington and Bogota with USA and Colombian government officials.
25. On the certification process, see Testimony by **Rand Beers, Assistant Secretary for International Narcotics and Law Enforcement Affairs,** Before the Western Hemisphere, Peace Corps, and Narcotics Subcommittee of the Senate Foreign Relations Committee (Washington, DC: March 1, 2001).
26. Bert Ruiz, *The Colombian Civil War* (London: McFarland and Company Publishers, 2001), 222.
27. Harvey F. Kline, *Chronicle of a Failure Foretold: the Peace Process of Colombian President Andrés Pastrana* (Tuscaloosa: University of Alabama Press, 2007), 44.
28. For these examples Ruiz, *The Colombian Civil War* (2001), 21, 249.
29. Assessment as quoted in Douglas Farah, "Colombian Rebels Seen Winning War; US Study Finds Army Inept, Ill-Equipped," Washington Post, April 10, 1998.
30. Anonymous SOUTHCOM official, interview with author, Bogota, Colombia, October 2012.
31. For an excellent analysis of Pastrana's views on prior attempts to negotiate, see Borda, *The Internationalization of Domestic Conflicts* (2009), 62–64.
32. Coletta A. Youngers, "Collateral Damage" (2004), 142.

33. Official transcript of the joint press conference by President Clinton and Colombian President Pastrana as released by the White House, Office of the Press Secretary, October 28, 1998.
34. As quoted in Anthony Boadle, "US Closer to Boosting Military Aid to Colombia," *Reuters*, October 6, 1999.
35. John Diamond, "Capitol Hill Divided Over Colombian Aid appeal," *Chicago Tribune*, September 23, 1999.
36. Agence France-Presse, "Colombian president plays down rebel ultimatum," November 9, 2001.
37. This included "to restructure [and]…to focus on its mobility, its sustainability, its intelligence capabilities, its command, and control." Douglas Farah, "US Aid to Colombian Military: Drug-dealing rebels Take Toll on Army," *Washington Post*, December 27, 1998.
38. Recommendations included replacing voluntary conscripts with professional soldiers, retraining soldiers in skills specific to the current threat profile, and shifting the Air Force's mandate to support for military and police units. Ruiz, *The Colombian Civil War* (2001).
39. This included "funding to stand up a 950-strong Colombian army counter-narcotics battalion, support to the National Police in funding, training, and arms…[and] a "CIA-sponsored" intelligence center in the Amazon region." Douglas Farah, "US to Aid Colombian Military," *Washington Post*, December 27, 1998.
40. As cited in LeoGrande and Sharpe (2000).
41. Discursos sobre la paz, "De la retórica de la paz a los hechos de paz," August 11, 1998.
42. Dates from www.ciponline.org/colombia
43. Author interview, Colombian government official, Bogota, Colombia, October 2012.
44. Of 1873 and 540, respectively. See table in Annex for specific numbers of attacks at the end of this dissertation.
45. *Reuters*, "Colombia blames rebels for Bogota Club bomb," February 8, 2003.
46. As quoted in Ambassador Ann Patterson, "Las nuevas relaciones entre Estados Unidos y Colombia" in "La Revista de El Espectador," November 4, 2001, Bogotá.
47. Arlene B. Tickner, "Colombia and the United States: From Counternarcotics to Counterterrorism," *Current History* 102 (February 2003), 77–85.

48. As the National Security Strategy states: "In Colombia, we recognize the link between terrorist and extremist groups that challenge the security of the state and drug trafficking activities that help finance the operations of such groups. We are working to help Colombia defend its democratic institutions and defeat illegal armed groups...by extending effective sovereignty over the entire national territory." President George W. Bush, "The National Security Strategy of the United States—2002," (Washington, DC, 2002).
49. This language was initially included in and passed as House of Representatives resolution H.R. 358 that called on the white house to immediately support the government of Colombia to "protect its democracy from United States-designated foreign terrorist organizations." The full H.R. 358 is available at http://www.gpo.gov/fdsys/pkg/BILLS-107hres358eh/pdf/BILLS-107hres358eh.pdf. Accessed February 2012.
50. Thomas Ginsberg, "Latin Battleground—The U.S. is joining its anti-terror fight with the war on drugs in Colombia. It could be a success, or a mess," *Philadelphia Inquirer*, Sunday, December 1, 2002.
51. Rochlin, *Social Forces and the Revolution in Military Affairs* (New York: Palgrave MacMillan, 2007), 46.
52. "El Embrujo Autoritario: Primer Ano de Gobierno de Alvaro Uribe Velez," *Plataforma Colombiana de Derechos Humanos, Democracia y Desarollo* (Bogota, Colombia: 2003).
53. The DSP outlined the following tactics among others: (1) provide adequate equipment and training to soldiers, (2) increase intelligence capacity to identify the opposition, (3) increase defense spending, and (4) gain control over major national roads. As presented by Alejandro Arbelaez, Deputy Minister of Defense for President Alvaro Uribe, in interview with author. Washington, DC, June 12, 2012.
54. These were Guaviare, Meta, Caquetá, and Putumayo Departments. For an overview of operations, see Ramsey III, "From El Billar" (2009), and Spencer et al., *Colombia's Road to Recovery* (2011).
55. Ramsey III, "From El Billar," (2009), 109–110.
56. In 2002 the US Congress voted to approve $93 million in counter-terrorism funding devoted to protecting an Occidental Petroleum pipeline in Arauca.

57. This included adding mountain battalions Kline *Showing Teeth* (1999), 42.
58. Jennifer S. Holmes, "Drugs, Terrorism, and Congressional Politics: The Colombia Challenge," Ralph G. Carter, ed. *Contemporary Cases in U.S. Foreign Policy*, (Washington, DC: CQ Press, 2005), 33–64.
59. Newly equipped and trained Colombian Special Forces, reportedly with support from US Special Forces units, began targeting high- and mid-level commanders. Spencer et al., *Colombia's Road to Recovery* (2011).
60. Pastrana extradited 65 Colombians. Uribe by mid-2005 extradited 215 and 500 by 2007. Crandall, *Driven by Drugs* (2002), 155.
61. As part of the NCP, US SOUTHCOM and Colombia's Ministry of Defense created "Integrated Action." For an overview, see Adam Isacson and Abigail Poe, "After Plan Colombia: Evaluating Integrated Action—The Next Phase of U.S. Assistance," Center for International Policy, December 2009.
62. Murillo, *Colombia and the United States* (2004), 126.
63. Kline, *Showing Teeth* (1999), 41.
64. "Colombia's Uribe wins second term," *BBC News*, May 29, 2006.
65. Steven David makes this point in (1991b) "Explaining Alignment in the Third World," 239. See also David (1992) "Why the Third World Still Matters."
66. For an excellent discussion of state development in Latin America, see Miguel Angel Centeno, *Blood and Debt: War and the Nation-State in Latin America* (University Park, PA: University of Pennsylvania Press, 2002). See also Harvey F. Kline, *Chronicle of a Failure Foretold: the Peace Process of Colombian President Andrés Pastrana* (Tuscaloosa: University of Alabama Press, 2007), 5.
67. Ana Maria Bejarano, *Precarious Democracies—Understanding Regime Stability and Change in Colombia and Venezuela* (Notre Dame: University of Notre Dame Press, 2011), 227–228.
68. Ana Maria Bejarano and Eduardo Pizarro, "Colombia: The Partial Collapse of the State and the Emergence of Aspiring State-Makers," in *States within States—Incipient Political Entities in the Post-Cold War Era*, Paul Kingston and Ian Spears, eds. (New York: Palgrave MacMillan, 2004), 113–114.
69. See Robert H. Dix, *The Politics of Colombia* (New York: Praeger Publishers, 1986).

70. Arlene Tickner, "Colombia: An Ambiguous Foreign Policy," Presentation to Annual Conference of the Latin American Studies Association (LASA) (Washington, DC, 2001).
71. Governors are relevant due to their role in administering affairs in departments where the government balances armed actors, yet interacted less with the USA. The Ministry of National Defense coordinates and oversees all actions of the National Army, Air Force, National Police, and the National Armada (the Naval branch of the military) and the Ministry of Justice and Law, which is responsible for prosecuting criminals and all other matters pertaining to the law.
72. On the Colombian military's autonomy and its influence onto government policy, see Bejarano, *Precarious* Democracies (2011), 150.
73. Bejarano, *Precarious* Democracies (2011), 144.
74. Bejarano, *Precarious* Democracies (2011), 150.
75. Bejarano, *Precarious* Democracies (2011), 150.
76. Bejarano, *Precarious* Democracies (2011), 154.
77. Barbara Geddes, *Politician's Dilemma: Building State Capacity in Latin America* (Berkeley: University of California Press, 1994), 7.
78. For an excellent and perhaps the seminal analysis of patron-client relations and clientelism in Colombia, see Francisco Davila Ladron de Guevara and Andres Leal Buitrago, *Clientelismo: el sistema político y su expresión regional* (Bogota, Colombia: Universidad de Los Andes Press; 2010). See also Eduardo Diaz Uribe, *El clientelismo en Colombia: Un estudio exploratorio* (Bogota, Colombia: Ancora Editores, 1986). On corruption in Colombia as rooted in clientelism, see Fernando Cepeda Ulloa, *La Corrupcion en Colombia* (Bogota, Colombia: TM Editores, 1997). See also Andres Leal Buitrago, *Estado y Politica en Colombia* (Bogota, Colombia: Siglo Veintiuno de Colombia, 1989). Additionally, see John D. Martz, *The Politics of Clientelism—Democracy and the State in Colombia* (London: Transaction Publishers, 1997).
79. Fernando Cepeda Ulloa, Interview with Author, Bogota, Colombia, October 2012.
80. Grace Livingstone, *Inside Colombia: Drugs, Democracy and War* (New Brunswick: Rutgers University Press, 2004), 35.
81. Livingstone (2004), 35.
82. Kline, *Chronicle of a Failure* (2007), 7.

83. Martz, *The Politics of Clientelism* (1997), 70.
84. Philip Mauceri, "State, Elites, and the Response to Insurgency," in *Politics in the Andes—Identity, Conflict, Reform*. Jo-Marie Burt and Philip Mauceri, eds. (Pittsburgh, PA: University of Pittsburgh Press, 2004), 155.
85. In the 1980s and 1990s, the government of Colombia enacted political and fiscal decentralization reforms aimed to grant subnational units more authority over the use of their resources as well as individuals in these areas the ability to select those officials who would serve in public office. For an overview of these, see Kent Eaton, "The Downside of Decentralization: Armed Clientelism in Colombia," *Security Studies* 15, No. 4 (2006), 533–562.
86. Eaton, "The Downside of Decentralization," (2006), 553.
87. Martz, *The Politics of Clientelism* (1997), 47.
88. Kline, *Chronicle of a Failure* (2007), 23.
89. Mario A. Murillo, *Colombia and the United States—War, Unrest and Destabilization* (New York: Seven Stories Press, 2004), 49–50.
90. Geoff Simons, *Colombia: A Brutal History* (London: Saqi Publishers, 2004).
91. The annual death toll from 1988 to 2008 ranged from 1330 to 4038. See Jorge Restrepo and Juan F. Vargas, "The Severity of the Colombian Conflict: Cross-Country Datasets versus New Micro Data," Seminar paper presented at the 8th ECAAR Conference on Economics and Security, Bristol, UK, July 2004. The elements and death toll of the war satisfy the definition of a civil war used in this dissertation. Meredith Reid Sarkees "The Correlates of War Data on War: An Update to 1997," *Conflict Management and Peace Science*, Vol. 18, No. 1 (2000), 123–144.
92. See Manuel Jose Bonnet Locarno, *Estrategia General De Las Esfuerzas Militares Por La Seguridad de la poblacion y sus recursos*, December 1997, as quoted in Spracher in Zackrison, *Crisis? What Crisis?*
93. The links between the Colombian military are well-documented. See also "The Ties That Bind: Colombia and Military-Paramilitary Links," *Human Rights Watch* (Washington, DC: February 2000).
94. Steven Dudley, *Walking Ghosts: Murder and Guerrilla Politics in Colombia* (New York: Routledge, 2004).
95. David Myhre, *Colombia: Civil Conflict, State Weakness, and (In)security* (Princeton: Princeton University Press, 2003), 88.

96. See Richani, *Systems of Violence* (2002), 59.
97. On the ELN, see Richani, *Systems of Violence* (2002).
98. The M-19 were a third (but less formidable) insurgent group.
99. On this topic see Francisco E. Thoumi, *Illegal Drugs, Economy, and Society in the Andes* (Washington, DC: Woodrow Wilson Center Press, 2003); see also Collette Youngers and Eileen Rosin, *Drugs and Democracy in Latin America: the impact of U.S. Policy* (Boulder: Lynn Reiner, 2004).
100. Author interview, US government official involved in counter-narcotics operations, Washington, DC, July 2012.
101. On the cartels, see Ronald Chepusiuk, *The Bullet or the Bribe: Taking Down Colombia's Cali Drug Cartel* (New York, NY: Praeger, 2003); see also US Drug Enforcement Agency.
102. Patricia Bibes, "Transnational Organized Crime and Terrorism: Colombia, a Case Study," *Journal of Contemporary Criminal Justice* Vol. 17, No. 3 (2001) 243–258.
103. Author interview, Colombian government official, Bogota, Colombia, October 2012.
104. As quoted in "Colombia May Get U.S. Aid in Civil War," *Washington Times*, October 13, 1997.
105. Author Interview, Former US Ambassador to Colombia, Myles Frechette, Washington, DC. On FARC financing, see Alfredo Rangel Suarez, "Parasites and Predators: Guerrillas and the Insurgent Economy of Colombia," *Journal of International Affairs* 53:2 (2000): 582.
106. Dudley, *Walking Ghosts* (2004), 53, and Author interview, former Ministry of Defense Official, Washington, DC. January 2012.
107. William L. Marcy, *The Politics of Cocaine: How US Foreign Policy Has Created a Thriving Drug Industry in Central and South America* (Chicago, IL: Lawrence Hill Books, 2010), 120–30.
108. Statistics provided in Passage, "The United States and Colombia" (2000).
109. M. Klare, "Detras del petroleo colombiano: intenciones ocultas," *Agencia Latinoamericana de Informacion*; and US Department of State, "Preliminary Report, Colombia Survey Team, Colonel Landsdale," February 23, 1960. Accessed via www.icdc.com; Peter Pace, "Advance questions for Lieutenant General Peter Pace. Defense Reforms," US Senate Committee on Armed Services, 2000. Accessed via www.senate.gov

110. On FDI in Colombia, see Stephen J. Randall, *Colombia and the United States—Hegemony and Interdependence*, (Athens, GA: University of Georgia Press, 1992); see also Office of the United States Trade Representative US Census Bureau—Foreign Trade—Colombia. Available at http://www.census.gov/foreign-trade/balance/c3010.html
111. See David Passage, "The United States and Colombia: Untying the Gordian Knot," (Washington, DC: Strategic Studies Institute, March 2000).
112. On the Reagan administration's view of the FARC/traffickers as one in the same, see George Shultz, "A Forward Look at Foreign Policy" (Washington, DC: US Department of State, October 19, 1984).
113. Interview with author, Colombia Ministry of Interior Official, Bogota, Colombia, October 2012.
114. The "war on drugs" was made official by the US Congress passing the Defense Authorization Act.
115. Marcy, *The Politics of Cocaine* (2010), 123.
116. National Security Decision Directive 221, "Narcotics and National Security," issued 1982, accessed March 2013. Published on the Federation of American Scientists, Intelligence Resource Program Website. Available here: https://www.fas.org/irp/offdocs/nsdd/nsdd-221.pdf
117. Harvey Kline, *Colombia: Democracy Under Assault* (New York, Westview Press: 1995), 124.
118. Specifically, in the Guajira area. Kline, *Colombia: Democracy Under Assault* (1995), 124.
119. Randall, *Colombia and the United States* (1992), 251.
120. Kline, *Colombia: Democracy Under Assault* (1995), 124.
121. Juan Gabriel Tokatlian, "National Security and Drugs: Their Impact on Colombian-U.S. Relations," *Journal of Interamerican Studies and World Affairs* Vol. 30, No. 1 (1988), 147.
122. In 1988 Reagan received passage of the Anti-Drug Abuse Act. Marcy, *The Politics of Cocaine* (2010).
123. National Security Decision Directive 71, Issued November 30, 1982, "U.S. Policy Toward Latin America In the Wake of the Falklands Crisis." Published on the Federation of American Scientists, Intelligence Resource Program Website. Available here: https://www.fas.org/irp/offdocs/nsdd/nsdd-71.pdf

124. National Security Directive 23, "US Relations with the Soviet Union," issued September 22, 1989, published on the Federation of American Scientists, Intelligence Resource Program Website. Available here: http://www.fas.org/irp/offdocs/nsd/nsd23.pdf
125. "Latin America and the Caribbean: Illicit Drug Trafficking and U.S. Counterdrug Programs" (Washington, DC: Government Accountability Office [GAO], August 2010), 10–11.
126. Additionally, NSDD 18 made the Department of Defense (DoD) the lead entity in the US counter-narcotics efforts worldwide and in doing so broadened its mandate to cooperate with governments in their such efforts. National Security Directive 18, available via the George W. Bush Presidential Library. Accessed March 18, 2013. http://bushlibrary.tamu.edu/research/pdfs/nsd/nsd18.pdf
127. Rafael Pardo, 1997.
128. He was an advocate for more forceful government action against the narco-traffickers.
129. Ruiz, *The Colombian Civil War* (2001), 174–175.
130. Interview with Author, Fernando Cepeda Ulloa, Minister of Governments under President Barco and Minister of the Interior under Gaviria, Bogota, Colombia, October 2012.
131. Anonymous former Colombian government official, Interview with Author, citing his own scholarly work, Bogota, Colombia, October 2012.
132. Javier Almario, "The FARC attacks, the government negotiates, and Colombia disintegrates," *EIR News Service*, May 8, 1998.
133. Interview with author, Colombian government official, Bogota, Colombia, October 2012.
134. Ricardo Vargas, "The Revolutionary Armed Forces of Colombia (FARC) and the Illicit Drug," *The Transnational Institute*, June 7, 1999.
135. Statistics cited in George H. Franco, "Their Darkest Hour: Colombia's Government and the Narco-Insurgency," *Parameters* (Summer 2000), 83–93.
136. Javier Almario, "The FARC attacks, the government negotiates, and Colombia disintegrates," *EIR News Service*, May 8, 1998.
137. Bruce Bagley, "Drug Trafficking, Political Violence and U.S. Policy in Colombia in the 1990s," Working Paper (Miami, FL: School of International Studies, University of Miami, February 7, 2001).

138. Bagley, "Drug Trafficking," (2001).
139. For a discussion of corruption in the Colombian government, see "Corruption and Drugs in Colombia: Democracy at Risk" (Washington, DC, Senate Committee on Foreign Relations, 104th Cong., 2nd session, 1996).
140. Mauceri, "State, Elites," (2004), 150.
141. David E. Spencer et al., *Colombia's Road to Recovery: Security and Governance 1982–2010* (Washington, DC: Center for Hemispheric Defense Studies, National Defense University, June 2011), xii.
142. Spencer et al., *Colombia's Road to Recovery* (2011), 12.
143. Bert Ruiz, *The Colombian Civil War* (London: McFarly and Company Publishers, 2001), 164.
144. Bejarano, *Precarious* Democracies (2011), 217–230.
145. Geoff Simons, *Colombia: A Brutal History* (London: Saqi Books, 2004), 62.
146. Interview with Author, Anonymous US Official, Washington, DC, July 2012.
147. Bowden, *Killing Pablo* (2001).
148. Gabriel Marcella and Donald Schulz, "Colombia's Three Wars: US Strategy at the Crossroads" (Washington, DC: Strategic Studies Institute, March 1999), 18.
149. As quoted in Max G. Manwaring, "Non-State Actors in Colombia: Threats to the State and to the Hemisphere," *Small Wars & Insurgencies*, Vol. 13, No. 2 (2002), 15.
150. As quoted in Ruiz, *The Colombian Civil War* (2001), 91.
151. *Reuters*, "Rebels Accuse Colombian Army of Highway Robbery," May 19, 1999.
152. Interview with former Colombian government official, Bogota, Colombia, October 2012.
153. Harvey F. Kline, *Statebuilding and Conflict Resolution in Colombia, 1986–1994* (Tuscaloosa: University of Alabama Press, 1999), 38.
154. William L. Marcy, *The Politics of Cocaine—How U.S. Foreign Policy Has Created a Thriving Drug Industry in Central and South America* (Chicago, IL: Lawrence Hill Books, 2010), 64.
155. Livingstone *Inside Colombia* (2005), 58.
156. As recounted in an interview, though, even before this official reinstatement, though, he had already directed his Minister of Justice to continue with extraditions. Interview with Author, Fernando Cepeda Ulloa, Minister of Governments under President Barco

and Minister of the Interior under Gaviria, Bogota, Colombia, October 2012.
157. Interview with author, Rafael Pardo, former Minister of Defense of Colombia, Bogota, Colombia, October 2012.
158. Following Escobar's escape, the USA and Colombia worked closely to track him down and kill him, demonstrating the ability of the USA and Colombia to closely cooperate and coordinate their policies and activities. The effort involved collaboration by the CIA, DEA and their counterparts in Colombia. Interview with author, Rafael Pardo, former Minister of Defense of Colombia, Bogota, Colombia, October 2012.
159. Interview with Author, Fernando Cepeda Ulloa, Minister of Governments under President Barco and Minister of the Interior under Gaviria, Bogota, Colombia, October 2012.
160. Robert Gelbard, Assistant Secretary of State for International Narcotics and Law Enforcement, Testimony before the US House of Representatives, International Relations Committee, Subcommittee on the Western Hemisphere, "Certification for Drug Producing Countries in Latin America." March 7, 1996. Accessed February 9, 2012 at the Drug Enforcement Agency website: http://www.justice.gov/dea/pubs/cngrtest/ct960307.htm
161. United States House of Representatives, Committee on Government Reform and Oversight, hearings on counter-narcotics efforts in Colombia, July 9, 1997.
162. Interview with Author, US Ambassador to Colombia Thomas McNamara, Washington, DC, August 2012.
163. Interview with Author, Alejandro Arbelaez, Deputy Minister of Defense for President Alvaro Uribe, Washington, DC, June 12, 2012; Anonymous former Colombian government official who worked in Minister of Interior under Samper, Interview with Author, Bogota, Colombia, October 2012.
164. For a summary of these resources, see Spencer et al., *Colombia's Road to Recovery* (2011). 29; Clinton recertified Colombia via a national security waiver despite contrary demands from Congress. Waiver of Restrictions on US Assistance to Colombia, Unclassified, Action Memorandum, c. February 25, 1997, 7. Downloaded from the Digital National Security Archive, March 23, 2013.
165. See Mauricio Reina, *Las Relaciones entre Colombia y Estados Unidos* (Bogotá, Colombia, CEI, 1990), 41.

166. Bruce Bagley and Juan Tokatlian, "Colombian Foreign Policy in the 1980s: The Search for the Leverage," *Journal of Inter-American Studies and World Affairs*. 27, Issue 3 (Autumn, 1985).
167. Patricia H. Micolta, "Illicit Interest Groups" (2004).
168. Interview with Author, US Ambassador to Colombia, Thomas Boyatt, Washington, DC.
169. For example, he joined the Non-Aligned Movement (NAM). Drexler, *Colombia and the United States* (1997).
170. As noted by a (1998) US State Department document, the USA aimed to "enhance the Colombian military's ability to counter both the insurgents and traffickers" because there was a "firepower imbalance" between the opposition and government that the USA determined needed to be addressed in order to empower the government to defeat the insurgents and therefore prevent its collapse. Quoted in Marcy, *The Politics of Cocaine* (2010), 124.
171. Amnesty was granted through Law 35. Kline, *Colombia: Democracy Under Assault* (1995), 124.
172. Kline, *Colombia: Democracy Under Assault,* (1995), 58.
173. Bagley and Tokatlian, "Colombian Foreign Policy in the 1980s" (1985).
174. See Sewall H. Menzel, *Cocaine Quagmire: Implementing the US Anti-Drug Policy in the North Andes* (Boston, MA: University Press of America, 1997).
175. William Aviles, *Global Capitalism, Democracy, and Civil-Military Relations in Colombia* (Albany, NY: State University of New York Press, 2007), 41.
176. Peace talks with the guerrillas also broke down around this same time, due to lack of political will by the guerrillas as well as the military's advocacy against the negotiations and for a military solution to the conflict. Ruiz, *The Colombian Civil War* (2001), 160–165.
177. Sandra Borda, *The Internationalization of Domestic Conflicts: A Comparative Study of Colombia, El Salvador, and Guatemala* (University of Minnesota, Dissertation, 2009), 52.
178. Juan Tokatlian, "Colombia at War: The Search for a Peace Diplomacy, *International Journal of Politics, Culture, and Society*, Vol. 333 (2000), 339.
179. Bagley and Tokatlian, "Colombian Foreign Policy in the 1980s" (1985). 48.

180. Rafael Pardo, "La Politica Exterior de la Administracion Barco," *Análisis Político* N° 2 Agosto-Diciembre (1987).
181. On the Barco administration's strategy vis-à-vis the guerrillas see Kline, *Statebuilding* (1999), 33–43.
182. Kline, *Colombia: Democracy Under Assault* (1995), quoting "Realizaciones del programa de cambio: El gobierno cumple con Colombia" (report of the presidency to the National Congress, December 16, 1989), 139–140.
183. As quoted in Gerald M. Boyd, "Reagan accuses Soviet Union, Cuba of Aiding Latin terrorists," *Times-News*, January 3, 198, 9.
184. They did so mainly because he was an advocate for more forceful government action against the narco-traffickers.
185. See table on Strength of Insurgent Forces.
186. Kline, *Statebuilding*, (1999), 38.
187. The other development was the guerrilla-orchestrated kidnapping of a presidential candidate.
188. Quote from Juan Gabriel Tokatlian, "The Drug Problem in US–Colombian Relations," (Washington, DC: CSIS Americas Program Report, August 15, 1994), citing Juan G. Tokatlian, "La política exterior de Colombia hacia Estados Unidos, 1978–1990 : El asunto de las drogas y su lugar en las relaciones entre Bogotá y Washington," in Carlos G. Arrieta, Luis J. Orjela, Eduardo Sarmiento, and Juan G. Tokatlian, *Narcotráfico en Colombia* (Santafé de Bogotá: Ediciones Uniandes/Tercer Mundo Editores, 1990).
189. The death of Galan prompted the Barco government to declare (with the enthusiastic support of the [H.W.] Bush Administration) a "War on Drugs." Police and military forces arrested more than 11,000 people in raids on ranches, homes, companies. Ruiz, *The Colombian Civil War* (2001), 174–175.
190. Barco also enacted various decrees aimed to target the finances of drug dealers including making it easier to extradite narcos (at this time, a treaty was necessary) as well as making it easier for law enforcement officials to seize property (including real estate or other material goods) from suspected traffickers if they could not, within five days, prove how they were able to pay for (legally) these items. Suspects of drug trade or terrorism could also now be held for seven as opposed to one day. *Cromos*, August 29, 1989.

191. Grace Livingstone, *Inside Colombia: Drugs, Democracy and War* (New Brunswick: Rutgers University Press, 2004), 58.
192. On US training and help creating this Search Bloc see Bowden, *Killing Pablo* (2001), 79.
193. Military support was primarily in the form of arms transfer and training to units charged with attacking the cartels and FARC. US Special Forces provided training to the Colombian military as well as assisted with planning missions.
194. "Colombia Purges 2075 Police Officers for Bribery." *St. Petersburg Times.* October 5, 1989.
195. Kline, *Statebuilding*, (1999), 60.
196. The White House, "New National Security Policy of the United States" (Washington, DC: United States Government Printing Office, August 1991).
197. To keep politically vital campaign promises to influential sectors, Gaviria coupled negotiations with military action to decrease guerrilla violence. Talks eventually broke down, however, due to guerrillas' intransigence and Military efforts to undermine the process including attacking primary FARC headquarters without Presidential authorization. Interview with author, Ministry of Defense Official, Bogota, Colombia, October 2012.
198. Saying in March 1992: "the response of the government is to strengthen our security capabilities, our armed forces, to be sure that the outcome of the peace process being carried out in Mexico does not matter." As quoted in *La Prensa*, April 2, 1992.
199. Kline, *Statebuilding* (1999), 113.
200. Gaviria issued Executive Decree 416 that created a "war tax" to generate revenues for "expenses related to fortifying internal security" including better intelligence gathering capabilities for armed forces as well as establishing two 1500 solider mobile brigades and additional army companies to patrol pipelines. As summarized by Kline, *Statebuilding* (1999), 86, from *Semana* Magazine (Bogota, Colombia), August 28, 1990; on military elements of Gaviria's strategy, Drexler, *Colombia and the United States* (1997), 156.
201. At the invitation of Minister of Defense Pardo, late in 1990 a team of defense and military advisers from US Southern Command (SOUTHCOM) traveled to Colombia to provide Gaviria's regime with recommendations on how to reorganize the military's intelligence to better combat the internal threat. Based on advice

received from this team, the military developed a strategic plan to "combat 'escalating terrorism by armed subversion' from narcos and guerrillas." Ruiz, *The Colombian Civil War* (2001), 181.
202. See David E. Spencer et al., *Colombia's Road to Recovery: Security and Governance 1982–2010* (Washington, DC: Center for Hemispheric Defense Studies, National Defense University, June 2011), 9.
203. While authorized and intended as assistance to better equip the military and police to combat then increasingly influential drug cartels, by extension and due to few restrictions (at the subnational level) on how the Colombian government used the monies, the Colombian military also used funds and resources to combat the FARC and ELN. Bruce Bagley and William Walker III, eds. *Drug Trafficking in the Americas* (New Brunswick: Transaction Publishing, 1994). For an excellent overview and analysis of the US support to Colombia's effort to kill Pablo Escobar, see Bowden, *Killing Pablo* (2001), 64–65.
204. Under prior administrations, US Special Forces were limited to a training and advisory role. H.W. Bush secured a change to the Posse Comitatus Act that enabled Special Forces and Green Beret units to directly participate in operations in other countries that were deemed as "law enforcement" and part of the counter-narcotics effort, which had previously required congressional approval. Ronald J. Ostrow, "Ruling Allows Wider Action By U.S. Military," *Los Angeles Times*, December 18, 1989; also Michael Isikoff, "Bush decides military can take law agency role," Austin American-Statesman, December 16.
205. As quoted in William R. Long, "Colombia's New Leader Says He'll Pacify Nation: Gaviria takes office with a tough position against the Medellin drug cartel," *Los Angeles Times*, August 8, 1990.
206. Gaviria viewed the issue (divergent from Barco) as comprising cartel violence ("narco-terrorism") and production/trafficking of cocaine ("narco-trafficking"). See Kline, *Statebuilding* (1999).
207. Regarding the threat from cartels, he pursued a softer-line by indicating that if they "submitted to justice," they would not be extradited to the USA. See Bowden, *Killing Pablo* (2001).
208. Interview with Author, Government official in Gaviria administration, Bogota, Colombia, October 2012.

209. More than 100 were injured in the El Chico neighborhood attack. Bowden, *Killing Pablo*, (2001).
210. Bowden, *Killing Pablo*, (2001), 138.
211. Presidential Decision Directive 14, Accessed March 2013. Published on the Federation of American Scientists, Intelligence Resource Program Website. Available here: http://www.fas.org/irp/offdocs/pdd/pdd-14.pdf
212. Ruiz, *The Colombian Civil War*, (2001), 21.
213. On the certification process, see Testimony by **Rand Beers, Assistant Secretary for International Narcotics and Law Enforcement Affairs,** Before the Western Hemisphere, Peace Corps, and Narcotics Subcommittee of the Senate Foreign Relations Committee (Washington, DC: March 1, 2001).
214. See Crandall, *Driven by Drugs* (2002).
215. See Crandall, *Driven by Drugs* (2002), and Spencer et al., *Colombia's Road to Recovery* (2011).
216. As codified in Samper's Presidential Decree 2010, enacted in 1995. Spencer et al., *Colombia's Road to Recovery* (2011), 26, fn 86.
217. Spencer et al., *Colombia's Road to Recovery* (2011), 26, fn 86.
218. BBC News "Colombia Seizes 'key Farc Data'" September 23, 2008; and Government Accountability Office, Report Number 09-71 (Plan Colombia) to Committee on Foreign Relations, US Senate, October 2008. The AUC also grew during this period.
219. James Brittain, "The FARC-EP in Colombia: A Revolutionary Exception in an Age of Imperialist Expansion," *Monthly Review*, Vol. 57 (2005), 4.
220. Interview by author, via telephone, Anonymous official from Ministeria de Defensa, February 20, 2010; see also Colombian Ministry of Defense Report, "Logros de la Política de Consolidacíon de la Seguridad Democratica, February 2009," February 2009.
221. Brittain, "The FARC-EP in Colombia" (2005), 4.
222. Angel Rabasa and Peter Chalk, "Colombian Labyrinth, The Synergy of Drugs and Insurgency and Its Implications for Regional Stability," RAND Corporation Report (2001), p. 32.
223. Restrepo and Vargas, "The Severity of the Colombian Conflict" (2004). See tables in Annex.
224. Downes, "Landpower and Ambiguous Warfare" (1999), 2.
225. Ramsey III, "From El Billar" (2009), 1.

226. John Otis, "Colombian Army Suffers One of its Worst Defeats in Fight with Rebels," *Houston Chronicle*, March 8, 1998, and Douglas Farah, "Colombian Army Fighting Legacy of Abuses," *The Washington Post*, February 18, 1999.
227. *El Tiempo*, November 4, 1998.
228. Richani, *Systems of Violence* (2002), 59.
229. Richani, *Systems of Violence* (2002), 59.
230. Quote from Ambassador Myles Frechette in Larry Rohter, "Armed Forces in Colombia Hoping to Get Fighting Fit," *New York Times*, December 5, 1999.
231. Ramsey III, "From El Billar" (2009), 17.
232. Ramsey III, "From El Billar" (2009), 18.
233. Anonymous interview, Official from Colombian Ministry of Defense, via Skype, 28 February 2010.
234. Tom Long, *Convincing the Colossus: Latin American Leaders Face the United States* (Washington, DC: American University School of International Service—Ph.D. Dissertation, June 2013), 312.
235. On Pastrana's hesitation to pursue negotiations, then decision to do so as a ploy to win election, see Kline, *Chronicle of a Failure* (2007), 50.
236. As quoted in Laura Brooks, "Colombian President Inaugurated," *Washington Post*, August 8, 1998.
237. For an excellent analysis of Pastrana's views on prior attempts to negotiate, see Borda, *The Internationalization of Domestic Conflicts* (2009), 62–64.
238. For an excellent overview of the details and analysis of the effects of the economic crisis, see Livingstone, *Inside Colombia* (2004).
239. Ruiz, *The Colombian Civil War* (2001), 156.
240. Arguably, the event that consolidated this shift was the FARC's 1998 attack onto El Billar.
241. Juan Forero, "Colombia Fires 27 From Army Over Killings," *Washington Post*, October 30, 2008.
242. "Colombia's Anti-Drug Chief Fired in Corruption Case." *Buffalo News*. May 6, 1999.
243. Ruiz, *The Colombian Civil War* (2001).
244. ElGammal, Mai Maher. "Fighting Corruption, Lessons Learned from International Experiences: Colombia." *World Academy of Science, Engineering and Technology*, Vol. 56 (2011).

245. Gamarra Vergara, Jose R. *Agenda Anticorrupcion en Colombia: Reformas, Logros y Recommendaciones*. Banco de la Republica: Centro de Estudios Economicos Regionales (CEER): Cartegena. November 2006. See also Gobierno de Colombia. "Programa Presidencial de lucha contra la corrupcion," February 26, 2010.
246. John C. Dugas, "The emergence of Neopopulism in Colombia? The case of Alvaro Uribe," *Third World Quarterly*, 24, No. 6 (2003), 1134 and 1126.
247. Kline, *Showing Teeth* (1999).
248. "Colombia re-election ban lifted," *BBC News*, October 20, 2005.
249. "Para Pedir Solidaridad Debemos Ser Solidarios," quoted in *El Tiempo*, March 21, 2003.
250. As reported in *El Tiempo*, March 27, 2003.
251. Hynds, "Colombia: President Alvaro Uribe Implements New Restrictions Under State Of Unrest," *NotiSur*, September 20, 2002.
252. Per comments by Undersecretary of State Marc Grossman: Quoted in Susannah A. Nesmeth, "U.S. Declares Support for Colombia," *Associated Press*, August 15, 2002.
253. Reflective of this general opposition, see "New Escalation in Repression," Colombia Solidarity Network. October/December 2002.
254. Author confidential interview with Colombian ministry of Defense official, Bogota, Colombia, October 2012.
255. Rob Edmond, "Former Colombia Police General sentenced to 13 years in U.S. Prison." *Colombia Reports*. December 14, 2012.
256. Bargent, James. "Ex-Colombian Intelligence Head Gets 13 Years Prison for Drug Ties." *InSight Crime*. December 4, 2012.
257. "Colombia Issues New Anti-Corruption Law" *Xinhua News Agency CEIS*. January 11, 2004.
258. Hoggard, Shiloh. "Preventing Corruption in Colombia: the Need for an Enhanced State-level Approach." *Arizona Journal of International & Comparative Law.* Vol. 21, No. 2. (2004).
259. Due to defections (2000 for these statistics, see table on level of threat in the Annex.
260. From 529 in 2002 to 1300 in 2004 to 1558 in 2006 and, finally, 11,615 in 2009. Statistics compiled by the Programa de Atencion Humanitaria al Desmovilisado, at www.mindefensa.gov.com. Accessed 31 October 2011.

261. *BBC News*, "Top Farc leader killed by troops," March 1, 2008.
262. This data according to a security analyst based on Bogota and the Colombian Ministry of Defense.
263. BBC News "Colombia Seizes 'key Farc Data'," September 23, 2008; see also Government Accountability Office, Report Number 09-71 (Plan Colombia) to Committee on Foreign Relations, US Senate, October 2008.
264. As reflected in the associated table on level of threat.
265. Colombian Ministry of Defense, Vice Minister of Strategy and Planning, Sectorial Studies—"Public Forces Operational Results—Violence and Criminality—Terrorism." www.mindefensa.gov.co
266. Fundación Pais Libre (FPL), Estadisticas Secuestro, 1996–2006; FPL's statistics are largely mirrored in the Colombian Ministry of Defense Report, "Logros de la Política de Consolidacíon de la Seguridad Democratica, February 2009," February 2009. The number of kidnappings declined from 2000 to 2001, and then from 2002 to 2008. However, kidnapping slightly increased between 2001 and 2002 before decreasing again.
267. T. Christian Miller, "US Troops Answered Oil Firm Pleas," *Los Angeles Times*, December 30, 2004.
268. Interview by author, via telephone, anonymous official from Ministeria de Defensa, February 20, 2010; see also Colombian Ministry of Defense Report, "Logros de la Política de Consolidacíon de la Seguridad Democratica, February 2009," February 2009.
269. John Otis, "After dominating southern Colombia for years, numerous setbacks deal serious blows to FARC; Putting rebels on the run," *Houston Chronicle* (South America Bureau), June 15, 2008.
270. Interview, Colombian Ministry of Defense official, Bogota, Colombia, October 2012.
271. Meta, Huila, Caqueta, Nariño, and Cauca. Interview, Colombian Ministry of Defense official, Bogota, Colombia, October 2012.
272. Ramsey III, "From El Billar" (2009), 106.
273. See table on FARC strength.
274. Ramsey III, "From El Billar" (2009), 1.
275. For information on increases in size of Colombia's armed forces, see "The effectiveness of the Colombian Democratic Security and Defense Policy," Presidency of the Republic-Ministry of Defense, Republic of Colombia.www.mindefensa.gov, and "Presupuesto Defensa de Colombia de Este Año Será de 3.600 Millones de

Dólares," Agencia EFE news (Spain), February 20, 2003, and "Recursos para seguridad y defensa superarán por primera vez los de educación," *El Espectador* (Colombia), October 21, 2009.
276. For an overview of this assistance, see Ramsey III, "From El Billar" (2009). 160.
277. On these intelligence gathering capabilities, see Spencer et al., *Colombia's Road to Recovery* (2011), 29.
278. Connie Veillette, "Plan Colombia: A Progress Report" (Washington, DC: Congressional Research Service, January 11, 2006), 8.

CHAPTER 3

US–Afghanistan Internal Threat Alliance (2001–2012)

This chapter applies the theoretical framework presented in Chap. 1 to the US–Afghanistan internal threat alliance. It traces US–Afghanistan cooperation to defeat Taliban insurgents and secure associated US interests. It shows that the Afghan government of President Hamid Karzai sought US assistance to thwart rising threats to his survival from Taliban militants, while the USA aligned in order to ensure terrorists could not again use Afghanistan as a base to plan and launch attacks (as they did on September 11, 2001) and ensure access to natural resources in the region. Regarding bandwagoning, the chapter shows that while some elements of the Afghan Army fought against the Taliban (balanced), others actively cooperated with them (bandwagoned). Similarly, while some subnational governors and elements of the national police resisted Taliban incursions, others aligned with the worst of the terrorist organization. Finally, the chapter shows that the alliance was largely ineffective due to insufficient resources and Karzai's insufficient efforts to stop elements of his regime from colluding (bandwagoning) with the belligerents. The chapter begins with a brief historical overview of the alliance and discussion of the characteristics of the Afghan state. It then examines the formation, bandwagoning within, and effectiveness of the alliance in order to evidence the theoretical framework's core arguments.

US–Afghanistan Internal Threat Alliance (2001–2012):
Historical Overview

The events that precipitated the US–Afghanistan alliance—the attacks on September 11, 2001—have their roots in the war-torn country's prior decades of conflict and strife. This arguably begins with the 1978 Saur Revolution, where the People's Democratic Party of Afghanistan (PDPA), with support from the Afghan military, toppled President Mohammed Daoud Khan's government. Seeking to expand its influence and acting in the context of the Cold War paradigm, the Soviet Union soon thereafter began providing support to the PDPA government and its pursuit of socialist goals. The PDPA regime's policies and persecution of dissenters spurred opposition elements to form militia groups (*mujahedeen*) and attempt to overthrow the government and reincorporate Islamic principles into the state.[1] With the *mujahedeen* increasing in force due largely to support from the USA and Pakistan, the Soviet Union occupied Afghanistan in 1979 to shore up the PDPA government.[2] Nine years later, worn down by the *mujahedeen's* insurgent campaign and abetted by its domestic economic demise, the Soviet Union began withdrawing troops. In 1992, the mujahedeen ousted the PDPA and replaced it with an Interim government.[3]

Building on popular resentment of the nascent government, religious leader Mullah Omar in 1994 established the Taliban ("religious students"), a politico-religious movement comprised of former *mujahedeen* and religious scholars. Leveraging an increased flow of supporters and government financial support from Pakistan, the Taliban expanded its goal from removing Kandahar province's governor to overthrowing the central government and taking control of the state.[4] The Taliban eventually captured Kabul and installed Islamic policies.[5]

This development had implications for Afghans and regional/global security alike. For the people of Afghanistan, it brought the rise of a repressive regime whose strict interpretation of Sharia law meant punishing "un-Islamic" behavior with barbaric acts (including public stonings) as well as forcing women to wear the *burqa* (a garb that covers the entire body and face) and forbidding them from pursuing education and other basic opportunities.[6] Given the Taliban regime's brutal nature, only three states recognized the government during its rule, which lasted from 1996 to 2001. In response to the Taliban's ascent to power and in opposition to its repressive rule, regional powerbrokers ("warlords" or commanders) affiliated with a particular ethnicity or faction joined remnants of the deposed regime in order to reclaim Afghanistan from the Taliban. Commonly referred to as the "Northern Alliance," these militias were led by the ousted government's Defense Minister.[7] With follow-on effects for regional and global security, the Taliban welcomed the terrorist organization Al-Qaeda and its leader, Osama bin Laden, into Afghanistan. With the government's permission, bin Laden established training camps in Afghanistan[8] from which he extended Al-Qaeda's "operations around the world."[9]

Five years after the Taliban came to power, on September 11, 2001, Al-Qaeda hijacked airplanes in the USA and flew two into the World Trade Center in New York City and one into the Pentagon just outside of Washington, DC. The attacks were master-minded by bin Laden. In response to the 9/11 attacks, US President George W. Bush declared a global "war on terrorism."[10] As part of this, he launched Operation Enduring Freedom—Afghanistan through which the USA cooperated with the Northern Alliance opposition to remove the Taliban government and capture or kill bin Laden and his Al-Qaeda affiliates.[11] In October 2001 and as part of this operation, the USA collaborated with NA commanders and other prominent leaders controlling militias (including Hamid Karzai) to rout the Taliban and capture/kill bin Laden.[12] By December the USA and this "anti-Taliban front" of "warlords, strongmen, and political factions"[13] had defeated the Taliban and killed Al-Qaeda operatives or forced them into Pakistan (though bin Laden escaped).[14]

As the Taliban fell and Al-Qaeda was routed from Afghanistan and across the border into Pakistan, a grouping of Afghan and international leaders assembled in Bonn, Germany, to develop a transitional political process for Afghanistan (the Bonn Agreement) and select an Interim leader. They chose Hamid Karzai, a Pashtun leader who worked with the Northern Alliance opposition to defeat the Taliban. In June 2002 and per the Bonn Agreement, a grand council (*Loya Jirga*) of elders elected Karzai to a two-year term as Interim president, marking the official start to his regime.

With Karzai in office, the USA began weighing options for safeguarding his administration and ensuring Al-Qaeda would not again use territory there to launch attacks. Ultimately, the USA selected a "light footprint" approach and in 2002 deployed 8,000 troops to Afghanistan with the objective of killing Taliban and Al-Qaeda fighters and training the Afghan National Security Forces (ANSF)—comprised of the Afghan National

Army (ANA) and Afghan National Police (ANP).[15] Other states pledged assistance and the United Nations established a Mission (UNAMA).[16]

The USA soon became increasingly preoccupied with its pending invasion of Iraq. This limited American resources available for Afghanistan. In accordance with its light footprint approach, due to competing priorities in Iraq, and in line with the US focus on Al-Qaeda (versus Karzai's preoccupation with a Taliban regrouping in Pakistan), the USA devised and pushed Karzai to accept what later became known as the "warlord strategy" for balancing threats in the country.[17] After the collapse of the Taliban, the Northern Alliance commanders and "warlords" the USA had worked with to oust the repressive regime reclaimed the subnational "fiefdoms" they ruled before the Taliban came to power.[18] These regional powerbrokers were largely "considered U.S. allies" and, by paying these individuals "to not fight one another" and "maintain stability in their outlying areas," a means by which the USA could ensure stability without more American boots on the ground. Accordingly, the alliance strategy involved deploying US Special Forces to hunt Al-Qaeda throughout Afghanistan while "relying on the warlords to keep *Pax Americana* in the countryside."[19]

Building from this initial alignment, the USA and Karzai's presidential administration were able to work together to agree on strategy, tactics, and activities. As James Dobbins, US envoy to Afghanistan following 9/11, told me in an interview: "Once the Karzai interim government had been installed, it was fully cooperative and willing to do anything it could, within its capabilities, to advance our agenda."[20] The US Special Presidential Envoy for Afghanistan, Zalmay Khalilzad, worked closely with Karzai to forge all aspects of alliance strategy, with "no significant decision made by Karzai during this period without his involvement."[21]

It soon became clear that the warlords-cum-government actors were more interested in solidifying control over subnational strongholds than balancing threats and securing alliance goals. Rather than using alliance capabilities to fight insurgents, for example, the warlords fought *each other* over control of territory and associated spoils.[22] These purported "extensions" of the central government "were not reconciled to the Karzai presidency and remained potential threats" to his rule.[23] By 2003, they "were becoming stronger while the Karzai regime lacked the resources to compete."[24]

Due in part to warlord bandwagoning and the flow of insurgents back into Afghanistan from havens in Pakistan, the international community's initial triumphant sense of "victory" gave way in 2003 to dire assessments of resurgent attacks throughout Afghanistan. Whereas US Vice President Dick Cheney had exultantly declared in October 2001 that the "Taliban is out of business, permanently,"[25] the insurgency was soon thereafter clearly *back in* business and continued to mount attacks that threatened the Karzai administration's survival and US interests.[26] This wave of violence prompted further concerns in Washington that the Karzai regime might collapse, with dire consequences for US interests. As Khalilzad said at the time in remarks to the US Senate Committee on Foreign Relations: a "lack of success" to include a "renewed civil war, a narco-state, a successful Taliban insurgency, or a failed state" would "undermine efforts in the global war on terrorism and could stimulate an increase in Islamic militancy and terrorism."[27]

It was in this context that the allies looked toward holding the 2004 Afghan presidential elections. Recognizing that threats were rising and the election was a watershed moment in the Bonn process,[28] Bush called for a "Marshall Plan" for Afghanistan and in 2003 approved what would become the alliance's new strategy. This "Accelerated Success" strategy diverged from its "warlord" predecessor by adding the Taliban and insurgents as principal threats (in addition to Al-Qaeda) and including tactics to strengthen the regime's capacity to reclaim "ungoverned spaces" where target actors could operate. The new strategy's *military component* consisted mainly of US and Afghan Army forces conducting operations against insurgents as well as training and equipping the army and police to grow their size and capacity. The strategy's *non-military component* included strengthening the capacity of the Karzai administration and central government to have "a monopoly over the legitimate use of physical force throughout the country."[29] This included training/funding to agencies relevant to alliance goals, activities to reduce poppy production and drug-trafficking (to remove a form of insurgent financing),[30] and establishing Provincial Reconstruction Teams (PRTs) in subnational areas[31] to work with Afghan government actors "to extend its authority" and "develop a stable and secure environment."[32]

Through the 2005 parliamentary elections, continued high levels of threat and allies' dependence on each other to balance it pushed the USA and Karzai together and (by and large) to cooperate on alliance goals and strategy. Reflecting this, in 2005 the allies agreed to the "Joint Declaration of Strategic Partnership,"[33] to "strengthen U.S.-Afghan ties to help ensure Afghanistan's long-term security" so as to facilitate "common efforts to cooperate in the war against international terror and the struggle against violent extremism." The allies agreed to "organize, train, equip, and sustain Afghan forces" and "continue intelligence sharing" among other initiatives.[34]

To be sure, Karzai's need for the US military to balance rising insurgent violence pushed the "mercurial leader" closer to Bush and facilitated their ability to work together (enhanced cohesion). However, Karzai was also eager to collaborate because he recognized that the alliance—and US leverage and largesse that came along with it—was a key asset to solidifying *his* political power and influence. In particular after US back-room dealing during the 2002 *Loya Jirga* partly assured Karzai was named Interim president, he recognized that US influence could (1) help him win the 2004 presidential elections and (2) install an electoral system (options were being weighed at the time) that would consolidate and reduce checks against Executive authority and thereby enhance his power/influence.

Following Afghanistan's 2005 parliamentary elections, the threat remained. Insurgent attacks increased by approximately 300 percent through 2006[35] and a CIA assessment that year said the insurgency was a greater threat "than at any point since late 2001."[36] In response, US/Afghan officials began to "openly ask" just "how long the regime could survive,"[37] recognized that more resources were needed to push back the insurgents, and agreed that the Afghan Army should further increase in size and effectiveness. With "few other countries"[38] willing to contribute, the USA was "compelled to invest substantially more of its own troops and considerably more funds to stem the Taliban tide."[39] This included transferring $2 billion in weapons and armaments to the Afghan Army beginning in 2006.[40]

Karzai's need for US resources to dampen unrelenting violence pushed him to collaborate with US President Bush to implement joint operations against insurgent forces[41] and agree to the "Afghanistan Compact" in 2006. The Compact outlined a strategy to decrease political violence in order to "contribute to national, regional, and global peace and security"[42] and an agreement to increase the army's size, allow Afghanistan to take more "ownership" of the army and police, and to focus efforts on "building lasting Afghan capacity" in the security sector. Partly due to mounting US concern about government actors colluding with the insurgents (e.g., by diverting alliance funding to them), the Compact also included efforts to "combat corruption and ensure public transparency and accountability."[43] Even though Karzai's *central* regime and some army elements initially cooperated with the USA to implement the Compact and military operations against insurgents, other regime components were at the same time diverting resources and aiding insurgents or turning their weapons on and killing regime forces in "green-on-blue" attacks.

In spite of continued military assistance and alliance efforts to quell violence, at the end of Bush's term and as Barack Obama prepared to assume the US presidency, "nearly all indicators of progress" were "trending downward," "Al-Qaeda remained active," the "Taliban were spreading their wings," and "suicide bombings terrorized Kabul."[44] At this point, Karzai recognized that his central regime remained under siege and therefore continued to press the army to collaborate with the USA; however, with an eye toward re-election in 2009, he simultaneously complied progressively less with US demands (and alliance strategy) to curb corruption or enact reforms related to alliance goals. Karzai increasingly prioritized his interests and power over the Afghan national interest and alliance goals. This started in the twilight of Bush's second term and metastasized during US President Barack Obama's administration.

Linked to Obama's campaign pledge that cast Afghanistan as a "war of necessity" and responding to an escalating threat, the USA conducted two reviews of its Afghanistan strategy and associated military tactics.[45] These shared a similar conclusion as distilled by one of their final reports: "the overall situation is deteriorating" as the insurgency is "resilient and growing."[46] The USA recognized that it needed to adjust alliance strategy accordingly; however, its core policy-makers had two competing views on preferred alliance strategy. On one side, members of the US military[47] argued the alliance could fail unless Taliban momentum was reversed with a "comprehensive counterinsurgency (COIN) strategy" that required a "surge" of 44,000 additional troops[48] based on the premise that if the USA retained its current strategy of "chasing terrorists in remote valleys," the "Taliban would continue to seize more territory" and "if insurgents toppled Karzai's government, it would open the door for al Qaeda's return."[49] Securing US interests required reaching the point "where the insurgency no longer threatens the viability of the state."[50] On the other side, policy-makers argued the USA should secure its objectives through "Counter Terror-Plus": Special Forces attacks onto terrorists combined with growing/training the ANA.[51] Obama's administration would eventually select the former approach.

In the midst of and informing this strategy debate, reflecting a decline in cohesion, and Karzai's turn to fully prioritizing *his* regime's political prospects over what was best for the alliance, the USA was increasingly skeptical if Karzai was reliable as an alliance partner and asking: "Could we live with this situation for another presidential term? Did the international community have a solid interlocutor in the presidential palace?" And in answering these questions, the USA "had serious doubts."[52] In a 2008 cable to then US Secretary of State Hillary Clinton, for example, US Ambassador to Afghanistan Karl Eikenberry listed six reasons why the surge/COIN would not be successful including that "Karzai is not an adequate strategic partner" and "continues to shun responsibility for any sovereign burden" including sacking corrupt officials.[53] Citing further concerns with the Karzai regime, he said in a later cable that a "credible partner in Kabul" was required for the COIN strategy but a "variable" he lacked confidence in.[54]

In contrast to the Karzai administration's view before the 2004 elections (close collaboration with the USA was an *asset* to cementing regime power), in the run-up to the 2009 presidential election it viewed non-military aspects of the strategy as a *liability* to winning and consolidating power for the long term. In particular, Karzai was concerned with the 2006 agreement whereby he was supposed to "combat corruption" within his government (curb bandwagoning) to ensure proper use of alliance resources and bolster Afghan state capacity.[55] For Karzai, appointing ("corrupt") clients to regime positions, turning a blind eye to their diversion of alliance funds, and himself using regime monies (alliance or non-alliance) as patronage were vital to garnering support sufficient to win the election. US-Afghan alliance strategy called for the central regime to curb these forms of collusion because doing so was in the better interests of Afghanistan writ large and necessary to stop flows of financing to insurgents; however, for Karzai this was contrary to what would facilitate remaining in power. Consequently, as the election approached Karzai's administration violated these aspects of alliance strategy in order to grease the wheels of its get-out-the-vote machine and in doing so hindered cohesion and effectiveness.[56]

As reflected in a classified version of US–Afghanistan strategy at the time, Karzai's actions were not lost on the USA, which viewed him as a liability to securing American interests: "The implication is clear: Karzai is not our man in this upcoming election."[57] Doubting whether another five years with Karzai as president would best position the USA to secure its interests, the USA quietly urged other (more pro-USA) candidates to run against Karzai.[58] News of these US actions soon reached and incensed Karzai, who accused the USA of a "British-American plot" to oust him from office.[59] After the USA recognized that its push to promote alternate candidates was futile, it shifted support back to Karzai, who eventually won the 2009 presidential contest.[60]

The consequences of events surrounding the election for US–Afghanistan relations were palpable: "Even as Obama committed far more resources to Afghanistan in his first two years in office than Bush did over eight years in two terms, the Afghan leader grew convinced that the new US president was out to get him. *He began to fear for his political survival* [emphasis added]."[61] The USA no longer viewed Karzai as a reliable ally and Karzai no longer viewed the partnership as serving his interests but, instead, as a direct challenge to them.

Reflecting the United States's need to continue preserving Karzai's regime, however, the COIN alliance strategy rolled out in full after the 2009 elections sought to "deny safe haven to al Qaeda and to deny the Taliban the ability to overthrow the Afghan government."[62] Deploying 30,000 additional troops to fight with and train regime army/police to "reverse the Taliban momentum" demonstrated the USA continued need to safeguard the regime and, as Obama said in 2009, "seize the initiative."[63]

Having secured re-election, however, the Karzai administration's willingness to work with its ally and implement strategy declined. No longer relying on the USA to cement long-term political power, "Karzai was finally free to be Karzai," a former US diplomat said, and "it wasn't long before his behavior toward the coalition would change."[64] Like its position vis-à-vis the 2006 Compact, the Karzai regime viewed aspects of the COIN strategy as potential threats to its political interests, specifically, the tactic which called for building "more credible" institutions at the subnational level and in so doing supplanting the patron-client power relationships vital to maintaining his power.[65] Even though a high threat level remained and should arguably have pushed the allies closer, Karzai's regime "was not a willing partner in America's grand plans"[66] and began to openly disagree and act contrary to alliance strategy.

The rift between the USA and Karzai's administration had by November 2012 grown so wide that the *Wall Street Journal* editorialized: "Afghanistan is now a two-front war: a military struggle against the Taliban and a bitter political rift with the Afghan president."[67] This encapsulates alliance dynamics at this juncture and the distinct characteristics of internal threat alliances: parts of the Afghan government were working with the USA in its "military struggle" to balance the insurgents, while other actors *in the same regime* (including Karzai himself) were engaged in bandwagoning to further their political/personal agendas.

Through Obama's first term and the period examined here, alliance effectiveness was moderate to low. In spite of $US billions in resources pooled through its alliance with the Karzai regime, the threat from an active insurgency remained.

Characteristics of the Afghan State: Internal Fragmentation, Multiple Actors, and Competing Interests

In Afghanistan, patron-client relationships are key to power and regime actors prioritized them over alliance goals.[68]

Before proceeding to examine the dynamics of this alliance, it is first necessary to explore the characteristics of the weaker state. As noted in Chap. 1, neoclassical realism holds that *states (in particular those outside of the West) are frequently* not *cohesive but, rather, fragmented and in some cases prone to instability* because they lack a monopoly on the legitimate use of force within their borders.[69] As such, the internal composition of these fragmented states—and the factors motivating actors therein—will influence their foreign policy decision-making.

In line with the characteristics of weak states involved in internal threat alliances, Afghanistan lacks strong institutions, firm control over those agencies that exist, or a writ that extends throughout its complex topography. This lower level of development is rooted in a state formation process plagued by external intervention and subnational factions competing for power. As a result of its geopolitically advantageous location, for centuries Afghanistan was the "playground" for the "Great Game" fought between Russia and Britain.[70] Through this period Afghanistan became a "rentier state" whose central regime relied on largesse from great powers to maintain internal order and balance demands from ethnic groups and "elite, patronage-based networks" competing for power and influence. Due to this combination of invasion and insufficient attempts (or resources) to stand up a robust government, Afghanistan's central state became "defined more in its relation to outside players and the negotiation of a complex web of kinship-based patronage than any internally generated sense of national unity among the ethnic, national, and tribal units within its borders."[71]

Despite external and internal challenges, Afghanistan's rulers over the course of decades developed central agencies charged with maintaining a monopoly on the use of force. In doing so and driven by their core desire to maximize power/influence, rulers endeavored to centralize authority in the capital (and executive office) and establish sway over outlying areas. However, they were able to "consolidate their power" at the national level only by "playing [ethno-regional] groups against each other." Even then, control over territory remained "precarious."[72] In some respects, the Bonn Agreement sought to strike a balance between prior attempts[73] to consolidate authority by constructing central institutions reflecting Afghanistan's multiethnic makeup while devolving some authority to subnational (mainly provincial) actors; however, subsequent efforts to flesh out institutional protocols and funding streams arguably re-balanced authority in favor of the center.[74] The 2004 constitution further consolidated central (presidential) authority. Despite these and other efforts to centralize power, though, deeply imbedded competing loyalties and "tribal and religious resistance to central government authority" continued to make central control of subnational areas feeble.[75]

The products of this stylized synopsis of Afghanistan's state formation process relevant to alliance dynamics would be threefold—first, bureaucratic agencies that were weak, corrupt, and did not always act to advance the regime's interests and a central government that could not control their actions; second, a fragmented nation characterized by subnational systems of political and economic power, the actors in which prioritized *their* interests (patron-client, survival, or a share in the spoils of victory) over the central regime (and eventually alliance strategy); and third, a central regime tightly entangled in these elite-based, ethno-regional patronage networks that strongly informed its decisions and actions, particularly related to alliance dynamics. In sum, these three products of state formation meant that the state under Karzai was "on the whole an empty shell occupied by forces which claim to be acting in the name of the state but are in fact pursuing their own ends, whether individual, familial, tribal or ethnic."[76]

For the period examined, Afghanistan's *central regime* was comprised of the president and his cabinet.[77] These actors worked with the USA to align their security policies and agree to alliance strategy and tactics. Analogous to peripheral states needing to form internal threat alliances, the central regime can be conceptualized as "neopatrimonial" wherein the leader "maintains authority through personal patronage, rather than ideology or law and" occupies their office "less to perform public service than to acquire personal wealth and status."[78] To remain in power and maximize influence, Afghan leaders must appease regionally based ethnic-patron networks and use the spoils of government to do so: the "matters and resources of state" are "treated by the ruler as his personal affair."[79] Since the 2004 constitution, the Executive has been one of the more powerful branches of government. In his dual role as head of state and commander-in-chief, the president formulates (and can quickly alter) foreign and defense policy and appoint (or remove) governors and ministers. As applied to alliance dynamics, the regime's core motivations meant Karzai's decisions on policy/strategy were linked to the option that would best augment his influence; and presidential authority enabled him to change these policies quickly and as needed, to secure these interests.

The *core bureaucratic agencies* involved in devising alliance strategy and carrying out tactics were the Ministries of Interior and Defense—and the Afghan National Army (ANA) and Afghan National Police (ANP) they oversee, respectively. Provincial governors are relevant in so far as they control ANP forces and oversee government agencies in their area of authority.[80] Technically, Executive authority should include sway over agency policies and actions. Afghanistan's level of development and political history combined to grant them greater autonomy in terms of policy planning and activities. As former US Ambassador to Afghanistan Dr. Robert Finn told me in an interview: "Karzai was President and people in and out of government and throughout the regions recognized that, but then did what they wanted."[81] In prioritizing their interests and instead of unshakably implementing central government guidance, regime agencies "defend[ed] their bureaucratic turf" and aimed "first to preserve the interests of stakeholders, which usually center on patron-client relations."[82]

In addition to this de facto autonomy from the central regime, Afghanistan's particular political context further fragmented agencies' *internal* structures to in essence yield ministries consisting of various *component parts*. Competing loyalties to ethno-regional fealties that permeate Afghan society and institutions create factions *within* government agencies in general and security forces (army and police) particularly. These can be viewed as sub-components of the key ministries and are particularly pronounced in the armed forces: "With ethnic frictions and political factionalism undercutting institutional loyalty," the army "remains a fragmented force" that serves "disparate interests."[83] As summarized by an Afghan security official, "you do not have a *national* army or a *national* police" but rather a "factionalized army and police" that "are fighting for their factions, not the country."[84] Rather than pursuing alliance objectives, the security forces (from ministers to lower officers) were "little more than pawns in an elaborate game of chess between multiple regional powerbrokers."[85] Leveraging this de facto autonomy from the central regime, the military and police (and sub-components therein) throughout the alliance took actions to pursue *their* primary interests and not alliance goals: "Despite the billions of dollars spent, the army's expansion is likely to yield diminishing returns because of the government's failure to check ethnic factionalism, with senior military commanders, backed by powerbrokers, engaged in dangerous political rivalries."[86]

In sum, the regime's fragmented character meant that agencies (and components therein) leveraged autonomy, made decisions, and used government resources to advance their personal interests—maximize resources flowing into their coffers, solidify patronage ties, or to benefit their ethnic kin—over alliance goals. What is more, the further *intra*-fragmentation of regime ministries and security forces meant that specific agency components (e.g., police unit A) may be balancing the threat, but others (for instance, police unit B) could simultaneously be bandwagoning.

Various scholars of Central Asian politics have documented patron-client relations (clientelism) in Afghanistan and its effect onto the nation's politics, governance, and economic development.[87] A full review of these texts is beyond the scope of this chapter; however, a brief outline of the root causes and main manifestations of clientelism in Afghanistan is necessary in order to demonstrate its impact onto alliance dynamics.

Rather than any sense of or allegiance to a national identity, Afghans' "primary loyalty" has always been to their "own kin, village, tribe, or ethnic group" ("Qawn"), ethno-factional "solidarity groups" generally concentrated in a particular subnational region.[88] These patron-client networks with associated motivations permeated agencies and associated actions and "regularly trumped any loyalty to the central state or national interest."[89] In so far as regime actors affiliated with and loyal to an ethno-regional network run government agencies, these political institutions were and "remain deeply rooted in Afghan cultural values and social organizations"[90]; and actors therein prioritized these fealties over the national interest or other considerations. Concurrent with consolidation of subnational power bases rooted in these allegiances, attempts by Afghan rulers to establish control outside the capitol laid a foundation for patronage-based power dynamics between the center (Kabul) and periphery (subnational regions) where in the latter "concepts of patriotism, citizenship, or indeed any sense of political obligation to the state was almost entirely absent."[91]

During the Soviet occupation, the contours of patron-client relations changed in two ways. First, aligning with an outside power "to obtain resources to solidify local power bases, only to then contravene that agreement," was institutionalized.[92] Second, the center-periphery disconnect was solidified and "the collapse of a functioning central government led to the formation of parallel power structures at the local level, often headed by local commanders."[93] By the late 1990s, such "regional and ethnic power brokers had emerged that stood in opposition to Kabul-based elite"[94] and acted to advance the power/influence of their competing elite networks. This laid a foundation for inter-elite network competition that later dominated Afghan politics. As the Soviet-based regime crumbled, Afghanistan consisted of a central regime that needed to cement power and to do so employed great power-provided patronage to gain favor with and control subnational powerbrokers and an array of regional powerbrokers who sought not to serve the center but, instead, solidify and expand their subnational power bases. After international actors routed the Taliban, the scope and manifestation of patron-client relations morphed further.

The Bonn Agreement altered the power dynamics of clientelism by mandating space for representatives of competing networks *within* government/regime positions and agencies relevant to the alliance. As the Interim regime took shape, two broad "political constructed ethno-regional" networks "principally defined along ethnic lines" emerged to compete for power and influence within the state: a broad patchwork assembly of former Northern Alliance commanders and the other headed by Hamid Karzai.[95] The "distribution of government ministries on the basis of a spectrum of political representation" essentially "resulted in the establishment of ethnic fiefdoms in the ministries that quickly set up networks of nepotism, bribery and corruption."[96] Instead of establishing a viable form of administrative government, then, the Bonn Agreement "set into motion a fierce internal competition between different elites within the government"[97] with bureaucratic agencies (and parts therein) motivated principally to serve patron-client ties based on such elite networks.[98] The resources introduced via the US-Karzai alliance swelled the revenues and thus patronage (influence) these elite networks could compete for to divert and distribute as patronage to actors in exchange for their support and associated influence.[99] This influx of alliance monies also enlarged the pool of resources insurgents could extort from subnational officials and further incentivized attempting to press regime elements to bandwagon.

The detailed trajectory of Afghanistan's variant of clientelism aside, this process yielded two products that pushed Afghan government actors to choose patron-client relations over loyalty to the national interest (and thus colluding with the enemy vice working to defeat it) during the alliance and are directly relevant to examining its dynamics. First, it firmly entrenched prioritizing increasing power/influence over alliance goals and therefore bandwagoning over balancing: "Rather than thinking of... effective or enabling decisive decision-making, Afghans consider all their actions in terms of kinship, patronage networks, and the complex society of which they are a part."[100] And second, regionally based power structures emerged where ensuring and maximizing personal power/influence via fealty to patron/client trumped loyalty to the central regime (and alliance). In Afghanistan this created "sub-state political communities" (Chowdhury and Krebs 2009), "micro-societies of tribal power" (Sharan 2011), or "de facto states controlled by regional power-holders" (Wilder and Listed 2011)."[101] These subnational bases of power comprise a mix of the elite-based networks fused with government positions and the "local leaders and ethnic regional strongmen" that are "resistant to the project of building a nation-state" whose power is based on "financial and military strength, as well as personal, factional and historical loyalties."[102]

In sum, Afghanistan was a fragmented nation characterized by subnational bases of political/economic power; relationships therein incentivized actors involved in the alliance to go against orders of the central presidential administration.

Having provided an overview of the alliance period and characteristics of the Afghan state, the following sections apply the theoretical framework to the case. In so doing, it evidences the three main parts of the framework related to alliance formation, bandwagoning, and alliance effectiveness.

Alliance Formation

If the Afghan government falls to the Taliban or allows al Qaeda to go unchallenged, that country will again be a base for terrorists who want to kill as many of our people as they possibly can.[103]

The purpose of this section is to evidence the theoretical framework's first core argument: that internal threat alliances will form in response to a threat that *is domestic in origin* and imperils the survival of a weak state's leadership regime. The weaker state's leadership will seek cooperation because it needs military or economic resources to thwart challenges to its existence, while the great power will become involved in order to safeguard interests linked to the regime's stability or survival. To address each part of this argument, the section first demonstrates that the USA and Afghanistan formed an alliance in response to a threat consisting of a high level of political violence generated by insurgents. It then demonstrates that the core motivation underlying US/Afghanistan alignment was to ensure the regime's survival and the great power's interests associated with it. In so doing, the discussion below demonstrates that by 2002 the USA and Karzai had formed an alliance based on a *common* threat from *within*

Table 3.1 US–Afghanistan Internal Threat Alliance Formation

	Threat/Motivation for USA	Threat / Motivation for Afghanistan	Type of Alliance
2001–2008 (AFG): Karzai (USA): Bush	(Threat): Political violence from insurgents (Motivation): Ensure regime survival to prevent terrorist attacks, ensure natural resource access	(Threat): Political violence from insurgents (Motivation): Obtain capabilities to ensure physical/political survival	Internal threat alliance
2008–2012 (AFG): Karzai (USA): Obama	(Threat): Political violence from insurgents (Motivation): Ensure regime survival to prevent terrorist attacks, ensure natural resource access	(Threat): Political violence from insurgents (Motivation): Obtain capabilities to ensure physical/political survival	Internal threat alliance

the weaker state: the Karzai administration needed military and economic capabilities to balance threats from insurgents and remain in power, while the USA needed to ensure terrorists could not again use Afghanistan as a base to plan and launch attacks. To safeguard these interests, it needed to make sure its ally regime did not fall. The table below provides a summary of these motivations disaggregated by presidential administration (Table 3.1).

Profile of the Internal Threat: *Insurgents Imperiling Regime Survival and US Interests*

The threat that spurred the USA and Afghanistan to bring their security policies into close cooperation and begin pooling resources consisted of political violence from insurgents that imperiled regime survival (physical and political) and the consequences such instability and regime failure posed to US interests.

This political violence can be disaggregated into two periods. The first is the period of internal war (mid-1990s through 2001) that *enabled* Al-Qaeda to carry out the 9/11 attacks (reviewed above in the Historical Overview section) and witnessed the advent of insurgent or militia actors that re-merged after the alliance onset and attempted to topple Karzai's regime. The second period and focus of this case includes the continuation of and escalation in political violence after Karzai came to power, when insurgent groups returned to Afghanistan to topple and replace the regime with a "more Islamic" state.

In sum, three sets of actors emerged from and through these periods of conflict that fomented political violence and imperiled the regime and associated US interests: (1) insurgent groups of Afghan and foreign fighters aiming to overthrow the Karzai regime and rout foreign forces. These included the Taliban, Haqqani network, Hezb-i-Islami, and Al-Qaeda, among others; (2) factional militias controlled by regional "warlords" who used violence to control "subnational fiefdoms" and associated power; and (3) narco-criminal bands who exploited a weak and pliable government to traffic opium in Afghanistan.[104] Militias and narco-criminal elements generated violence but were not the alliance's main focus. For the purpose of this analysis, then, the principal threat to the USA/Afghanistan is what I broadly refer to as "insurgent forces."

The Insurgent Threat

After Karzai was named Interim president, various insurgent outfits that had regrouped in Pakistan began to re-enter Afghan territory and mount attacks against the regime.[105] Collectively, the insurgents comprised "a xenophobic, anti-secular, anti-Western, ethno-linguistically Pashtun opposition."[106] The belligerents lacked a common command structure or unified ideology but "maintained a radical Islamist line" and shared a core overlapping objective: to jettison foreign forces from Afghanistan and overthrow the Karzai regime in order to replace it with a "more Islamic" regime (the Taliban's motive) or recover "occupied" Muslim territory (Al-Qaeda's desire).[107]

While insurgents attacked the regime, the aforementioned regional powerbrokers engaged by the alliance to maintain stability were also churning up violence.[108] These warlords were concerned primarily with increasing their power/influence rather than alliance objectives and used these resources not to not *dampen* political violence but instead act with "contempt for the government and its international backers"[109] and "create further mayhem in the countryside."[110]

Collaborating with belligerents and corrupt regime actors, drug traffickers increased the production and trafficking of opium in Afghanistan and in so doing indirectly endangered regime survival by providing insurgents with an additional source of financing. The Taliban and others relied on opium-related revenues for 70 percent of operational costs, leading the allies to conclude that Afghanistan's opium trade "fueled the Taliban insurgency."[111]

In sum, brazen attacks, assassination attempts, and other forms of violence and illicit activity carried out by insurgents and warlord militias endangered the regime's survival. Lacking the military/economic resources necessary to maintain its hold on power, the Karzai regime aligned and worked with the USA to obtain capabilities necessary to do so.

Why the USA and Afghanistan Aligned: *To Safeguard the Regime and US Interests Associated With It*

Responding to the threat profile outlined above, the US and Afghanistan decided to cooperate to weaken and defeat the various non-state actors generating violence. For Karzai's regime, insurgents threatened its survival and hold on political power. Without sufficient capabilities to balance the threat, the regime sought US assistance. For the USA, these groups threatened their ally's survival and sowed instability that could enable terrorist organizations to again use Afghanistan as a staging ground for future attacks as well as imperiled American access to Eurasian energy stores. Therefore, the USA had an interest in helping amass capabilities to weaken the insurgents and ensure regime survival. For the USA, insurgents threatened their ally's survival and sowed instability that imperiled two strategic imperatives related to Afghanistan that drove alignment.

First, Afghanistan is located amidst energy-rich polities and is a transit point for moving gas and oil stores from Eurasia to the US market.[112] Recognizing this, the USA has since the 1990s sought to construct an oil/gas pipeline across Afghanistan to reduce US dependence on Arab oil and forego using Iranian or Russian pipelines in the region. By jeopardizing US ability to do so, and making it harder to extract other resources from Afghanistan, political violence there hinders its ability to reduce dependence on Gulf oil.

The second and more primary reason that Afghanistan is strategically important to the USA is that it served as a staging ground for terrorist organizations (namely, Al-Qaeda) to attack American interests and territory. Instability within Afghanistan as an enabler for attacks onto US interests increasingly became a threat in 1996, when the Taliban government allowed Al-Qaeda to establish training camps in its territory.[113] From its base there and as part of its global jihad, Al-Qaeda recruited and trained members as well as implemented attacks against US targets across the globe including Embassies in Tanzania and Kenya (1998), a US Navy destroyer stationed in Yemen's port of Aden (2000), and the attacks on 9/11.[114]

In addition to killing 2,753 US residents, the 9/11 attacks wrought damage and destruction that sapped American resources and capabilities including but not limited to $55 billion in physical damage, $123 billion in lost economic opportunities and business devaluations, and a six-day closure of the New York Stock Exchange.[115] As facilitated by Afghanistan's "ungoverned spaces" (and pliable Taliban regime), Al-Qaeda's terrorist acts represented a threat to the USA because they killed American civilians and destroyed US military installations and strategic assets at home and abroad. Continued instability within Afghanistan generated by political violence, then, represented a threat to US interests and needed to be balanced.

Before and after Karzai was named Interim president and thus marking the start to his regime—instability that could facilitate terrorism represented a threat to the USA. After Karzai assumed power, however, US ability to balance this threat became intimately linked to his regime's survival. As insurgent attacks onto the regime increased from 2003 onward, then, so too did the risk to US interests.

The discussion below analyzes policy documents and statements by policy-makers to demonstrate that why the great power/regime aligned was clear and in line with the core motivations for formation of internal threat alliances.

George W. Bush (2001–2009) and Hamid Karzai: *Regime Survival to Balance Terrorism*

Statements by US President Bush and his foreign policy team concerning America's engagement in Afghanistan and alignment with the Karzai regime clearly demonstrate that the core factor motivating the USA to align was to balance perceived threats stemming from instability in the Central Asian state. In order to prevent another 9/11, the USA needed to make sure Afghanistan was stable and devoid of "safe havens" terrorists could use to launch attacks, and preserving the Karzai regime's survival was required to do so. As a senior official serving in the first Bush administration told me in an interview: "we knew terrorists could use those mountains/valleys to launch attacks and to make sure it didn't happen, Karzai needed to be able to stand up; we needed to make sure he didn't fall back down."[116]

Reflecting this threat perception, on October 7, 2001 Bush explained the motivation for US "carefully targeted actions" in Afghanistan as "designed to disrupt the use of Afghanistan as a terrorist base of operations, and to attack the military capability of the Taliban regime."[117] In doing so, the USA would "make it more difficult for the terror network to train new recruits and coordinate their evil plans."[118] Further to this point, Paul Wolfowitz, US Deputy Secretary of Defense, summarized the threat to the USA and the strategy it should pursue to balance it as not only "capturing people and holding them accountable" but "removing the sanctuaries, the support systems, ending states who sponsor terrorism."[119]

Propping up the Karzai administration was crucial to removing safe havens terrorists could use to attack the homeland. As the US National Security Strategy for 2002 holds, the USA was "threatened less by conquering states than by failing ones" and therefore needed to make sure the regime sitting atop the Afghan polity did not crumble.[120] This core incentive for US alignment remained relatively constant through the end of Bush's two terms. The 2005 State Department counter-terrorism strategy holds, for example, that "denying terrorists safe haven plays a major role in undermining terrorists' capacity to operate effectively" and therefore is why the USA in Afghanistan "is helping to build a safe, stable society" that "eliminates an environment in which terrorist groups have flourished."[121] Similarly, the March 2006 US National Security Strategy states that the USA "must deny the terrorists control of any nation that they would use as a base and launching pad for terror"[122] and goes on to state regarding Afghanistan specifically:

> The terrorists' goal is to overthrow a rising democracy; claim a strategic country as a haven for terror…and strike America…with ever-increasing violence. This is why success in Afghanistan is vital, and why we must prevent terrorists from exploiting ungoverned areas.[123]

The USA needed to safeguard Karzai's regime to mitigate future terrorist attacks. This is reflected in Vice President Dick Cheney's 2008 statement regarding the US-Afghan alliance: "All future success will hinge on the defeat of the extremists and the terrorists who want to pull this country back to the dark ages…the commitment of the United States is firm and unshakable."[124] A senior US official who served in the second Bush administration and was involved in Afghanistan policy echoed this statement when he told me in an interview that "like it or not, we needed to keep him [Karzai] stable. He was "our man" in Kabul, and routing terrorists meant we needed to keep him/his people alive."[125]

Various statements by the Karzai regime demonstrate that it aligned in order to obtain capabilities needed to thwart attacks from insurgents and remain in power. When asked about the importance of US engagement in 2002, for example, he noted that "the cost of the U.S. not staying committed is too high" and that without continued US capabilities "Afghanistan could slide back into lawlessness and anarchy."[126] He lacked a national army to combat increasingly active insurgents and depended on "international security forces in Kabul to stay in power."[127] Absent reliable body guards and with a fragmented Defense Ministry (elements of which, discussed below, lusted after his seat), Karzai asked the USA in July 2002 to replace his Afghan protectors with US Special Forces.[128] That Karzai relied on the American soldiers for his personal security detail "was a stark reminder of this weakness."[129] Without security forces to thwart attacks, the regime relied on US capabilities devoted to the alliance to balance the threat. This remained relatively constant through 2005 when Karzai said, after being asked what would happen if US forces left, that his country would "go back immediately to chaos" and would "not make it as a sovereign, independent nation able to stand on its own feet."[130]

This continued through the end of Bush's second term. Through 2007 Karzai was "heavily" dependent on the US presence "for his safety and consolidation of his government"[131] and in a 2008 press conference with Bush said his regime needed "to continue our cooperation" with the US "until we have defeated terrorism and extremism and the threat that emanates from them to us."[132] Afghanistan, he said, would "not allow the international community to leave before…we are strong enough to defend our country."[133] There was "no way" his regime could "let [the U.S.] go" before "we have taken from President Bush and the next administration billions and billions of more dollars."[134] Though this statement reportedly drew laughter from the crowd in the Afghan presidential palace, it is indicative of how the regime's survival continued to depend on its great power ally and therefore underscores the core factor motivating its decision to align.

Barack H. Obama (2008–2012) and Hamid Karzai: *Regime Survival to Balance Terrorism*

> *We will prevent the Taliban from turning Afghanistan back into a safe haven from which international terrorists can strike at us or our allies. This would pose a direct threat to the American homeland, and that is a threat that we cannot tolerate.*—President Barack Obama, December 2009

The Obama administration's threat perception and associated motivation for continued alignment with the Karzai regime was like that of Bush. Soon after assuming office, Obama stated that the US objective in Afghanistan remained to "disrupt, dismantle and defeat al Qaeda" and to "prevent their return in the future" and that the Karzai regime's survival was vital to achieving this objective: "If the Afghan government falls to the Taliban or allows al Qaeda to go unchallenged, that country will again be a base for terrorists who want to kill as many of our people as they possibly can."[135] This view is further evidenced in comments made by James Jones, Obama's National Security Advisor, who said in June 2009 that "If we're not successful here…you'll have a staging base for global terrorism all over the world."[136] These core motivations for US alignment are formally reflected in the 2009 "Terms Sheet" outlining the Obama administration's US Strategy for Afghanistan:

> The United States goal in Afghanistan is to *deny safe haven to al Qaeda* and *to deny the Taliban the ability to overthrow the Afghan government* [emphasis added]. The strategic concept for the United States...is to degrade the Taliban insurgency while building sufficient Afghan capacity to secure and govern their country...This approach is tied more tightly to the core goal of disrupting, dismantling, and eventually defeating Al Qaeda and preventing al Qaeda's return to safe havens in Afghanistan.[137]

The US need to safeguard Karzai's regime against overthrow in order to guard against safe havens informed Obama's decision to escalate the total number of US forces in Afghanistan through two "surges" in force deployments: 17,000 troops before Afghanistan's 2009 presidential elections and a further 30,000 soon thereafter, bringing the total to more than 100,000 by 2010.[138] As described by the US Senate Foreign Relations Committee, safeguarding Karzai's regime also guided the use of non-military alliance capabilities devoted to "stabilizing" the country: "The goal of our assistance...is to create the conditions for a more stable, democratic government capable of resisting attempts by Al Qaeda and other insurgent groups from returning and establishing safe havens from which to launch attacks on the U.S. homeland."[139] Insurgents posed direct and indirect threats to US national security and needed to be weakened or defeated.

The Karzai regime's core motivation for aligning with the USA remained constant from the Bush to Obama administrations: to secure capabilities he lacked yet were required to ensure his regime's political and physical survival. Speaking at a press conference with US Secretary of Defense Robert Gates in 2009, for example, Karzai said there was a "realism on our part that it will be some time before Afghanistan is able to sustain its security forces entirely on its own."[140]

BANDWAGONING

I described this is a Mafia state. We see the Afghan state on one side, and the Taliban on the other. But the reality is they work together.—Peter Galbraith, UN Special Representative for Afghanistan.[141]

It is now clear that the USA and Afghanistan were engaged in an internal threat alliance. But, how did elements of the Afghan regime act after the alliance formed? Did all of these entities adhere to alliance strategy and seek to defeat (balance) the insurgents, or did some elements of the Afghan state collude (bandwagon) with the threat? Through examining these questions, this subsection evidences the portion of the theory which argues that balancing (resisting the target threat) and "bandwagoning" (appeasing the target threat) will occur *simultaneously* during internal threat alliances. Actors within the weak state will bandwagon to survive, share in the victor's spoils, or advance patron-client relationships.

The discussion below will demonstrate that elements of the Afghan regime in the capital or subnational areas, including police, military, governors, and other actors, violated alliance strategy and colluded (bandwagoned) with the insurgents in order to survive, "for profit" (share in the spoils of victory), or to maximize their own power/influence (as rooted in patron-client relations). Even as the US and Hamid Karzai's presidential administrations collaborated to defeat insurgents, various Afghan agencies (and components parts therein) were *simultaneously* colluding with these actors.

Bandwagoning to Survive: *Defections and Diverting Alliance Resources*

As part of their repertoire of action aimed at toppling the regime, insurgents threatened civilian and security sector regime actors to the point where they agreed to collude with the insurgents in order to survive. This bandwagoning took many forms yet two were most prominent: first, army or police components defected to the insurgents to protect themselves or their families, and, second, insurgents extorted regime actors by forcing them to give up alliance resources (money, arms, etc.) in exchange for living or permission to operate in a given area.

Representative of security force defections as a form of collusion in exchange for survival, in response to "the threat of death" from insurgents in July 2008, various police officers in Nuristan and Faryab provinces "defected" to the Taliban in order to save their own lives or those of their families.[142] Instances of extortion by insurgents were more widespread (or regularly reported) than security force defections to survive and include, for example, a Jalalabad provincial official paying the Taliban

($2,000 to $4,000) monthly in exchange for the group not killing him and his family. As the official recounted: "We pay so they don't kill us. And the Taliban are happy with the sum and leave us alone."[143] As a US official who worked in Paktika province told me in an interview: "government officials' survival relied on keeping the Taliban satisfied, and that often meant giving them what they wanted—money."[144] Similar collusion in exchange for survival occurred in Kandahar, as a Senior US official who worked there told me: "Provincial officials were holding money and skimming it off of the top. They had to give a cut to who held that territory (Taliban or other insurgents) to make sure they survived."[145] Much the same occurred in Kunar province, where "insurgents pushed local government officials to give them a cut of resources used in their area" under "threat to them and their families." It was "abundantly clear" that "insurgents were extorting government officials."[146] And in Nangarhar, regime representatives did "what was necessary to stay alive" and this often "was opposite to what was agreed at the center and involved colluding with the opposition."[147]

In addition to threatening and forcing Afghan government representatives to hand over alliance monies to survive, insurgents targeted foreign organizations working with (and viewed as an extension of) the central Karzai regime. As a US military official who worked in Helmand province told me, these actors "paid the Taliban in order to prevent attacks on their workforce," and there was "no doubt money was making its way into opposition hands and buying weapons for them to use against us."[148] Insurgents pressing actors to bandwagon in this manner swelled to the point where the Taliban established an office in Kabul to receive such payments in exchange for "clearance" to work in an area.[149] In Kandahar, this "fee for survival," as one interviewee dubbed it, ranged from 10 to 20 percent of an activity budget.[150] A separate investigation concluded that "handing cash out to insurgents to keep them from attacking projects was a common practice."[151] "Like their co-conspirators in the Afghan government," another analysis concluded, "the insurgents learned how to score U.S. taxpayer money for their own purposes."[152] Regime actors were actively colluding by diverting alliance capabilities to insurgents who used said monies to fund anti-regime operations. After insurgents extorted funds from regime actors and organizations working on a construction project, for example, they used them to purchase weapons then used against US and Afghan security forces.[153]

International and regime representatives corroborated that this form of bandwagoning occurred throughout Afghanistan. As a senior ISAF official who managed such funds told me in an interview in Kabul, "we were under the illusion that increasing resources would reduce violence in some areas" but instead "the opposite happened and in many cases the number of violent attacks actually increased because insurgents were extorting funds and then using them against us."[154] Senior US representatives were also aware of this bandwagoning. A report to the US Congress indicated that funds paid to the Taliban for "security" (safe passage through a given area) were "a significant source of funding for the insurgents."[155] US Secretary of State Clinton said in 2009 testimony to the Senate Armed Services Committee that "siphoning off contractual money from the international community" is a "major source of funding for the Taliban."[156] The US Special Representative for Afghanistan and Pakistan came to a similar conclusion: "American and coalition dollars help finance the Taliban. And with more development, higher traffic on roads, and more troops, the Taliban would make more money."[157] And the UN, as reflected in comments by its Kabul-based representative, came to similar conclusions: "Money disappears into the hands of wealthy Afghans" and was paid "to the Taliban to ensure safe passage."[158]

Non-governmental officials and the insurgents themselves also substantiate that belligerents pressed regime actors and their foreign organization extensions to divert resources and collude with the insurgents in order to survive. As an NGO worker with more than ten years' experience in Afghanistan told me in an interview, after opium "most people consider aid project taxing to be the most important source of revenue for insurgents."[159] And as a former Taliban foreign affairs official said, implying the insurgents relied on extorting regime elements: "The Americans have been deceiving themselves" by "saying the Taliban has been getting all of their money from drugs."[160]

This form of bandwagoning had become so widespread in the alliance's later years that the US and Karzai administration established Task Force 435 to investigate and devise mechanisms to stop it. In July 2011 this unit concluded that insurgents had extorted an estimated $2.16 billion in alliance capabilities.[161] As one journalist covering Afghanistan found, it was "an accepted fact" that "the U.S. government funds the very forces American forces are fighting."[162] The US and central regime agreed to pool resources and weaken insurgents partly through a strategy of "winning hearts and minds"—but instead, as an army captain would tell me, "because these guys were defecting or handing stuff over to the Taliban," resources were instead used to purchase *bombs and mines* used against alliance forces.[163]

Bandwagoning for Profit: *Switching to the Winning Side to Share in Spoils of Victory*

Regime actors also bandwagoned "for profit." This is in line with Afghanistan's "culture of defection" wherein the "art" of "opportunistic betrayal is as old as Afghanistan itself."[164] The "ultimate aim" of Afghans is "to survive in their unstable land by joining the winning side."[165] Bandwagoning to share in the spoils of victory manifested in two main forms. Examples below should be viewed as distinct from those presented above insofar as Afghan government actors contravened alliance strategy because they believed the insurgents may win.

The first form of bandwagoning for profit included defecting to the insurgency and can be seen as a function of the Taliban's structure of supporters within the population and regime, which can be disaggregated into two broad networks: "hard core militants" and "networkers." The former (*Talib*) fervently supported the insurgency and consistently remained "aligned to it" even after the alliance routed the Taliban. The "networkers," by contrast, were "local leaders" and other regime actors "of various kinds" who practiced "flexible alignment politics" that were contingent "upon the balance of threats, rewards and solidarity factors."[166] Where the *Talib* unswervingly supported the insurgency after initial US-Karzai alignment, the networkers largely defected (at least overtly) from the movement and "sat on the fence in the intervening years" until the Taliban returned and started to attack the regime.

As there appeared to be "momentum behind the insurgency" (and victory looked probable), "networker" elements proceeded to "join the anti-government forces" because there was "something in it for them."[167] Police, army, and other actors decided to actively aid (and bandwagon with) the Taliban at this juncture not out of fear for survival but because they had hedged their bets, decided the insurgents were the most likely winning coalition, and sought to share in the spoils of its (at that point) likely victory. In eastern Afghanistan in July 2008, for example, "collusion took place" between the national police chief and governor in a specific district with the insurgents that enabled the belligerents to carry out a surprise attack against alliance forces.[168] These regime actors were to provide actionable information to and work with alliance authorities to balance insurgents but instead shared information on planned military operations with the insurgents, which then conducted a deadly counteroffensive. As an army assessment found: "the district police chief and district governor were complicit in supporting the attack."[169] Similarly, regime elements allocated non-military activity budgets to individuals known to financially support the Taliban. Kapisa's governor, for example, allocated alliance funds to individuals with proven ties to the insurgency who in turn gave "a part of the funds allocated" to "HiG and Taliban commanders in Kapisa province and Sorobi District (Kabul province)."[170] One year later, the insurgency ballooned in these areas.

"Green-On-Blue" Bandwagoning

The second form of collusion for profit involved Afghan Army or police actors carrying out "green-on-blue" attacks wherein they (in "green" uniforms) attacked other non-regime alliance personnel (in "blue" uniforms") and in some cases Afghan security forces who were working to combat the insurgents. This is arguably the most conceptually pure form of bandwagoning in that it involved regime actors slaying other regime actors (or US soldiers) in order to assist the insurgents' campaign to topple the regime. Since alliance actors began tracking this phenomenon in 2008, there have been 80 (reported) incidents of green-on-blue bandwagoning, and the frequency of such attacks has progressively increased by 50 percent from 2008 to 2009, by 220 percent from that year to 2011, and by 175 percent from 2011 to 2012.[171]

Afghan Army and Police components were most responsible for these incidents of bandwagoning. To cite but a few examples of each, in November 2010 a soldier killed two US Marines at a base in Helmand and then "fled to the Taliban."[172] The following year, a police representative killed two alliance soldiers in Helmand, and a few months later a soldier killed two and wounded seven US soldiers in Kandahar.[173] In July 2011, an Afghan soldier killed an ISAF soldier in Helmand while on a joint patrol.[174] Though concentrated in southern Afghanistan, green-on-blue bandwagoning also occurred elsewhere.[175] In April 2011, for example, a soldier killed several US soldiers in Kabul airport and in 2012 a soldier killed two US soldiers in Nangrahar province, other army members assassinated two American advisors inside the Ministry of Interior, and a police officer in Paktia killed nine officers. This bandwagoning (particularly in the south) occurred at the same time as other regime actors were carrying out activities (in the same areas) to *balance* insurgents.[176]

Bandwagoning for Power and Patron: *Self-Interest over National Interest*

Distinct to internal threat alliances, fear for survival or a share in the spoils of victory cannot account for all instances of regime bandwagoning during this period. Indeed, central and subnational regime elements also colluded with the enemy to maximize their power or influence (mainly financial).[177] Bandwagoning motivated by this priority seems to have been the most widespread, yielding "a grand collusion between the insurgents and the Afghan authorities" that resulted in a "pattern repeated over and over" where "traditional enemies are working together wherever there's a chance to make money."[178] Actors who bandwagoned in this manner occupied posts at all levels and included warlords used to maintain security outside of Kabul, ministers and their staff, as well as army soldiers/officers and those of similar rank in the police.[179]

This type of bandwagoning had tangible implications for the alliance's ability to achieve its goal: "Corruption has become a factor contributing to terrorism, insurgency, and narcotics. It has done more damage to Afghanistan than much of the violence."[180] The following are additional examples of bandwagoning to advance power or patron-client ties.

Bandwagoning Enables bin Laden's Escape
In October 2001 US and Northern Alliance allies had driven a large contingent of Taliban and Al-Qaeda operatives (including bin Laden) to the mountainous region known as Tora Bora.[181] The USA paid various Afghan commanders thought to be reliable allies to ensure the belligerents could not escape into Pakistan—some of these Afghan commanders actively pursued (and balanced) opposition elements, but others were simultaneously colluding with Al-Qaeda and helping them escape. In exchange for payments amounting to a reported $6 million,[182] specific Afghan commanders aligned with the USA helped 800 Al-Qaeda fighters and bin Laden escape into Pakistan. Even as the US and some NA commanders *balanced* opposition elements, "Bin Laden could count on other Afghan helping hands" that guaranteed his escape.[183] Capturing bin Laden "was the single most important objective," and this collusion prevented the allies from achieving it "precisely because the United States' new Afghan allies refused to

stand in their way."[184] This bandwagoning enabled Taliban and insurgent actors to flee and later return to mount campaigns against Karzai's regime and was also a sign of further balancing/bandwagoning to come.

"Warlords" Bandwagon to Safeguard Subnational Fiefdoms

> *Encouraged by their own ambitions and U.S. support, the warlords refused to disband their private armies, and routinely engaged in armed clashes over control of territory...The most senior and well known warlords served as provincial governors, but refused to accept direction from Karzai's central government in Kabul.*[185]

An element of initial strategy was to give arms and cash to regional powerbrokers ("warlords") to dampen political violence in their subnational regions; and viewed as extensions of the regime, they were expected to apply these capabilities to carry out alliance activities against the insurgents. During this time, some warlords operated according to alliance strategy and balanced opposition elements. "We could rely on some of them to track down the insurgents," a former US official told me.[186] At the same time and particularly by 2002, however, rather than unswervingly implementing agreed strategy (and balancing), the warlords were bandwagoning by running "their enclaves like private mini-states, often without regard for the central government."[187] Instead of ensuring stability per alliance strategy, they had instead "stolen peoples' homes, arbitrarily arrested their enemies, and tortured them in private jails." And rather than actively working with US and Afghan forces to track down, kill, or capture insurgents, the warlords had through 2004 "focused much of their efforts on drugs, extortion, and intimidation, using their relationships with U.S. soldiers to frighten local civilians and advance their own greed."[188]

Actions by Ismail Khan, the alliance warlord in Herat (2002–2004), are illustrative of such bandwagoning. Instead of maintaining stability in his area of influence, Khan deployed militia forces to clash with another (Pashtun) warlord. Rather than yielding a pacified subnational territory according to alliance strategy, then, Khan's bandwagoning to cement control over more territory meant that "the central government was faced with the threat of a major inter-ethnic war."[189] Assumed and intended to serve as an extension of the regime and implement strategy (and produce stability), Khan instead prioritized increasing his power/influence and acted accordingly (and generated violence).[190]

In addition to using alliance resources for their own gain, warlords such as Khan directly contravened specific regime requests associated with alliance tactics. In October 2002, for example, the alliance ordered warlords to hand over their militia forces for incorporation into regime forces or disband their militias. Instead, many warlords "defied" the central government and acted to advance their interests: by retaining (instead of dissolving) militia forces to guard against the "internecine struggles between and among them" (only 16 percent of militia forces had disbanded by 2004).[191]

Thus, the USA and Karzai during these initial years were juggling alliance dynamics that included regime elements balancing agreed targets while others were colluding with them. The implications of bandwagoning were clear: "as the factional militias have wreaked havoc among the general population, the Taliban have started to recover and regroup, especially in the south and east."[192] These forms of bandwagoning confounded alliance assumptions at the time arguably rooted in logic underpinning traditional military alliances (all forces will balance) yet were in line with internal threat alliance dynamics: regime actors are primarily inclined to pursue their own objectives, even if doing so violates alliance goals.

To reign in this behavior and as part of the Bonn political processes, the alliance decided to incorporate warlords into the government by giving them positions in the cabinet or other agencies.[193] Rather than bringing warlords and militias under the central regime's writ, this "created a situation where those with a vested interest in keeping central government institutions weak and ineffective, and their own personal power and regional fiefdoms strong, were placed in positions of authority over the very institutions that needed to be strengthened."[194] Accordingly, instead of implementing alliance strategy and following Karzai regime orders, warlords (now in positions of power) chose to "flout his authority" by aiding (directly or indirectly) actors within their region generating political violence or using new positions to expand their networks' hold on power.[195]

In some cases they directly challenged Karzai, while in others they used alliance resources to cement control over subnational bases of power and the associated spoils.[196] Regarding direct challenges to Karzai, before Fahim Khan (then Defense Minister) was sacked he nearly implemented a plot to forcibly overthrow Karzai and "only the presence of international forces in the capital prevented a coup."[197]

The warlord-cum-government officials leveraged their new positions to cement wealth and power by engaging in narco-trafficking: "the opium-trading warlords quickly figured out how to use the U.S.-backed Afghan government to their advantage" and through their regime positions lay "the foundation for the corrupt nexus between drugs and political power that soon pervaded Afghanistan."[198] It was not long before "narco-kleptocracy" had "extended its grip around President Karzai," who by 2003 was "regarded by some as increasingly isolated by a cadre of corrupt officials."[199] As Karzai, the US, and other regime elements sought to curb narco-trafficking and stem the violence it fueled, these warlords and other regime elements were simultaneously *colluding with* the traffickers to amass revenue and solidify or expand their respective power bases.

Rather than steadfastly carrying out this mandate and balancing threats, however, many warlords chose to prioritize maximizing their personal influence and solidify their power subnationally. They did so and bandwagoned, while other warlords or regime actors worked with the USA to decrease the threat by pursuing Al-Qaeda or Taliban insurgents. This desire to enhance power and influence (rooted in patron-client ties) also pushed agencies (and components therein) to bandwagon.

Ministries of Interior (and Police) and Defense (and Army) Bandwagoning

> The inflow of billions in international funds has cemented the linkages between corrupt members of the Afghan government and violent local commanders—insurgent and criminal, alike.[200]

Over the course of the alliance and as one US official told me, ministry and police elements worked with the US to carry out strategy and balance: "the Ministry and National Police had some credible, reliable people and units who helped stabilize areas and cut down drug flows."[201] In accordance with the distinct dynamics of internal threat alliances, however, while these government elements were seeking to defeat the insurgents, other components from the lowest (Afghan Auxiliary Police) to highest (deputy Minister of Interior) levels were colluding with the enemy to advance their patron-client linkages. This took two forms.

First, they *accepted bribes in order to aid or turn a blind eye to insurgent activity*. Instead of implementing agreed alliance policy, for example, police would "often do the bidding of whoever paid them the most money."[202] The "deeply corrupt" Ministry of Interior was one of the two "fatal weak points" in Afghanistan's government."[203] The implication for the alliance was that "without effective and honest" administrators and police, the regime "can do little to provide internal security."[204] This assessment was echoed by Senior US Representative for Afghanistan Holbrooke, who said that Ministry and "Provincial and police chiefs are deeply on the take."[205] Drawing a similar conclusion, another analysis indicated that police elements were so prone to collusion that they are "almost extensions of militias and cannot be relied on to subdue them."[206] And a 2010 analysis indicated that "regular officers as well as the border police, pose even larger problems as corruption are rampant in the ranks."[207]

The Afghan National Auxiliary Police, formed to dampen violence at the village level, was a component particularly prone to this form of collusion. Rather than carrying out its alliance mandate of "effectively combatting the insurgents or protecting the local population," it was "more concerned with extracting revenue for themselves and doing their local patrons' bidding."[208] In addition to aiding actors fomenting violence, components of the Ministry in specific areas "became a center for drug trafficking with police posts in opium-growing regions being auctioned to the highest bidder."[209]

And second, Interior Ministry and Police officials bandwagoned by *diverting alliance capabilities from their intended purpose and to oneself or their patronage network*. Such bandwagoning "occurred along tribal lines" (motivated by patron-client ties) and was "perpetrated by actors serving in government positions."[210] Where alliance capabilities were amassed with the purpose of "benefiting the populace or calming the insurgency," they instead "flew out of the country."[211] Capabilities provided to the Interior Ministry to balance threats were (in full or part) not used for their intended purpose and instead diverted to actors fomenting violence. In 2003, for example, regime representatives in Mazar-i-Sharif were "to ensure the flow of resources from the center to the police headquarters" but, instead, "became party to their diversion." As one scholar notes of this example and form of bandwagoning more broadly: "diversion of resources through corruption in the Afghan government was a major constraint" because it reduced capabilities available to balance.[212]

The Ministry of Defense and its forces engaged in similar bandwagoning. Components of the Afghan Militia Forces (AMF), for example, were "ostensibly under the defense ministry's control" yet were in actuality "often more loyal" to "a local commander than to national priorities," resulting in "a weak chain of command…plagued by high desertion rates and low operational capacity."[213] Rather than balancing insurgents in a unified manner, AMF components violated central regime guidance, worked for powerbrokers, and diverted alliance resources.[214]

Bandwagoning was not limited to lower level officials or soldiers, however, and extended to the highest levels and the Defense Minister himself.[215] Rather than focusing on coordinating forces to balance insurgents, the Minister used resources to expand his subnational "fiefdom" and played "a double game" by "pledging loyalty to Karzai and the Americans" but at the same refusing orders to dissolve his militia forces and using regime security forces to protect his stake in the drug trade. This bandwagoning fueled an "escalating rivalry" that threatened "to further destabilize Afghanistan's shaky government."[216] Similar incentives pushed governors and provincial-level actors to bandwagon.

Powerful Provincial Figures Bandwagon to Expand Power, Influence

> *In much of the country…the government was at best a reluctant partner… Most governors…Instead of trying to win over the population, sat in their lavish homes and brokered personally enriching deals.*[217]

One prominent form of bandwagoning by provincial officials was their diverting alliance capabilities and then using these resources as a form of patronage to help solidify control over subnational "fiefdoms." Part of alliance strategy included allocating resources to regime actors to "build government institutions" in subnational areas based on the assumption that doing so would reduce violence in ("stabilize") them. The strategy was therefore contingent on the regime actors applying resources accordingly.[218] Instead, a "consistent theme" in many provinces "was that a select group of tribally affiliated strongmen took advantage to secure government positions and gain access to government and development funds" which they used as a form of "patronage to reinforce one's own position and marginalize others" to "consolidate political and economic power among their own people."[219] As one leader in Paktia province indicated, this was widespread: "Millions of dollars are stolen. If you increase the amount of money it will also be useless because the government will simply steal more."[220] Governors in five separate provinces (Helmand, Kandahar, Uruzgan, Paktia, and Ghazni) engaged in this form of bandwagoning.

Rather than employing funds according to alliance strategy to "build institutions" and "provide other basic services," for example, Helmand's governor (Akhundzada) used them and his authority "to reestablish his family's dominance over the drug trade" and "pocketed much of the profit."[221] Reflecting the extent of this bandwagoning, the USA viewed the governor as "part of the problem, not the solution," and pressed Karzai to replace him. Eventually Karzai sacked the governor, but before this occurred, Akhundzada sent his militia forces to work with the Taliban. In exchange for accepting and paying these men (many were the governor's clients or linked to politically important actors), the Taliban was able to put "its tentacles into [Akhundzada's] drug trade" and obtain "tens of millions of dollars every year to expand its guerrilla war."[222] Kandahar's governor Agha Sherzai engaged in similar bandwagoning. Rather than using resources gained through the alliance to stabilize the province, Agha Sherzai employed them "to solidify his power at the expense of Hamid Karzai's central government."[223] Much the same occurred in Uruzgan, where the governor leveraged his position "to exert tight control over the province" for personal gain and did so by diverting and distributing alliance resources as patronage.[224]

The governors of Paktia and Ghazni bandwagoned by diverting funds to insurgents. Regarding Paktia, a 2009 cable from the US Embassy in Kabul says the governor's "Hezb-i-Islami Gulbuddin (HiG) [insurgent] connections...leadership of a province-wide corruption scheme, and suspected contacts with insurgents make him detrimental to the future of Afghanistan" and therefore alliance goals.[225] While other regime elements were balancing target threats, this governor was violating alliance strategy by diverting resources ("corruption scheme") and colluding with insurgents ("HiG connections"). A cable from the same year indicates that Ghazni's governor (Usmani) and his staff engaged in comparable bandwagoning: "[they] routinely embezzle government funds and international aid money intended for public administration and humanitarian assistance."[226] Ghazni's governor and his regime representatives were a "criminal enterprise masquerading as public administration."[227] During the period examined, then, key provincial-level regime actors colluded with non-state actors responsible for violence. They did so while other actors were balancing the common threat and in order to solidify control over their subnational area of influence (governors of Helmand

and Kandahar) and/or actively aid insurgents (governors of Paktia and Ghazni).

The above section demonstrated that elements of the Afghan state colluded with the alliance's primary threat (insurgents) rather than working to defeat these actions. The following section explains how this influenced the alliance's effectiveness.

Alliance Effectiveness

Your enemies will make you laugh and your friends will make you cry—Traditional Dari and Pashto euphemism.

It is now clear that the USA and Afghanistan were engaged in an internal threat alliance and that components of the Afghan state were actively colluding with the enemy, rather than implementing alliance strategy and seeking to defeat it. But, did the alliance achieve its objectives? Why, or why not, were the USA and Afghanistan able to weaken the insurgents? How did Hamid Karzai's interests (e.g., patron-client ties and political priorities) influence his administration's willingness to work with the USA and therefore alliance cohesion and effectiveness?

Through examining these questions, this subsection evidences the portion of the theory which argues that effectiveness of internal threat alliances will depend on whether allies have military resources sufficient to weaken their common enemy *and* are able to control subnational bandwagoning. The principal determinant of internal threat alliance effectiveness will be allies' ability to bring together capabilities sufficient to weaken or defeat the threat. And only when the great power and regime are able to agree on goals, strategy, and tactics and to coordinate activities directed toward those ends (enjoy high alliance cohesion) will they be able to collectively amass resources sufficient to weaken or defeat their common menace. However, alliances will not be effective if the weaker state's leadership is not willing and able to stop their bureaucratic actors from colluding with the enemy. Capabilities *and* curbing bandwagoning must be the recipe for success. In evidencing this argument, the section demonstrates that political priorities or patron-client ties may complicate a central leadership circle's willingness ability to work with their great power ally to define a strategy and associate tactics and thus decrease cohesion. To evidence this argument, the section cites examples from 2001 to 2012 and during the

Karzai administration [2001–2012] and US presidential administrations of Bush [2001–2008] and Obama [2008–2012].

Karzai and Bush, Early Days: *Regime Priorities Smooth Path for Strategy Agreement*

As Karzai took office as Interim president, political violence had lessened but the threat to his regime remained, leading him and the USA to agree on the "warlord strategy."[228] As with traditional alliances, a high threat level and the Karzai regime's military dependence pushed it to agree to this strategy and (for the moment) put aside its view that any strategy needed to take into account Pakistan's role in enabling violence.[229] With an "empty treasury and no security force of his own," Karzai conceded and agreed to rely on warlords to provide stability throughout the country.[230] However, another factor distinct to internal threat alliance cohesion also pushed Karzai to agree to this strategy: recognizing that the USA could help advance *his* primary/core priority of consolidating power in his office and maximizing political/financial power and influence. Two examples demonstrate the USA helping him do so and that it needed to preserve his regime.

First, during the 2002 *Loya Jirga*, the US envoy to Afghanistan convinced the main challenger to Karzai, Zahir Shah, to withdraw and support Karzai.[231] After other prominent candidates withdrew, delegates selected Karzai as Interim leader.[232] And second, in early 2003 the USA helped Karzai ensure that Afghanistan's constitution being drafted at the time would establish a presidential rather than a parliamentary system of government. Where the former would maximize Karzai's authority to make politically valuable appointments and institutionalize other powers in his office, a parliamentary system would have diluted central authority and established additional checks on it (such as a prime minister). Throughout the drafting process, the US Ambassador to Afghanistan (Khalilzad) actively lobbied for a constitution that enshrined strong presidential powers.[233] Partly due to Khalilzad's back-room dealing, and recommendations from a US advisor helping write the constitution, a presidential system was approved in January 2004.[234] This was a "win-win" for the USA and Karzai. For the USA and reflecting its core need to preserve the regime, it "would retain the benefit of having a clearly identifiable Afghan partner whom it would know well and indeed preferred."[235] And for Karzai, he received the protection he needed while laying the foundation for his regime's long-term political survival and influence.

Karzai's Desire to Consolidate Authority Drives Him Closer to Bush (2004–2006)

In the run-up to the 2004 elections, a surge in threat from insurgents and dependence on each other to balance it drove the allies together, pushed them to agree to a new strategy ("Accelerated Success"), and maintained cohesion through much of Bush's two terms. However, two regime-specific motivations also drove them together during this period: Karzai recognized that US influence could (1) help him win the 2004 presidential elections and (2) install an electoral system that would consolidate and reduce checks against Executive authority and thereby enhance his power/influence.

With regard to the 2004 elections, Karzai recognized US funding and influence could help him win. The recently arrived US Ambassador had a $1.4 billion budget and was to spend a "significant portion" before the elections on building schools and an array of other highly visible public works. Karzai's administration recognized that such projects would garner support from the populace and his "core network of patron supporters" and help win the election. As a former US official told me in an interview, "Karzai came close" and agreed to cooperate across all alliance strategy components "because the money we brought in was going to win him key votes."[236] Further, even after receiving credible reports that the poll would be flawed (in Karzai's favor), the USA did not send election observers or push the UN to do so. The decision was made to avoid criticizing "the election of the only candidate who stood any chance of stabilizing the nation" and securing American interests.[237] Karzai won the election and did so "buttressed with a great show of American support and largesse."[238] The USA needed to keep a (thus far) reliable ally in office; and Karzai wanted to remain in power and reap associated spoils ("for him and his network of cronies," as an interviewee described it).[239] This increased cohesion.

Regime-specific motivations to install a pro-center electoral system also drove Karzai closer to the USA. In early 2005 Afghanistan was considering two system options, one known to hinder development of viable opposition parties/alliances (single nontransferable vote or SNTV) and the other to encourage their formation (proportional representation or PR).

Wanting to maximize his authority and minimize checks against it, Karzai strongly preferred SNTV[240] because it would splinter the opposition and help his "strategy to streamline power in the executive branch by fragmenting the parliament and weakening the opposition."[241] Accordingly, as applicable Afghan bodies weighed these options, Karzai actively campaigned against PR and in favor of SNTV because, and corresponding to motivations of regimes in internal threat alliances, he was "not so much interested in institution-building" (the national interest) "as in the centralization of patronage" (and consolidating his power).[242]

Where domestic Afghan stakeholders and foreign actors (United Nations and European Union) backed the PR option because it was "better for the country and its future,"[243] the USA actively supported Karzai's campaign for SNTV by bankrolling and widely distributing a report advocating against PR (and for Karzai's preferred SNTV). Khalilzad also advocated for SNTV in meetings on system options, including declaring that President Bush had said "SNTV is the choice. SNTV is going to happen."[244] At least partly due to US pressure and Karzai's back-room dealing, legislators approved an SNTV-based system and parliamentary elections soon thereafter (run on the new system) yielded Karzai's desired results: a largely disjointed parliament devoid of any block of individuals/parties to challenge his policy decisions or (politically important) appointments. American support again helped consolidate Karzai's authority and pushed him closer to the USA.

The allies were largely able to agree on strategy and tactics through 2006—in part evidenced by their signing the "Joint Declaration of Strategic Partnership in 2005 and the "Afghanistan Compact" in 2006—because a high level of threat (and their common need to balance it) pushed them together. Additionally, however, Karzai's desire to consolidate power (and US help in doing so) pushed him closer to the Bush administration and increased cohesion through 2007. This is reflected in remarks by each leader that year. Bush said that the USA was "proud to call you [Karzai] an ally in this war against those who would wreak havoc" and the presidents were "working closely together" and weekly spent a "fair amount of time talking about our security strategy."[245] For Karzai, he said that his regime would continue to "fight terrorism" and was "committed" and hoped US "assistance will continue."[246] Continued violence against Karzai, Bush then said, made it "in the interests of" the USA "to tip the scales of freedom your way."[247]

The USA might have shifted the "scales of freedom" in favor of Afghanistan but in doing so also ensured that the *political* scales were tilted in Karzai's favor. American support facilitated Karzai's triumph in the 2002 *Loya Jirga*, US monies aided his victory in the 2004 presidential contest, and US backing helped Karzai push through an electoral system that hindered opposition alliance development and consolidated central regime power. By largely agreeing to US alliance strategy and thus balancing (albeit while other regime components bandwagoned), Karzai achieved many of his core objectives. To this point, implementing all alliance tactics (and balancing) was an *asset* to the Karzai regime's political survival and drive to consolidate authority. With many regime-specific priorities secured, however, Karzai began to view comprehensively implementing all alliance tactics as less of an *asset* and more of a *liability* to safeguarding regime interests. This began to manifest in Karzai contravening non-military aspects of alliance strategy and diverting alliance resources to important clients and refusing to enact desired reforms, among other acts. As former Ambassador to Afghanistan Ronald Neumann told me in an interview regarding this juncture, the regime "was less concerned with implementing our agreed strategy and more focused on their own political/personal survival, based in patron-client relations, and used the assistance accordingly."[248]

Karzai's Political Interests Undercut Alliance Gains (2006–2008)

Following Afghanistan's 2005 elections, insurgent violence kept alliance cohesion relatively high, but signs began to emerge that Karzai was becoming less willing to cooperate across all alliance areas. Given that Karzai's central regime relied on the alliance to combat insurgents seeking his overthrow, it remained in its interests to work with the USA (militarily) and *balance*. At the same time, Karzai had attained most items required to consolidate power and influence and therefore began making decisions that would help guarantee re-election in 2009 but also violated non-military aspects of the alliance. This included diverting (and using as patronage) alliance resources and appointing corrupt officials to bolster patron-client links key to re-election: "Political criteria became increasingly evident. Karzai sought to co-opt potential rivals, rebels or critics by appointing them as special advisors and distributing positions in the provinces."[249]

As Kai Eide, Senior UN representative for Afghanistan, said regarding this time period, the regime "seemed not to listen any more" and "the British and Americans were his main targets."[250] As one interviewee told me, Karzai "began to slide off the rails" by refusing to sack corrupt regime elements, firing US-favored officials, and appointing individuals the US opposed including a person previously imprisoned for drug charges to head regime anticorruption efforts.[251] Rather than using authority to make provincial appointments to promote "civil service reform," an alliance tactic to thwart threats in subnational areas, Karzai "increasingly used" them "as a strategy of political survival."[252] These actions hindered allies' ability to implement tactics. And US praise for Karzai as "indispensable" changed to "disparagement of his weak leadership."[253]

Starting from this juncture, then, the USA was aligned with a central regime cooperating with some alliance tactics (and balancing) but violating others because doing so was not in Karzai's political and patron-client interests. Where rising threats to traditional alliances drive allies together to preserve the national interest, the Karzai regime's priorities related to political survival pulled the great power/regime apart. All the while, other regime agencies (and components therein) were also colluding with the enemy.

Karzai and Obama: *"Bandwagoning for Ballots" Drives Allies Apart*

After President Obama assumed office and conducted two strategy reviews, his administration decided to send a "surge" of 30,000 troops to Afghanistan and fully shift its military strategy to COIN. As demonstrated through reservations voiced by senior US officials (see Historical Overview section), the USA was increasingly questioning the viability of Karzai as an ally. These reservations informed the strategy review process, demonstrate the lower state of alliance cohesion at the time, and illustrate how Karzai was increasingly playing a "double game." Karzai's remarks clearly demonstrate his regime's opposition to the strategy. When asked his opinion of COIN, for example, he said in 2008 that "sending more troops to the Afghan cities, to the Afghan villages, will not solve anything."[254] If Karzai was acting only with alliance goals in mind, he would have responded to the high threat level and cooperated in order to balance an insurgency that remained robust and imperiled the country's fabric—

instead, he publicly denounced the alliance and waivered on tackling the insurgents in order to secure the regime's core priority: winning the 2009 presidential elections. Events surrounding the election reflect decreased alliance cohesion and show that a regime will do what is necessary to remain in power (including contravening alliance agreements).

In contrast to the Karzai regime's view before the 2004 elections (close collaboration with the USA was an *asset* to cementing regime authority) in the run-up to the 2009 contest, it viewed non-military aspects of the strategy as a *liability* to winning and consolidating power for the long term, specifically, the 2006 agreement that Karzai "combat corruption" to ensure proper use of alliance resources and bolster Afghan state capacity.[255] For Karzai, appointing ("corrupt") clients to regime positions, turning a blind eye to their diversion of alliance funds, and himself using regime monies (alliance or non-alliance) as patronage were vital to garnering support sufficient to win. Alliance strategy called for the central government to curb these forms of collusion because, in part, it would reduce financial flows going to insurgents; however, restraining such bandwagoning was contrary to what would facilitate his remaining in power. As a result, as the election approached, the regime violated these aspects of alliance strategy in order to grease the wheels of its get-out-the-vote machine and in doing so hindered alliance cohesion.[256]

During this period, Karzai "cut deals" with "a number of unsavory Afghan politicians" in order to "ensure his re-election." He was "determined to win re-election" and therefore "looked to the political past to maintain his power even at the cost of weakening the state structure."[257] For example, the USA asked Karzai to deny a warlord's request to re-enter Afghanistan given the likelihood he would sow (not dampen) political violence. Rebuffing this demand and to cement his election victory, Karzai allowed Dostum's homecoming in exchange for the warlord's "assistance to have the votes he needed from the Uzbeks in the north."[258] This included appointing to regime posts (or pardoning) individuals linked to the drug trade, Taliban, or other actors in exchange for support/assets valuable to the presidential campaign. For example, Karzai attempted to replace Helmand's governor with "a crony of questionable administrative and anti-corruption credentials"[259] and went so far as to "release criminals from prison so they can campaign for him."[260] The disconnect on strategy and what was in Karzai's personal interest is aptly summarized here:

While some embassies were thinking in terms of gradually building or rebuilding institutions and staffing them, or at least were claiming to be doing so, the political instinct of Karzai and of most groups in government was to establish their own patronage network which they could control and use for their own political purposes, including re-election.[261]

Karzai's administration was increasingly "unpredictable" and issuing "decrees pointing in a specific direction at one moment and then abruptly turning in the opposite direction the next." This disconnect became so profound that the USA worried Karzai "might, without Washington's knowledge, conduct secret negotiations with Taliban leaders on a reconciliation formula that might not work.[262] Even though the threat remained and Karzai should have been more inclined to implement alliance strategy and tactics, he was *less* willing to implement strategy and tactics because doing so, he determined, would imperil re-election prospects. The impact on cohesion was to "make coordination with his government difficult."[263]

This decline in cohesion due to central regime motivations escalated as the election approached. Concerned primarily with winning re-election to retain his post atop Afghan's state apparatus and the patronage available for distribution therein, Karzai increasingly defied US requests, violated (mainly non-military) alliance tactics, and siphoned off alliance resources for use as patronage. In a move to shore up votes but opposed by the USA (which viewed it as a "serious setback") and contrary to alliance strategy, Karzai selected former Defense Minister Fahim as his vice presidential running mate.[264] Rather than selecting a reform-oriented individual devoted to advancing alliance objectives, Karzai chose a corrupt powerbroker in "an important tactical move to mobilize the votes" he needed to remain in power.[265] To be sure, Karzai's priorities drove a decline in cohesion.

U.S. Tries to "Make Nice," but Karzai Continues to Bandwagon

Karzai appeared at times to treat the United States as just one more faction to juggle in his balancing of contending Afghan and outside forces, not as a partner providing enormous support to him and his country.[266]—*US Ambassador to Afghanistan Peter Tomsen*

Following the 2009 election, the USA initiated its new COIN strategy. Having secured re-election, however, the Karzai regime's willingness to work with its ally and implement strategy declined markedly. No longer relying on the USA to cement long-term political power, "Karzai was finally free to be Karzai," a former diplomat said, and "it wasn't long before his behavior toward the coalition would change."[267] Additionally, the Karzai regime viewed aspects of the COIN strategy as potential threats to its political interests; specifically, the tactic of building "more credible" institutions at the subnational level that would supplant the patron-client power relationships vital to maintaining his power.[268] Even though a high threat level remained, Karzai's regime "was not a willing partner in America's grand plans"[269] and began to openly disagree with alliance strategy. Karzai's actions in Kandahar in 2009 reflect this pattern.

Karzai traveled with commander of US forces to Kandahar prior to military operations there because obtaining support from subnational actors for such actions was a tactic of the new strategy. Karzai was supposed to "urge elders to support the upcoming security operations."[270] Instead of cooperating in the interest of Afghanistan, in remarks to local leaders openly *opposed* the military operations: "We have to demonstrate our sovereignty," he said, and military operations would not occur until elders were "happy and satisfied."[271] Similarly, in April 2010 Karzai told elders in Marja he was "opposed" to the operation there.[272]

Although the overall threat level continued, and the allies remained dependent on each other to balance it, cohesion decreased because elements of the alliance strategy threatened the Karzai regime's interests. Attempts to "build local governance" were a direct affront to and "disrupting" the "natural system of self-regulating Pashtun governance"[273] that Karzai relied on for political power. To retain office and ensure political/financial influence after 2014 (when he would step down), Karzai needed to preserve (not upend) the subsystems of power the USA actively sought to modernize.

Despite US efforts to "Make Nice with Mr. Karzai," as the *New York Times* wrote,[274] such overtures again gave way to low cohesion and a "shaky and vulnerable" partnership.[275] Disagreements and associated decreased cohesion extended from tactics (Karzai opposed night raids because they incensed local leaders important to his influence) to overall alliance approach to the insurgents. Deviating from the alliance strategy of "reversing the momentum" of the Taliban, for example, Karzai said "he would seek to reconcile with top-level Taliban leaders" and intended "to convene a tribal *Jirga*" to "discuss how to bring the Taliban back into Afghan political life."[276] Karzai met representatives of HiG (an insurgent group), which presented a peace plan.[277] Reflecting that Karzai's actions contravened alliance strategy, Chairman of the Joint Chiefs of Staff, Admiral Mike Mullen, called the meetings "premature." The Karzai regime's actions vis-à-vis curbing bandwagoning—and specifically related to *effectiveness*—also evidence that regime priorities trumped the national interest.

Karzai's "Pendulum Approach" to Curbing Bandwagoning

The Karzai regime did not entirely ignore collusion and took some steps to curb it; however, these countermeasures were largely half-hearted and failed to ensure that all relevant government actors combatted the insurgents in a unified manner. For example, in 2003 following US pressure Karzai removed Agha Sherzai (Kandahar's governor) because he used alliance resources as patronage to cement control over his subnatioal area. Instead of jettisoning this bandwagoning-prone actor from the regime entirely, however, Karzai re-assigned him as the Minister of Urban Affairs. At face value, Karzai firing Sherzai can be seen as an attempt to replace an official who was not fully cooperating with someone who would be more inclined to implement the US-Afghan alliance strategy. At the same time, Karzai's decision must be viewed in the context of when it happened (when he needed US support to win the 2004 elections) and what transpired thereafter: Karzai replaced Sherzai with the warlord's cousin (allowing Sherzai continued influence in the region) and a mere two years later re-appointed Sherzai as governor,[278] because the votes Sherzai could rally were vital to Karzai's re-election.

In a similar move, in 2004 Karzai sacked Ismail Khan as Herat's governor.[279] On paper, this can be viewed as an attempt to curb government collusion by replacing a governor who misused alliance resources and regularly used private militia to "enforce his will" instead of curbing insurgent violence.[280] Like Sherzai's dismissal, though, Karzai curbed Khan's behavior less to advance alliance objectives and for Afghanistan's interest than to *secure his own* and win the upcoming presidential election. Replacing Khan a month before the poll "helped Mr. Karzai in the election by opening up the political scene and removing his [Khan's] political control of the region."[281] Further, with an eye toward the 2009 contest and needing Khan's support to win, Karzai did not remove Khan from the regime but re-shuffled him to the position of Minister of Energy and

Mines where he would again bandwagon by diverting alliance resources (by some estimates $70 million).[282]

The central regime's actions vis-à-vis such warlord-cum-governors can be viewed as a "pendulum approach" to curbing bandwagoning that reflects the motivations driving weak regime actions: Karzai curbed bandwagoning when doing so was in his interests—to get US help for the 2004 elections [Sherzai] or remove an actor that hindered re-election [Khan]—only to then swing back and reinstate bandwagoning actors because they were important to his political survival.

As the alliance wore on, the USA recognized insurgents were obtaining (via direct and indirect diversion) capabilities transferred to the alliance to defeat them.[283] In addition to creating American-led institutions to stop this from occurring, the USA pressed Karzai to stop Afghan government actors from diverting alliance aid resources to insurgents, which was fueling escalating violence.[284] Partly in response to this pressure, and according to alliance strategy (outlined in the Afghanistan Compact), Karzai in 2008 created the High Office of Oversight to investigate corruption claims; and soon thereafter, he established an inspectors-general office in each ministry to investigate and remove from office regime actors with "illicit" links to insurgents, narco-traffickers, or other entities fomenting violence.[285] One year later, Karzai launched a specialized task force in the national police to pursue organized crime within and outside of the Afghan government.

Initially, it looked promising that these new "anti-bandwagoning" bodies would help curb collusion. In 2010, for example, the task force arrested and jailed a key regime official on charges of corruption. The prospects of this anti-bandwagoning body making any real difference soon washed away, however, as Karzai took to his "pendulum approach" to bandwagoning and secured this individual's release. Of the dozens of cases started, a US official told me in an interview, "very few would yield results, and the spigot of resources flowing out because of this and to the bad guys wouldn't shut off."[286] Another analysis of Karzai's inaction vis-à-vis bandwagoning notes: "Karzai did not support his anti-corruption squads when they attempted to arrest corrupt ministers, and he was unwilling to remove corrupt governors who were friends."[287] By keeping in office actors prone to collusion, and sidestepping efforts to cull ministries of colluding elements,[288] Karzai's actions went against and alliance goals and hindered alliance effectiveness. As aptly encapsulated by Barfield (2010):

> Karzai was not really interested in building an institutionalized state structure. Despite the large sums that the international community was investing...Karzai's model of government was patrimonial...personal relationships determined everything from who would amass personal wealth to who would be thrown in jail. Karzai...used [the assets of the state] to create a patronage network of personal clients bound to him.[289]

These "personal clients" included regime actors that bandwagoned but also represented power and influence that would help Karzai remain in power. Accordingly, it was not always in Karzai's interests to push them to balance (as opposed to bandwagon). Reflecting this, in a meeting to decide how much the USA should increase military resources to secure alliance objectives, a senior US official argued that it was "premature to discuss resources until we have a very clear sense of how we" will "deal with corrupt and predatory Afghan governance."[290]

"Feathering His Own Nest": *Karzai Diverts Resources to Bolster Power*

The regime of Karzai has become a powerful, interlocking criminal enterprise.[291]

Not only did Karzai take insufficient measures to curb bandwagoning and "swing back" to undermine some actions he did enact, the leader and close central regime associates also allegedly engaged in corruption. In particular after Karzai had won the 2004 election and rammed through institutions to consolidate his power, alliance resources became attractive sources of patronage. Karzai "maintained his grip on power" and built a "body of personal patronage in support of his rule" by "capitalizing upon his position" as the "distributor of American and foreign aid, weapons and cash and the appointer of powerful government offices"[292] Karzai's actions were aptly described by US General Brent Scowcroft, who told me in an interview that the leader was "more interested in feathering its own nest" than "working closely with the U.S." for the betterment of Afghanistan as a whole.[293] The central regime's attempts to "feather its own nest" correspond with motivations determining actions by regimes in internal threat alliances. While engaged in these forms of bandwagoning, Karzai's central regime was also working with the USA to *balance* insurgents seeking its overthrow (because doing remained in its interests).

First, Karzai *abused Executive authority* in ways that violated alliance objectives and went against the Afghan national interest but advanced his own by maintaining or expanding patron-client links vital to staying in power. This included appointing (or refusing to fire) actors known to bandwagon in order to reap the patron-client benefits associated with them. A few weeks after being named Interim leader, for example, Karzai replaced the recently installed governor of Kandahar with the province's most powerful warlord (Agha Sherzai). Doing so helped Karzai retain influence in the region (benefiting prospects for the 2004 election) but hindered alliance effectiveness because Sherzai proceeded to collude with the enemy by ensuring a "high level" Taliban leader's (and target of a US-led manhunt) escape into Pakistan[294] and facilitating the departure from Afghanistan of Taliban leader Mullah Omar's deputy.[295] Routing the Taliban/Al-Qaeda was vital to improving the lives of Afghans as well as core alliance objectives—yet Sherzai's bandwagoning, enabled by Karzai's appointment, hindered allies' ability to realize them.

Nearly ten years later, Karzai continued to retain actors proven to bandwagon. For example, he refused to sack Ismail Khan from his position as Minister of Energy and Water over allegations he was diverting and using as patronage ($US millions) alliance resources to maintain his domestic influence. A US memo from 2009 refers to Khan as "known for his corruption and ineffectiveness at the energy ministry."[296] Karzai refused to remove Khan despite "repeated interventions directly with Karzai," the US memo says, because of "Karzai's deeply personal bonds with Khan." This "personal bond" was based in a mutually beneficial patron-client relationship defined mainly by Khan's pivotal role in helping Karzai win the 2009 presidential election (and what he received in exchange for this support).[297] Warlords-cum-regime actors such as Khan openly "pledged support" for Karzai's bid for re-election and actively drummed up votes in exchange, reportedly, for receiving new or retaining existing (as with Khan) lucrative cabinet-level posts.[298] Such actions led one historian to dub Karzai's 2009 re-election campaign the "warlord reunion tour": the president "paraded around" and promised these actors positions or financial payoffs in exchange for support in a given region.[299] By retaining such bandwagoning regime actors that would go on to compete fiercely for alliance resources and turf, however, Karzai facilitated collusion (and corruption) that increased violence: the "conflict over the state" between elite networks of bandwagoning actors "brought Afghanistan closer to interfactional political violence."[300]

In addition to using executive powers to appoint/retain bandwagoning regime actors, Karzai leveraged this authority to perform favors for actors who could help him remain in power. For example, and in violation of a prior agreement with the USA, Karzai facilitated the release of a prominent Taliban commander (Mullah Abdul Qayyum Zakir) in order to appease Sher Mohammed Akhundzada (former governor of Helmand) and receive this subnational powerbroker's support in the upcoming presidential election. Akhundzada wanted the commander released (due to his patron-client ties to the operative) and Karzai needed votes in Helmand. Events thereafter clearly demonstrate that Karzai's decision to prioritize patron over alliance objectives hindered effectiveness: Zakir returned to Pakistan, became a higher level Taliban military commander, and then returned to Afghanistan as the Taliban's commander in Helmand.[301] The decision clearly benefited Karzai (he won the election) but hindered alliance effectiveness: "the vast majority of U.S. military fatalities and injuries occurred in areas under Zakir's authority" in 2009.[302] Not only was the USA dealing with components of Afghanistan's army/police who were bandwagoning (while others cooperated/balanced) but also a central regime prone to bandwagon when it best suited his interests and to the point where deals beneficial to central regime power cost alliance lives.

Alliance Effectiveness Remains Low as Obama's First Term Ends
By the end of President Obama's first term, the internal threat level remained high and alliance effectiveness moderate to low. Various metrics demonstrate this. The number of insurgent forces aiming to topple the regime increased by 800 percent from 2002 to 2009 and reached 36,000 in 2010.[303] In tandem with this growth, the "organizational capabilities and operational reach" of the insurgents were "qualitatively and geographically expanding."[304] The insurgency had capacity sufficient to "sustain itself indefinitely" and retained access to a multiplicity of reliable sources for funding.[305] In tandem with this increase in size, the insurgent attacks onto regime and US targets escalated by 400 percent (2002–2006),[306] 51 percent (2007–2008),[307] with all but two provinces experiencing a rise in attacks over this period,[308] and a further 300 percent through 2009.[309] Weekly attacks in 2010 were the highest since the beginning of the alliance,[310] and average monthly attacks escalated by 41 percent over the next two years (and never below 1500).[311] Through the period examined attacks occurred with "much greater frequency" and in more "varied locations."[312]

Beginning around 2003 insurgents steadily increased presence in and *control of* territory, representing an escalation in threat to Karzai's regime—centrally and subnationally. In 2004, the UN designated 33 percent of the country as "high risk" for their staff. Northern provinces remained relatively stable, but the "situation in the south and southeast" was "more complex,"[313] with insurgents "operating openly" in Zabul and Uruzgan provinces, among others.[314] On the heels of the insurgency's further spread, in 2007 the regime controlled "a very small portion of Afghanistan" (Kabul and some southern/western areas) and "much of the country" was under the influence of either "armed local leaders" or insurgent forces.[315] The same year, the UN designated 84 percent of territory as "high risk" and[316] insurgents functioned "fairly freely" in Helmand, Uruzgan, Zabul, Paktia, and Kunar provinces, among others.[317] Challenging the regime's authority (national and subnational), the Taliban sought to establish alternative governments in Afghanistan's provinces; and these "shadow governors" increased by 200 percent from 2005 to 2009 (11/34–33/34 provinces).[318] Territory with a "permanent" insurgent presence also increased from 54 percent (2007) to 72 percent (2008) and then again in 2009 to 80 percent.[319] Early in 2010, the Taliban was active in more than one-third of Afghanistan's 400 districts, up from 2001 when they had a "negligible presence in the country."[320] Afghan government control over southern provinces (particularly Helmand and Kandahar) remained particularly tenuous,[321] and the Taliban had "gained de facto control over many outlying areas in Kandahar," leaving "Afghanistan's second-largest city…cut off from Kabul."[322]

Afghanistan's seat of government and Karzai himself also remained under duress. Attacks and assassination attempts in Kabul occurred regularly through 2012. Illustrating the proximity of threat to the central regime, by 2008 the insurgency had fronts in areas of provinces that are within a 60-minute drive of the presidential palace.[323] By 2009 at least 80 districts had to be secured "in order to weaken the insurgency enough that it would *no longer pose a threat to the central government* [emphasis mine]."[324] Insurgents continued reaping revenue from the opium trade that (by 2006) provided more than 70 percent of Taliban funding and (through 2010) roughly $150 million annually to insurgents.[325]

The efficiency and brazen nature of insurgent attacks also evidence that the threat to the regime remained consistently high. According to a 2006 CIA assessment, the insurgency was a greater threat "than at any point since late 2001."[326] The Taliban's response to "Operation Medusa"

(2006 in Kandahar) and the military assets uncovered thereafter bring to life this dire assessment. Over several days of fighting where more than 500 Taliban were killed and 160 captured, the insurgents discharged 4,000 rounds of ammunition, 2,000 RPGs, and 1,000 mortars. After the fighting stopped, ally forces uncovered 1 million rounds of ammunition, a fully stocked field hospital, and a facility for training suicide bombers.[327] Nearly ten years after the alliance began, insurgent forces could execute sophisticated and effective attacks in Kabul. In 2010, for example, insurgents battled Afghan forces for five hours a mere 200 yards from the presidential palace[328] in "one of the most dramatic attacks on Kabul" since the Taliban's demise" in 2001.[329] In September 2011, the Taliban staged a 20-hour siege on regime buildings in Kabul—located near the US Embassy—and soon thereafter orchestrated the elaborate assassination of the Chairman of the Afghan High Peace Council.[330] The week before this author visited Afghanistan, insurgents infiltrated the Ministry of Interior and assassinated top-level officials. These statistics and examples indicate that by the end of the period examined, the alliance was largely unable to weaken the threat to the point that it no longer endangered the regime and US interests.

Alliance effectiveness, therefore, remained low—for two reasons. First, as demonstrated through the above discussion, Karzai had not sufficiently curbed government collusion with narco-traffickers and insurgents. Whether internal threat alliances achieve their goal hinges not only on level of military resources aggregated but also the central regime's ability and willingness to corral their regime's component parts and push them to carry out agreed strategy (and balance). In the case of Afghanistan, it seems Karzai was largely unable or not willing to take these steps. The implication for alliance effectiveness was to essentially preclude unified balancing by regime actors against the insurgents. As former Afghan Finance Minister Ashraf Ghani said in 2009, it was not the insurgents who were the "largest threat" to Afghanistan but, rather, the "(Karzai) government" itself.[331]

And second, the USA and Afghanistan had not yet been able to amass sufficient resources to weaken the insurgents. As US Ambassador to Afghanistan said, "Afghanistan was a mission that in past years was poorly defined and under-resourced."[332] By the end of Obama's first term, the alliance had not aggregated capabilities sufficient to weaken actors threatening the regime's survival because those agencies and armed forces charged with balancing the internal threat lacked the force size and material to do so. Specifically, the alliance did not enhance the capacity of Afghan Army and Police forces to independently and consistently weaken actors threatening the regime's survival.[333]

Despite growing the Afghan National Army's (ANA) troop size by more than 2,000 percent, by 2010 the ANA remained unable to consistently thwart insurgent challenges due to "chronic shortfalls in training personnel, faulty equipment, slow infrastructural development, poor logistics, and the crippling army attrition rates."[334] Not a single army unit was assessed as "capable of conducting its mission" without US assistance as of September 2010. The proportion of army units capable of conducting "independent actions"[335] increased in 2012, though only to 7 percent of the total force. And according to a separate analysis, "the majority" of army units were by 2012 "unable to meet even the most basic operational benchmarks, particularly in the crucial areas of supply, logistics and air support."[336] Capacity shortcomings in turn "limit[ed]" the army's ability to "project force" beyond "large urban areas and logistical hubs."[337] Looking ahead, an assessment concluded it "highly improbable" the ANA would be able to alone safeguard the regime and balance insurgent threats.[338]

Like the army, the Afghan National Police (ANP) increased in size, but most assessments concluded that it remained too small to extend control across Afghanistan and ineffective to consistently balance threats.[339] By 2008, for example, not a single unit received a score/assessment of "fully capable" of ensuring stability and thwarting threats[340] and roughly 60 percent of units received the lowest possible score.[341] Toward the end of this period, the Afghan Minister of Interior bluntly said: "the Police is supposed to get to grips with terrorism, criminality, and narcotics" but is simply "not up to the job."[342] The picture remained largely the same through 2012, when 9 percent of police were deemed capable of "independent actions."[343] Collectively, capabilities aggregated were insufficient to shift the balance in favor of the regime and weaken the threat to the point it no longer represented a core threat to their security.

Case Conclusions

In this chapter I used the US–Afghanistan case to evidence the three main elements of the book's theoretical framework. The chapter traced US–Afghanistan cooperation to defeat Taliban insurgents and secure associated US interests. It showed that the Afghan government of President Hamid Karzai sought US assistance to thwart rising threats to his survival from Taliban militants, while the USA aligned in order to ensure terrorists could not again use Afghanistan as a base to plan and launch attacks (as they did on September 11, 2001) and ensure access to natural resources in the region. Regarding bandwagoning, the chapter showed that some elements of the Afghan Army fought against the Taliban (balanced), but others actively cooperated with them (bandwagoned) at the same time. Similarly, while some subnational governors and elements of the national police resisted Taliban incursions, others aligned with the worst of the terrorist organization. Finally, the chapter showed that the alliance was largely ineffective due to insufficient resources and Karzai's insufficient efforts to stop elements of his regime from colluding (bandwagoning) with the belligerents.

Notes

1. Antonio Giustozzi, *War, Politics and Society in Afghanistan, 1978–1992* (Washington, D.C.: Georgetown University Press, 2000).
2. Charles G. Cogan, "Partners in Time: The CIA and Afghanistan since 1979," *World Policy Journal* 10, No. 2 (Summer, 1993), 75.
3. Rais Ahmad Khan, "Pakistan in 1992: Waiting for Change," *Asian Survey* 33, No. 2 (1993), 129–140.
4. Kamal Matinuddin, *The Taliban Phenomenon, Afghanistan 1994–1997* (Oxford: Oxford University Press, 1999), 26.
5. Ahmed Rashid, *Taliban: Militant Islam, Oil and Fundamentalism in Central Asia* (New Haven: Yale University Press, 2001), 2–5.
6. On the Taliban's rule, see M. J. Gohari, *The Taliban: Ascent to Power* (Oxford: Oxford University Press, 2010).
7. Their official title was: the United Islamic Front for the Salvation of Afghanistan. See Ahmed Rashid, *Descent into Chaos—The U.S. and the Disaster in Pakistan, Afghanistan, and Central Asia* (New York, NY: Penguin Books, 2009), 15.

8. On Al-Qaeda's origins, see 9–11 Commission. *The 9/11 Commission Report: Final Report of the National Commission on Terrorist Attacks Upon the United States—Authorized Edition* (New York, W.W. Norton & Company, 2004), 58–59. See also "Bin Laden's Fatwa," *PBS NewsHour*, August 1996.
9. Rashid, *Descent into Chaos* (2009), 15.
10. For an overview of the objectives of the broader "War on Terror," see Belasco, "The Cost of Iraq, Afghanistan, and Other Global War on Terror Operations Since 9/11" (Washington, DC: Congressional Research Services, March 2011).
11. *CNN News*, "Transcript of President Bush's Address—September 20, 2011."
12. Rashid, *Descent into Chaos* (2009).
13. CNN News, "Transcript of President Bush's Address—September 20, 2011." September 21, 2001; Antonio Giustozzi, *Empires of Mud: Wars and Warlords in Afghanistan* (New York, NY: Columbia University Press, 2012), 89.
14. Charles Tenet, *At the Center of the Storm* (London, UK: Harper Collins, 2007).
15. Rashid, *Descent into Chaos* (2009).
16. Rashid, *Descent into Chaos* (2009).
17. This term was coined by Ahmed Rashid. See Ahmed Rashid, *Descent into Chaos—The U.S. and the Disaster in Pakistan, Afghanistan, and Central Asia* (New York, NY: Penguin Books, 2009), 127.
18. Ismael Khan controlled vast expanses in the West, while General Rashid Dostum controlled territory in the north. General Daud had control over three provinces in the northeast and Kunduz. In the south, Gul Agha Sherzai controlled four provinces. And in the center, Karim Khalili, Syed Akbari, and Mohammed Mohaqiq essentially controlled various territories. For an excellent overview of these warlords as well as their rivalries, motives, and activities, see Rashid, *Descent into Chaos* (2009), 127–130.
19. Rashid, *Descent into Chaos* (2009), 131.
20. Interview with author, US Envoy to Afghanistan James Dobbins, Washington, DC, July 10, 2012.
21. Rajiv Chandrasekaran, "Obama, Karzai: Not So Chummy," *Washington Post*, May 6, 2009.

22. In January 2002, for example, and representing passive bandwagoning, militiamen loyal to two warlords (Fahim and Dostum) fought each other in Mazar-i-Sharif; and in April of the same year, Hekmatyar attacked Fahim in Jalalabad.
23. This included Gul Agha Sherzai of Kandahar and former President Rabbani. Gulshan Dietl, "War, Peace and the Warlords: The Case of Ismail Khan of Herat in Afghanistan," *Alternatives—Turkish Journal of International Relations*, 3, No. 283 (2004), 51.
24. Rashid, *Descent into Chaos* (2009). 133.
25. Vice President Dick Cheney, "Remarks to Multinational Force of Observers: South Camp—Sharm el-Sheikh, Egypt," Wednesday, March 13, 2002.
26. See, for example, Rashid, *Descent into Chaos* (2009). xxxviii. In 2009 the USA and ISAF performed an assessment of the "state of the insurgency" in Afghanistan, the results of which were declassified the following year. ISAF Briefing, "State of the Insurgency: Trends, Intentions and Objectives," December 22, 2009. Also, Dexter Filkins, "The Great American Arm-Twist in Afghanistan," *The New York Times*, October 24, 2009, and Michael E. O'Hanlon and Hassina Sherjan, *Toughing it out in Afghanistan* (Washington, DC: Brookings Institution Press, 2010), 7.
27. Statement by Zalmay Khalilzad before the US Senate Committee on Foreign Relations on October 23, 2003. Statement made in hearing to consider his nomination to be Ambassador to Afghanistan. Accessed via US Senate Committee on Foreign Relations website and hearing.
28. For these figures and annual breakdowns, see relevant table for this chapter in the Annex at the end of the dissertation.
29. Sheri Berman, "From the Sun King to Karzai," *Foreign Affairs*, Vol. 89, No. 2 (March/April 2010), 2.
30. For an overview of US counter-narcotics programming, see "U.S. Counter-narcotics Strategy in Afghanistan—A Report by the Senate Caucus on International Narcotics Control" (Washington, DC: July 2010).
31. As stated by the USA, the purpose of the aid component of the intervention was to "support Afghanistan in its efforts to ensure economic growth led by the private sector, establish a democratic and capable state governed by the rule of law, and provide basic services for its people." United States Agency for International

Development, "USAID Assistance to Afghanistan 2002–2008," Press Release from March 27, 2008.
32. Islamic Government of Afghanistan, "Terms of Reference for the Combined Forced Command and ISAF PRTs in Afghanistan," January 27, 2005. As quoted in Oskari Eronen, "PRT Models in Afghanistan: Approaches to Civil-Military Integration," *CMC Finland Civilian Crisis Management Studies*, Vol. 1, No. 5 (2008).
33. Signed on May 17, 2005.
34. US Office of the Press Secretary, White House, "Joint Declaration of the United States-Afghanistan Strategic Partnership," May 23, 2005. Available for download here: http://georgewbush-whitehouse.archives.gov/news/releases/2005/05/20050523-2.html
35. During this period, suicide bombings increased from 27 to 139 (400 percent), the number of IEDs detonated from 783 to 1677, and there was a threefold increase in insurgent initiated attacks (from 783, in 2005, to 1677, in 2006. Seth G. Jones, "The Rise of Afghanistan's Insurgency State Failure and Jihad." *International Security* 32, No. 4. Spring 2008, 7–8.
36. As quoted in Walter Pincus, "Growing Threat Seen in Afghan Insurgency: Defense Intelligence Agency Chief Cites Surging Violence in Homeland," *The Washington Post*, March 1, 2006.
37. Rashid, *Descent into Chaos* (2009), 362.
38. Rashid, *Descent into Chaos* (2009), 203.
39. Tomsen, *The Wars of Afghanistan* (2011), 620.
40. This was a marked increase from prior annual allocations to the alliance—$797 million (2004) and $830 million (2005–2006). Statistics cited in Rashid, *Descent into Chaos* (2009), 203.
41. For an excellent review of military operations, see Seth Jones, *In the Graveyard of Empires: America's War in Afghanistan* (New York, NY: W Norton, 2010).
42. "The Afghanistan Compact," as released by NATO, available here: http://www.nato.int/isaf/docu/epub/pdf/afghanistan_compact.pdf
43. "The Afghanistan Compact," as released by NATO. To operationalize these agreements, the allies formed the first high-level interally coordination group since 2001. The group was part of the Joint Coordination and Monitoring Board (JCMB) and comprised of senior US military and civilian officials, major donors, and led by

Karzai, to discuss strategy and priorities monthly as outlined in "The Afghanistan Compact," as released by NATO.
44. Tomsen, *The Wars of Afghanistan* (2011), 590.
45. As described in Woodward, *Obama's Wars* (2010).
46. Stanley McChrystal, Commander US Forces and NATO International Security Assistance Force, Afghanistan, "Commander's Initial Assessment" (Kabul, Afghanistan: United States Army, August 30, 2009).
47. Ewan MacAskill, "Obama replaces top general in Afghanistan," *The Guardian*, May 11, 2009.
48. Stanley McChrystal, Commander US Forces and NATO International Security Assistance Force, Afghanistan, "Commander's Initial Assessment" (Kabul, Afghanistan: United States Army, August 30, 2009). Other proponents of COIN included General David Petraeus, then commanding US forces in Iraq.
49. Chandrasekaran, *The War Within the War for Afghanistan* (2012), 120.
50. And doing so required a new tactic—protecting population centers and helping the regime "earn the trust" of the Afghan people. Commander's Initial Assessment, as released via the *Washington Post*, August 2009.
51. Advocates of CT-Plus were Vice President Joe Biden and Karl Eikenberry (US Ambassador to Afghanistan), among others. See Toby Harnden, "Joe Biden: the worrying rise of Barack Obama's Mr. Wrong," *The Telegraph*, October 17, 2009.
52. Eide, *Power Struggle in Afghanistan*, 107–109.
53. The cable is summarized in Chandrasekaran, *The War Within the War for Afghanistan* (2012), 122–125.
54. The cable is quoted in Chandrasekaran, *The War Within the War for Afghanistan* (2012), 125–126.
55. Per the "The Afghanistan Compact," as released by NATO.
56. Richard Oppel Jr., "Afghan leader Courts the Warlord Vote, but Others Fear the Cost," *New York Times*, August 8, 2009.
57. Rajiv Chandrasekaran, "Administration Is Keeping Ally at Arm's Length," *The Washington Post*, May 06, 2009.
58. On US meetings with alternative candidates, see Eide, *Power Struggle in Afghanistan* (2012), 128.

59. Mainly, Karzai accused the USA of supporting Dr. Abdullah Abdullah. As quoted in Woodward, *Obama's Wars* (2010), 148.
60. This after some discrepancies regarding vote tabulation led to calls for a run-off between Karzai and the second-place finisher. "Karzai Re-elected Amid Turmoil," *CBS News*, November 2, 2009.
61. Rashid, "How Obama Lost Karzai" (2011), 82.
62. Memorandum drafted and released by Obama's National Security Advisor on November 29, 2009, entitled "President Obama's Final Orders for Afghanistan Pakistan Strategy, or Terms Sheet." "Terms Sheet" for Afghanistan Pakistan Strategy, November 29, 2009, as outlined in Woodward, *Obama's Wars* (2010)—Annex.
63. "Remarks by the President in Address to the Nation on the Way Forward in Afghanistan and Pakistan," Press Release from the Office of the Press Secretary, Whitehouse, December 1, 2009.
64. Cook, *Afghanistan: The Perfect Failure* (2012), 144.
65. Rashid, "How Obama Lost Karzai," (2011), 80.
66. Chandrasekaran, *The War Within the War for Afghanistan* (2012), 168.
67. "Our Man in Kabul?" *Wall Street* Journal, November 24, 2012.
68. Isby, *Afghanistan—Graveyard of Empires* (2010), 46–47.
69. Steven David makes this point in (1991b) "Explaining Alignment in the Third World," 239. See also David (1992) "Why the Third World Still Matters."
70. Barnett Rubin, *The Fragmentation of Afghanistan*. (New Haven, CT: Yale University Press, 1995).
71. Steve Hess, "Coming to Terms with neopatrimonialism: Soviet and American nation-building projects in Afghanistan," *Central Asian Survey*, 29, No. 2 (2010), 174.
72. Rubin, *The Fragmentation of Afghanistan* (1995), 47.
73. For summaries of prior state formation models in Afghanistan, see Alexander Thier and Jarat Chopra, "The road ahead: political and institutional reconstruction in Afghanistan," *Third World Quarterly* 23, No. 5 (2002), 893–907.
74. For an excellent overview of the Afghan government and associated powers, see Barnett Rubin, *Afghanistan from the Cold War through the War on Terror* (Oxford: Oxford University Press, 2013).

75. Peter Tomsen, *The Wars of Afghanistan: Messianic Terrorism, Tribal Conflicts, and the Failures of Great Powers* (New York: Public Affairs Books, 2011), 46.
76. Anatol Lieven, "The War in Afghanistan: Its Background and Future Prospects," *Conflict, Security and Development*, 9, No. 3 (2009), 344.
77. See Rubin, *Afghanistan from the Cold War* (2013).
78. Michael Bratton and Nicolas van de Walle, N., "Neopatrimonial regimes and political transitions in Africa," *World Politics*, 46, No. 4 (1994), 458.
79. Antonio Giustozzia and Dominique Orsini, "Centre–periphery relations in Afghanistan: Badakhshan between patrimonialism and institution-building," *Central Asian Survey*, 28, No. 1 (March 2009), 1 John L. Cook, *Afghanistan: The Perfect Failure—A War Doomed by the Coalition's Strategies, Policies, and Political Correctness* (New York: Xlibris Publishing, 2012), 46.
80. The ANP includes the Afghan Uniformed Police (AUP), Afghan Border Police (ABP), the Afghan National Civil Order Police (ANCOP), and the Counter Narcotics Police of Afghanistan (CNPA). The army consists of corps, the largest unit size, of which there are seven in Afghanistan—six are ground forces and one is the National Army Air Force. Each corps is divided into divisions, and divisions into brigades—similar to the US military after which it was modeled, brigades are divided into battalions, companies, and platoons.
81. Interview with author, US Ambassador to Afghanistan Robert Finn, via Skype, September 20, 2012.
82. Isby, *Afghanistan—Graveyard of Empires* (2010), 55.
83. "Afghanistan: Exit vs. Engagement," Crisis Group Asia Briefing N°115 (Brussels/Kabul: International Crisis Group, November 28, 2010), 7.
84. As quoted in "Afghanistan: The Long, Hard Road to the 2014 Transition," Crisis Group Asia Report N°236 (Brussels/Kabul: International Crisis Group, October 8, 2012), 17, fn. 16.
85. "Afghanistan: Exit vs. Engagement," Crisis Group (2010), 4.
86. "A Force in Fragments," Crisis Group (2010), 1.
87. On patron-client relations and clientelism in Afghanistan, see Thomas Barfield, *Afghanistan—A Cultural and Political History* (Princeton, NJ: Princeton University Press, 2010); see also Rubin,

The Fragmentation of Afghanistan (1995); Isby, *Afghanistan— Graveyard of Empires* (2010); and Edward Schatz, *Modern Clan Politics: The Power of 'Blood' in Kazakhstan and Beyond* (Seattle, WA: University of Washington Press, 2004), xxiii.
88. Barfield, *Afghanistan* (2010), 17–18.
89. Barfield, *Afghanistan* (2010), 18.
90. Barfield, *Afghanistan* (2010), 18.
91. Barfield, *Afghanistan* (2010), 63.
92. "The Afghan beneficiaries pledge allegiance to the ideology of their outside patron while avoiding any commitments that might limit their freedom of maneuver against local rivals. At an opportune time, they switch to other patrons, always with an eye to increasing their personal power and wealth and weakening their local rivals." Tomsen, *The Wars of Afghanistan* (2011), 58.
93. Astri Suhkre, "Reconstruction as Modernization: The Post-conflict Project in Afghanistan," *Third World Quarterly*, 28, No. 7 (2007), 1302.
94. Barfield, *Afghanistan* (2010), 12.
95. The two networks were: first, the former Northern Alliance (NA) jihadis, consisting mainly of the Panjsheris in Shura-yi Nezar, which is the military wing of the Jamiat Tanzim, and second, Hamid Karzai's elite network. Timor Sharan, "The Dynamics of Elite Networks and Patron-Client Networks in Afghanistan," *Europe-Asia Studies*, Vol. 63, No. 6 (2011), 1110.
96. Wolfgang Danspeckgruber and Robert Finn, "The Afghan Economy," in Wolfgang Danspeckgruber and Robert Finn, eds. *Building State and Security in Afghanistan* (Princeton, NJ: Liechtenstein Institute on Self-Determination at Princeton University, 2007), 150.
97. Sharan, "The Dynamics of Elite Networks" (2011), 1117. See also Schatz, *Modern Clan Politics* (2004), xxiii.
98. Naazneen H. Barma, "Peacebuilding and the predatory political economy of insecurity: evidence from Cambodia, East Timor and Afghanistan," *Conflict, Security & Development* 12, No. 3 (2012), 287.
99. As Mac Ginty argues, the alliance itself provided additional incentives for bandwagoning: "many of these warlords also benefited from the post-Taliban state-building process: exploiting reconstruction resources, seeking sponsorship from the US military,

accepting ministerial positions, etc. In other words, some of Afghanistan's warlords benefited from both state-building *and* state weakness." Roger Mac Ginty, "Warlords and the liberal peace: statebuilding in Afghanistan," *Conflict, Security & Development* 10, No. 4 (2010), 585.
100. Isby, *Afghanistan—Graveyard of Empires* (2010), 214.
101. Arjun Chowdhury and Ronald R. Krebs, "The Afghan Challenge Is Far Tougher," *Foreign Affairs* (July/August 2010), Vol. 89, No. 4.
102. Andrew Wilder and Sarah Listed, "State-building at the Subnational Level in Afghanistan: A Missed Opportunity," in Wolfgang Danspeckgruber and Robert Finn, eds. *Building State and Security in Afghanistan* (Princeton, NJ: Liechtenstein Institute on Self-Determination at Princeton University, 2007), 104.
103. The White House, "Remarks by the President on a New Strategy for Afghanistan and Pakistan," March 27, 2009. Available here: http://www.whitehouse.gov/the_press_office/Remarks-by-the-President-on-a-New-Strategy-for-Afghanistan-and-Pakistan/. Second portion of quote as stated in Woodward, *Obama's Wars* (2010), 113.
104. Combined with other actors, these three encompassed what Jones (2009) termed the "complex adaptive system" of actors representing the "threat environment" in Afghanistan. Dr. Seth G. Jones, "U.S. Strategy in Afghanistan," Testimony Before the Committee on Foreign Affairs Subcommittee on Middle East and South Asia, United States House of Representatives, April 2, 2009.
105. These included elements of the Taliban ("Neo"-Taliban), Al-Qaeda, and two groups that originated as *mujahedeen* and again took up arms to push a new (now American) occupation from Afghan soil: *Hezb-i-Islami* and the "Haqqani network." On these two insurgent groups, see Jones, "The Rise of Afghanistan's Insurgency" (2008).
106. David Isby, *Afghanistan—Graveyard of Empires: A New History of the Borderland* (New York, NY: Pegasus Books, 2010), 130.
107. Isby, *Afghanistan—Graveyard of Empires* (2010), 133, and Brian Glyn Williams, *Afghanistan Declassified: A Guide to America's Long War* (Philadelphia, PA: University of Pennsylvania Press, 2012), 144.

108. By 2002 these actors had re-solidified control in the following areas: Rashid Dostum (Mazar-i-Sharif), Daoud Khan (northeast), Karim Khalili (Center, in Hazara), Pacha Khan Zadran (southern areas, along the Pakistan border), Hazrat Ali (also in the south, in Nangarhar), and Gul Agha Sherzai (Kandahar). Rashid, *Descent into Chaos* (2009).
109. J. Alexander Their, "A Third Branch? (Re)establishing the Judicial System in Afghanistan," in Wolfgang Danspeckgruber and Robert Finn, eds. *Building State and Security in Afghanistan* (Princeton, NJ: Liechtenstein Institute on Self-Determination at Princeton University, 2007), 48–49.
110. Rashid, *Descent into Chaos* (2009). 131.
111. As paraphrased in Woodward, *Obama's Wars* (2010), 43–44.
112. On why the region has been considered important for US energy security, see "House Bill S.2749. To update the Silk Road Strategy Act of 1999," http://www.gpo.gov/fdsys/pkg/BILLS-109s2749is/pdf/BILLS-109s2749is.pdf
113. On Al-Qaeda's origins, see 9–11 Commission. *The 9/11 Commission Report: Final Report of the National Commission on Terrorist Attacks Upon the United States—Authorized Edition* (New York, W.W. Norton & Company, 2004), 58–59. See also "Bin Laden's Fatwa," *PBS NewsHour*, August 1996.
114. Kenneth Katzman, "Afghanistan: Post-Taliban Governance, Security, and U.S. Policy" (Washington, DC: Congressional Research Services, March 2011), 6. *CBC News*, "Bin Laden claims responsibility for 9/11," October 29, 2004.
115. Statistics drawn from two sources. Stock exchange figures taken from "9/11 by the Numbers," *New York Magazine*, September 2012. Other estimates taken from Shan Carter and Amanda Cox, "One 9/11 Tally: $3.3 Trillion," *The New York Times*, September 8, 2011.
116. Author interview, anonymous US government official involved in Afghanistan policy Washington, DC, August 2012.
117. George W. Bush, Address to the Nation, October 7, 2001.
118. George W. Bush, Address to the Nation, October 7, 2001.
119. Bob Woodward and Vernon Loeb, "CIA's Covert War with Bin Laden," *The Washington Post*, September 14, 2001.
120. The White House, "The National Security Strategy of the United States of America," 2002.

121. US Department of State, Office of the Coordinator for Counterterrorism, *Country Reports on Terrorism 2005*, April 2006, 6–33.
122. The White House, "The National Security Strategy of the United States of America," March 2006, 12.
123. The White House, "The National Security Strategy of the United States of America," March 2006, 12.
124. The White House, "Remarks by Vice President Cheney and President Karzai of Afghanistan in Press Availability," Gul Khana Palace, Kabul, Afghanistan. Available here: http://merln.ndu.edu/archivepdf/afghanistan/WH/20080320.pdf
125. Author interview, anonymous US government official involved in Afghanistan policy Washington, DC, August 2012.
126. Tim McGirk, "Lonely at the Top: An Interview with Hamid Karzai," *Time*, March 4, 2002.
127. Malcolm Garcia, "In a torn Afghanistan, leader's hold still shaky—Turmoil festers in Afghanistan," *Philadelphia* Inquirer, January 21, 2003.
128. "Karzai Fires Bodyguards, Calls in U.S. Soldiers for Protection," Associated Press, July 22, 2002.
129. Astri Suhrke, "Report: When More is Less: Aiding Statebuilding in Afghanistan" (Madrid, Spain: FRIDE, September 2006), 12.
130. As quoted in an interview Karzai provided on Voice of America, May 15, 2005. Available here: http://www.globalsecurity.org/military/library/news/2005/05/mil-050515-2c7d9c7d.htm
131. Sino, *Organizations at War* (2008), 259.
132. The White House, "President Bush Participates in Press Availability with Afghanistan President Karzai in Afghanistan," The Presidential Palace, Kabul, Afghanistan. December 15, 2008. http://merln.ndu.edu/archivepdf/afghanistan/WH/20081215.pdf
133. The White House, "President Bush Participates in Press Availability" (2008).
134. The White House, "President Bush Participates in Press Availability" (2008).
135. The White House, "Remarks by the President on a New Strategy for Afghanistan and Pakistan," March 27, 2009. Available here: http://www.whitehouse.gov/the_press_office/Remarks-by-the-President-on-a-New-Strategy-for-Afghanistan-and-Pakistan/.

Second portion of quote as stated in Woodward, *Obama's Wars* (2010), 113.
136. As quoted in Woodward, *Obama's Wars* (2010), 127.
137. White House "Terms Sheet" for Afghanistan Pakistan Strategy, November 29, 2009, as outlined in Woodward (2010).
138. Barack Obama, "Presidential Address on Afghanistan," West Point, NY, December 1, 2009.
139. "Evaluating U.S. Foreign Assistance to Afghanistan," A Majority Staff Report (Washington, DC: Committee on Foreign Relations, US Senate, June 8, 2011), 5.
140. Comments from joint press conference, as quoted in Richard A. Oppel and Elisabeth Bulmer, "Karzai Says Afghan Army Will Need U.S. Until 2024," *The New York Times*, December 8, 2009.
141. As quoted in interview, Wissing, *Funding the Enemy* (2012), 91.
142. The exact figures as reported are 14 police officers in Nuristan province and 15 in Faryab province. "Policing in Afghanistan: Still Searching for a Strategy," Crisis Group Asia Briefing N°85 (Brussels/Kabul: International Crisis Group, December 18, 2008), 3.
143. Douglas A. Wissing, *Funding the Enemy: How US Taxpayers Bankroll the Taliban* (New York, NY: Prometheus Books, 2012), 263.
144. Interview with author, USG official, via Skype, June 2012.
145. Interview with author, USAID DST Team member, via Skype from Kandahar, Afghanistan, June 2012.
146. Interview with author, USG official, Washington, DC, June 2012.
147. Interview with author, USG official, Washington, DC, June 2012.
148. Interview with author, USG official, Washington, DC, March 29, 2012.
149. Jean Wood, "Funding the Taliban," *Global Post*, August 7, 2008; See also Douglass Wissing, "It's a Perfect War. Everybody Makes Money," *Global Post*, January 19, 2010.
150. Anand Gopal, *The Battle for Afghanistan* (Washington, DC: New America Foundation, 2010), 29 and 42.
151. Rajiv Chandrasekaran, *The War Within the War for Afghanistan* (New York, NY: Alfred Knopf Publishing, 2012), 199.
152. Douglas A. Wissing, *Funding the Enemy: How US Taxpayers Bankroll the Taliban* (New York, NY: Prometheus Books, 2012), 90.

153. David Wood, "Allegation: Some Contractors in Afghanistan Paying Protection Money to the Taliban," *Politics Daily*, December 1, 2009.
154. Interview with author, Senior ISAF official, Kabul, Afghanistan, March 2012.
155. Aram Roston, "Congressional Investigation Confirms: US Military Funds Afghan Warlords," *Nation* June 21, 2010.
156. As quoted in Esther Kaplan, "Congress Launches Investigation into Taliban Payola," *The Nation*, December 17, 2009.
157. Holbrooke quote as paraphrased in Bob Woodward, *Obama's Wars* (New York, NY: Simon and Schuster, 2010), 225–226.
158. Kai Eide, *Power Struggle in Afghanistan—An Inside Look at What went Wrong—and What we can do to Repair the Damage* (New York, NY; Skyhorse Publishing, 2012), 52.
159. Interview with author, NGO worker, via Skype from Kabul, Afghanistan, February 2012.
160. Craig Whitlock, "Diverse Sources Fund Insurgency in Afghanistan," *Washington Post*, September 27, 2009.
161. Karen DeYoung, "US Trucking Funds Reach Taliban, Military-led Investigation Concludes," *Washington Post*, July 24, 2011; and Roston, "Congressional Investigation Confirms" (2010).
162. Roston, "How the US Funds the Taliban," (2009).
163. Interview with US Army captain who served in Afghanistan, via Skype, September 2012.
164. Williams, *Afghanistan Declassified* (2012), 171.
165. Williams, *Afghanistan Declassified* (2012), 101.
166. These "various kinds" of actors included "mullahs, tribal chiefs, ex-mujahedin and local commanders."
167. "Countering Afghanistan's Insurgency: No Quick Fixes," Crisis Group Asia Report N°123 (Brussels/Kabul: International Crisis Group, November 2, 2006), 11.
168. "Report Says Afghan Police Chief, Governor Aided Insurgents Attack," *FoxNews*, November 4, 2008.
169. US Army report on "post-intelligence" as quoted and summarized in "Report Says Afghan Police Chief, Governor Aided Insurgents Attack," *FoxNews*, November 4, 2008.
170. Shakeela Abrahimkhil, "Report Reveals Political Deals behind Governors Appointments," *Tolo News*, December 4, 2010.

171. These occurred mainly in the southern provinces of Helmand (19 attacks) and Kandahar (16 attacks) and accounted for 15 percent of US soldier deaths in 2012. These and other statistics as summarized and analyzed in Bill Roggio and Lisa Lundquist, "Green-on-blue attacks in Afghanistan: the data," *Long War Journal*, August 12, 2012.
172. Roggio and Lundquist, "Green-on-blue attacks" (2012).
173. Roggio and Lundquist, "Green-on-blue attacks" (2012).
174. Roggio and Lundquist, "Green-on-blue attacks" (2012).
175. The attacks were concentrated in Helmand (19 attacks) and Kandahar (16 attacks).
176. Roggio and Lundquist, "Green-on-blue attacks" (2012).
177. Wissing, *Funding the Enemy* (2012).
178. Peters, *Seeds of* Terror, 133, 136.
179. Isby, *Afghanistan—Graveyard of Empires* (2010), 48.
180. Isby, *Afghanistan—Graveyard of Empires* (2010), 203.
181. Rashid, *Descent into Chaos* (2009).
182. Other accounts indicate this was also motivated by tribal code dictating such collusion. Rashid, *Descent into Chaos* (2009).
183. Tomsen, *The Wars of Afghanistan* (2011), 609.
184. Barfield, *Afghanistan* (2010), 277.
185. Hafeez Malik, *U.S. Relations with Afghanistan and Pakistan* (Oxford, UK: Oxford University Press, 2008), 206.
186. Interview with author, former US official who worked on Afghanistan policy, Washington, DC, July 2012.
187. Dusan Stojanovic, "Karzai replaces guards with American troops," *Associated* Press, July 23, 2002.
188. Gannon, "Afghanistan Unbound" (2004), 44.
189. Williams, *Afghanistan Declassified* (2012), 133.
190. At minimum his decisions did not contribute to dampening violence in his area.
191. Gulshan Dietl, "War, Peace and the Warlords: The Case of Ismail Khan of Herat in Afghanistan," *Alternatives—Turkish Journal of International Relations*, 3, No. 283 (2004), 55–56.
192. Kathy Gannon, "Afghanistan Unbound," *Foreign Affairs* (May/June 2004), 40.
193. The government would go on to be comprised of "militarily strong Tajik, Uzbek, and Hazara factions and a weak Pashtun majority." Gannon, "Afghanistan Unbound" (2004), 44.38.

194. Wilder and Listed, "State-building" (2007), 105.
195. Kim Sengupta, "Afghan Warlord Agrees to Hand Over his Weapons to British Team," *The Independent*, December 4, 2003.
196. As Wilder and Listed (2007) argue: "rather than de-legitimizing their power and authority in the regions, giving militia commanders official positions in their areas of influence has legitimized their power." Wilder and Listed, "State-building" (2007), 109.
197. Astri Suhkre, "Reconstruction as Modernization: The Post-conflict Project in Afghanistan," *Third World Quarterly*, 28, No. 7 (2007), 1301.
198. Wissing, *Funding the Enemy* (2012), 63.
199. Anthony Loyd, "Corruption, Bribes, and Trafficking: A Cancer that is Engulfing Afghanistan," *Times*, November 24, 2007; and Peters, *Seeds of Terror*, 186.
200. "Afghanistan: Exit vs. Engagement," Crisis Group (2010), 1.
201. Interview with senior US government official, Washington, DC, August 2012.
202. Isby, *Afghanistan—Graveyard of Empires* (2010), 201.
203. Barnett R. Rubin, "Saving Afghanistan," *Foreign Affairs* (January–February 2007), 57–78.
204. Rubin, "Saving Afghanistan," (2007), 57–78.
205. As quoted during a lecture Holbrooke delivered at the Center for Strategic and International Studies in Washington, DC, August 5, 2008.
206. Abdulkader H. Sinno, *Organizations at War in Afghanistan and Beyond* (Ithaca, NY: Cornell University Press, 2008), 266.
207. Michael E. O'Hanlon and Hassina Sherjan, *Toughing it out in Afghanistan* (Washington, DC: Brookings Institution Press, 2010), 27.
208. According to various accounts, these very forms of collusion or bandwagoning spurred the alliance to disband the Auxiliary police in 2008. Isby, *Afghanistan—Graveyard of Empires* (2010), 325.
209. Rashid, *Descent into Chaos* (2009). 204.
210. Paul Fishtein and Andrew Wilder, *Winning Hearts and Minds? Examining the Relationships between Aid and Security in Afghanistan* (Boston, MA: Feinstein International Center, Tufts University, January 2012), 32.
211. On one day in July 2010, for example, $190 million in cash left Afghanistan and from 2007 to 2010 $3 billion left in suitcases via

the international airport." Wissing, *Funding the Enemy* (2012), 242.
212. Eckart Schiewek, "Keeping the Peace Without Peacekeepers," in Wolfgang Danspeckgruber and Robert Finn, eds. *Building State and Security in Afghanistan* (Princeton, NJ: Liechtenstein Institute on Self-Determination at Princeton University, 2007), 203.
213. "A Force in Fragments: Reconstituting the Afghan National Army," Crisis Group Asia Report N°190 (Brussels/Kabul: International Crisis Group, May 12, 2010), 7.
214. Schiewek, "Keeping the Peace" (2007), 192.
215. When the Interim government was formed soon after the USA effectively routed the Taliban, Mohammed Fahim was appointed as Minister of Defense in 2002 and served in this post through 2004, when the elected Afghan government took over for the Interim administration.
216. Susan B. Glasser, "Among threats to Karzai's control is country's own secret service," *The Washington Post*, August 4, 2002.
217. Chandrasekaran, *The War Within the War for Afghanistan* (2012), 79.
218. "Westerners, to a degree unique in history, invest their loyalty in institutions…[and] Western officials on the ground in Afghanistan were acting instinctively within this conceptual framework…But Afghanistan is not there yet. In Afghanistan, loyalties and allegiances are to individual" Sarah Chayes, *The Punishment of Virtue: Inside Afghanistan After the Taliban* (London, UK: Penguin Books, 2007), 169.
219. Fishtein and Wilder, *Winning Hearts and Minds?* (2012), 30.
220. Interview with local community leader and former *mujihadin* commander, Paktia Province, January 10, 2008. As described in Paul Fishtein and Andrew Wilder, *Winning Hearts and Minds? Examining the Relationships between Aid and Security in Afghanistan* (Boston, MA: Feinstein International Center, Tufts University, January 2012), Fn 60, p. 30.
221. "I sent 3000 of them off to the Taliban," Akhundzada was quoted as saying. As quoted in Rajiv Chandrasekaran, *The War Within the War for Afghanistan* (New York, NY: Alfred Knopf Publishing, 2012), 46–47.
222. "Chandrasekaran, *The War Within the War for Afghanistan* (2012), 46–47.

223. Chayes, *The Punishment of Virtue* (2007), 101.
224. Fishtein and Wilder, *Winning Hearts and Minds?* (2012), 32.
225. This U.S. Cable was written in December 2009 and then leaked and then published in full by *The Guardian* newspaper. See *The Guardian*'s series on the "U.S. Cables" and for this specific document "US embassy cables: Corrupt governor in eastern Afghanistan," *The Guardian*, December 10, 2010.
226. This U.S. Cable was written in December 2009 and then leaked and then published in full by *The Guardian* newspaper. See *The Guardian*'s series on the "U.S. Cables" and for this specific document "US embassy cables: Afghan provincial governor accused of widespread corruption," *The Guardian*, December 10, 2010.
227. This U.S. Cable was written in December 2009 and then leaked and then published in full by *The Guardian* newspaper. See *The Guardian*'s series on the "U.S. Cables" and for this specific document "US embassy cables: Afghan provincial governor accused of widespread corruption," *The Guardian*, December 10, 2010.
228. This term was coined by Ahmed Rashid. Rashid, *Descent into Chaos* (2009), 127.
229. On Taliban expansion into Pakistan, see Rashid, *Descent into Chaos* (2009), and Sino, *Organizations at War* (2008).
230. Ahmed Rashid, "How Obama Lost Karzai," *Foreign Policy* (March/April 2011), 80.
231. Shah had served as Afghanistan's King through 1973. As a delegate to the Loya Jirga wrote in the *Washington Post* soon thereafter, "a parade of high-level officials from the from the Interim government, the United Nations, and the United States visited Zahir Shah and eventually 'persuaded' him to publicly renounce his political ambitions." Omar Zakhilwal, "Op-Ed: Stifled in the Loya Jirga," *The Washington Post*, June 16, 2002.
232. BBC News, "Karzai elected Afghan leader," June 13, 2002.
233. That Khalilzad was intimately involved in this process was widely reported by international media. For an excellent review of the process through which the constitution was drafted, see Alexander J. Their, "The Making of a Constitution in Afghanistan," *New York Law School Law Review*, 51 (2006/2007).
234. Hamida Ghafour, Afghans Agree to New Charter, Los Angeles Times, January 5, 2004.

235. Barnett Rubin, "Crafting a Constitution for Afghanistan," *Journal of Democracy*, Vol. 13, No. 3 (2004), 12.
236. Interview with author, Anonymous US government official, July 2012.
237. Andrew Reynolds, "Constitutional Engineering and Democratic Stability: the Debate Surrounding the Crafting of Political Institutions in Afghanistan," in Wolfgang Danspeckgruber and Robert Finn, eds. *Building State and Security in Afghanistan* (Princeton, NJ: Liechtenstein Institute on Self-Determination at Princeton University, 2007), 55.
238. Astri Suhrke, *When More is Less: The International Project in Afghanistan* (New York, NY: Columbia University Press, 2011), 178.
239. Rashid, "How Obama Lost Karzai" (2011), 81.
240. "Afghanistan: The Long, Hard Road to the 2014 Transition," Crisis Group (2012), 9.
241. Suhrke, *When More is Less* (2011), 171.
242. Antonio Giustozzi, *Empires of Mud: Wars and Warlords in Afghanistan* (New York, NY: Columbia University Press, 2012), 96.
243. Interview with author, Anonymous Aid worker in Afghanistan during period in which electoral system was written, Via Skype, September 2012.
244. Suhrke, *When More is Less* (2011), 171.
245. Remarks by President George Bush, President of the USA, The President's News Conference With President Hamid Karzai of Afghanistan at Camp David, Maryland, August 6, 2007.
246. Remarks by Hamid Karzai, President of Afghanistan. The President's News Conference With President Hamid Karzai of Afghanistan at Camp David, Maryland, August 6, 2007.
247. Remarks by Hamid Karzai, President of Afghanistan. The President's News Conference With President Hamid Karzai of Afghanistan at Camp David, Maryland, August 6, 2007.
248. Interview with author, US Ambassador to Afghanistan Ronald Neumann, July 2, 2012.
249. Astri Suhrke, "Reconstruction as Modernization (2007), 1299–1300.
250. Eide, *Power Struggle in Afghanistan* (2012), 107.

251. Rajiv Chandrasekaran, *The War Within the War for Afghanistan* (2012), 88.
252. Astri Suhkre, "Reconstruction as Modernization," (2007), 1302.
253. Barfield, *Afghanistan* (2010), 310.
254. "Karzai faults coalition, says it is using 'thugs'—"Interview with Hamid Karzai," *Los Angeles Times*, December 23, 2008.
255. Per the "The Afghanistan Compact," as released by NATO.
256. Richard Oppel Jr., "Afghan leader Courts the Warlord Vote, but Others Fear the Cost," *New York Times*, August 8, 2009.
257. Barfield, *Afghanistan* (2010), 330.
258. Eide, *Power Struggle in Afghanistan* (2012), 156–157.
259. As quoted in Woodward, *Obama's Wars* (2010), 136.
260. Elizabeth Rubin, "Karzai In His Labyrinth," *New York Times Magazine*, Aug 9, 2009.
261. Antonio Giustozzia and Dominique Orsini, "Centre–periphery relations in Afghanistan: Badakhshan between patrimonialism and institution-building," *Central Asian Survey*, Vol. 28, No. 1 (March 2009), 1.
262. Tomsen, *The Wars of Afghanistan* (2011), 672.
263. Barfield, *Afghanistan* (2010), 330.
264. Eide, *Power Struggle in Afghanistan* (2012), 153.
265. Eide, *Power Struggle in Afghanistan* (2012), 153.
266. Tomsen, *The Wars of Afghanistan* (2011), 672.
267. Cook, *Afghanistan: The Perfect Failure* (2012), 144.
268. Rashid, "How Obama Lost Karzai" (2011), 80.
269. Chandrasekaran, *The War Within the War for Afghanistan* (2012), 168.
270. Chandrasekaran, *The War Within the War for Afghanistan* (2012), 164.
271. Chandrasekaran, *The War Within the War for Afghanistan* (2012), 165.
272. "Hamid Karzai's Rebellion," *The Nation*, April 26, 2010.
273. Chandrasekaran, *The War Within the War for Afghanistan* (2012), 165.
274. These included devising "a reinvigorated US–Afghanistan Strategic Dialogue" to develop a "shared vision and commitment to Afghanistan's future. White House, Office of the Press Secretary, "Joint Statement from the President and President Karzai of Afghanistan," May 12, 2010.

275. Eide, *Power Struggle in Afghanistan* (2012), 261.
276. "Hamid Karzai's Rebellion," *The Nation*, April 26, 2010.
277. "Hamid Karzai's Rebellion," *The Nation*, April 26, 2010.
278. Antonio Giustozzi and Noor Ullah, "The inverted cycle: Kabul and the strongmen's competition for control over Kandahar, 2001–2006," *Central Asian Survey*, Vol. 26, No. 2 (June 2007), 179.
279. "Afghan governor removed from power," *Baltimore Sun*, September 12, 2004.
280. Hoarding such revenue had become so widespread that Karzai deployed Finance Minister (Ghani) to Herat to demand that Khan hand over more tax revenues (Ghani flew back to Kabul with $20 million.) Gulshan Dietl, "War, Peace and the Warlords: The Case of Ismail Khan of Herat in Afghanistan," *Alternatives—Turkish Journal of International Relations*, Vol. 3, No. 283 (2004), 57.
281. Carlotta Gall, "Afghan Government Removes a Powerful Regional Leader," *The New York Times*, September 12, 2004.
282. Sadaf Shinwari, "Afghan water & energy minister accused of corruption," *Rawa News*, April 25, 2012.
283. The term "threat finance" began to be used within the government to describe the phenomenon whereby the Taliban and other insurgents—through direct and indirect means—obtained funds allocated for reconstruction or military efforts and use these capabilities to finance their operations and attempts to overthrow the regime. Passive bandwagoning in the form of extortion and corruption (diversion) of non-military alliance capabilities had escalated to the point where the USA adjusted aspects of the alliance's tactics and activities so as to curb it so as to "ensure dollars are not being diverted from their purpose by extortion or corruption." Evaluating U.S. Foreign Assistance to Afghanistan, A Majority Staff Report (Washington, DC: Committee on Foreign Relations, U.S. Senate, June 8, 2011), 3.
284. The USA established the Special Investigator General for Afghanistan Reconstruction (SIGAR) for this purpose.
285. Abubakar Siddique, "US Special Inspector: Afghan Corruption a 'Mix' of External, Internal Factors," *Radio Free Europe/Radio Liberty News Report*. November 12, 2009.
286. Interview with author, anonymous US government official, Kabul, Afghanistan, April 2012.

287. Williams, *Afghanistan Declassified* (2012), 197.
288. The USA determined by end of the period examined that of six ministries evaluated, none were able to "provide reasonable assurance of detecting significant vulnerabilities" that in turn, according to another report, "could result in the waste or misuse of US Government resources USAID evaluation as quoted and referenced in "Evaluating U.S. Foreign Assistance to Afghanistan," A Majority Staff Report (Washington, DC: Committee on Foreign Relations, U.S. Senate, June 8, 2011), 2.
289. Barfield, *Afghanistan* (2010), 304.
290. James L. Jones, as quoted in Woodward, *Obama's Wars* (2010), 165.
291. Cook, *Afghanistan: The Perfect Failure* (2012), 14.
292. Steve Hess, "Coming to Terms with neopatrimonialism: Soviet and American nation-building projects in Afghanistan," *Central Asian Survey*, Vol. 29, No. 2 (2010), 183.
293. General Brent Scowcroft, Interview with Author, Washington, DC, July 17, 2012.
294. Tomsen, *The Wars of Afghanistan* (2011), 617.
295. Scott Johnson, "U.S. Struggles to Find Honest Allies in Anti-Terror Hunt."
296. Memos cited were from 2009, as quoted in "Wikileaks: US officials pressured Karzai to remove former warlord Ismail Khan for "corruption and ineffectiveness," *Associated Press*, January 1, 2011.
297. Memos cited were from 2009, as quoted in "Wikileaks: US officials pressured Karzai to remove former warlord Ismail Khan for "corruption and ineffectiveness," *Associated Press*, January 1, 2011.
298. See, for example, Carlotta Gall, "Karzai Shows He'll Cast Lot With a Corps Of Warlords," *The New York Times*, June 8, 2004.
299. Barfield, *Afghanistan* (2010), 332.
300. Sharan, "The Dynamics of Elite Networks," (2011), 1114.
301. Later, his area of responsibility for the Taliban expanded to include Kandahar and other regions in southern Afghanistan.
302. Chandrasekaran, *The War Within* (2012), 289–290.
303. See table on Level of Threat to Afghanistan regime in the Index. These numbers are further corroborated by US government sources. Two illustrative examples are: (1) in 2009 and soon after beginning his 60-day Afghanistan review, as requested by Obama, McChrystal himself said that there "are 25,000" Taliban in

Afghanistan and that this figure was "higher than anything" he had previously estimated the number to be. As quoted in Woodward, *Obama's Wars* (2010), 133.; and (2) a US estimate published in 2009 put the number of insurgents in Afghanistan at 25,000, the highest number since initial engagement in 2001. Jonathan S. Landay and Hal Bernton, "While U.S. Debates Afghanistan Policy, Taliban Beefs Up," *McClatchy Newspapers Report*, October 16, 2009.

304. ISAF Briefing, "State of the Insurgency: Trends, Intentions and Objectives," December 22, 2009. Unclassified, slide 16.
305. ISAF Briefing, "State of the Insurgency," (2009).
306. These figures are summarized in Jones, "The Rise of Afghanistan's Insurgency" (2008), 7.
307. Figures from Jason H. Campbell and Jeremy Shapiro, "Afghan Index—2009—Tracking Variables of Reconstruction & Security in Post-9/11 Afghanistan," (Washington, DC: Brookings Institution, January 21, 2009). Accessed November 16, 2011.
308. Some provinces experienced a decrease in insurgent activity, but they were either relatively inactive previously (Sari Pul province, which decreased from 15 to 2 attacks) or experienced what we might consider rather marginal decreases (Balk province, where the total number of attacks decreased only by three from 44 to 41). These figures are drawn from Jason H. Campbell and Jeremy Shapiro, "Afghan Index—2009," Brookings (2009).
309. ISAF Briefing, "State of the Insurgency: Trends, Intentions and Objectives," December 22, 2009. Unclassified version.
310. This number was 1100. These figures are drawn from Ian S. Livingston and Michael O'Hanlon, "Afghan Index—March 2012" (Washington, DC: Brookings Institution, January 21, 2009). Accessed March 2012.
311. Author's calculation based on figures provided in Jason H. Campbell and Jeremy Shapiro, "Afghan Index—July 15, 2013 -," (Washington, DC: Brookings Institution, July 15, 2013). The Brookings Institution for this Index collects data via open source news, the US government and private firms it contracts to collect information. The Afghan Index and descriptions of its methodology is available at the following link: www.brookings.edu/Afghanindex. Accessed July 19, 2013.

312. ISAF Briefing, "State of the Insurgency: Trends, Intentions and Objectives," December 22, 2009. Unclassified, slide 16.
313. Barbara J. Stapleton, "The Failure to Bridge the Security Gap: the PRT Plan, 2002–2004," in Wolfgang Danspeckgruber and Robert Finn, eds. *Building State and Security in Afghanistan* (Princeton, NJ: Liechtenstein Institute on Self-Determination at Princeton University, 2007), 175.
314. Stapleton, "The Failure to Bridge the Security Gap" (2007), 173.
315. These "insurgent forces" included mainly the Taliban, Al-Qaeda, and Hezb-i-Islami. Abdulkader H. Sino, *Organizations at War in Afghanistan and Beyond* (Ithaca, NY: Cornell University Press, 2008), 262.
316. As another reflection of the change in threat level through 2007—where the UN agencies were able to operate freely throughout approximately 60–70 percent of the territory comprising southern Afghanistan from 2004 to 2005, in 2006 they were able to operate "freely" in only 6 (of 50) of the same region's districts. What is more, Taliban-initiated attacks and riots in the capital increased the proximity of threat to the regime in 2006. As quoted in Hafeez Malik, *U.S. Relations with Afghanistan and Pakistan* (Oxford, UK: Oxford University Press, 2008), 31.
317. Sino, *Organizations at War* (2008), 262.
318. "ISAF Briefing, "State of the Insurgency," (2009).
319. See table on Level of Threat to Afghanistan regime in the Index.
320. Michael E. O'Hanlon and Hassina Sherjan, *Toughing it out in Afghanistan* (Washington, DC: Brookings Institution Press, 2010), 78.
321. An analysis in 2012 based on extensive fieldwork, for example, concluded it had "become increasingly clear that ISAF is unable to dislodge the Taliban from its strongholds in the south and east." "Afghanistan: The Long, Hard Road to the 2014 Transition," Crisis Group (2012), 16.
322. Williams, *Afghanistan Declassified* (2012), 103.
323. Isby, *Afghanistan—Graveyard of Empires* (2010), 145.
324. Chandrasekaran, *The War Within the War for Afghanistan* (2012), 74.
325. See table in Annex on Level of Threat.

326. As quoted in Walter Pincus, "Growing Threat Seen in Afghan Insurgency: Defense Intelligence Agency Chief Cites Surging Violence in Homeland," *The Washington Post*, March 1, 2006.
327. Rashid, *Descent into Chaos* (2009), 364.
328. "Multiple Taliban attacks in Afghanistan," *PRI—The World*, January 18, 2010.
329. Lynne O'Donnell, "Kabul on high alert after brazen Taliban strikes," *AFP*, January 18, 2010.
330. "Afghan peace council head Rabbani killed in attack," *BBC News*, September 20, 2011.
331. This was in reference to the government 'losing' 80 billion in tax revenue due to corruption. As quoted in, Elizabeth Rubin, "Karzai In His Labyrinth," *New York Times Magazine*, Aug 9, 2009.
332. Ambassador Karl W. Eikenberry, testimony before the Senate Committee on Armed Services, December 8, 2009, 2.
333. Other assessments fault the USA for not deploying sufficient troops; and others argue that the (counterinsurgency) strategy was flawed from the beginning.
334. As quoted in "A Force in Fragments," Crisis Group (2010), 2.
335. "Report on Progress Toward Security and Stability in Afghanistan: United States Plan for Sustaining the Afghanistan National Security Forces", US Department of Defense, April 2012. Allen testimony, US Senate Armed Services Committee, 12 March 2012.
336. "Afghanistan: The Long, Hard Road to the 2014 Transition," Crisis Group (2012), 18.
337. The assessment lists the following improvements: According to an assessment performed by the US Defense Intelligence Agency, for example, by 2012 the security forces had "proven more capable and better coordinated in responding to sustained high-profile attacks in Kabul...and improved their capability to secure roads and critical transportation corridors in the country's north."
338. "Afghanistan: The Long, Hard Road to the 2014 Transition," Crisis Group (2012), 18.
339. For these figures and annual breakdowns, see Table in Annex—Size of Afghanistan's Security Forces and Annual Expenditures.
340. The score if achieved reflects ability to independently operate and comply with police standards and protocols. US Government Accountability Office, "Afghanistan Security: US Programs to Further Reform Ministry of Interior and National Police

Challenged by Lack of Military Personnel and Afghan Cooperation," (Washington, DC: GAO, March 2009).
341. US Government Accountability Office, "Afghanistan Security" (2009).
342. Mohammed Hanif Atmar, Minister of Interior, speech delivered at the Brookings Institution, Washington, DC, February 25, 2009.
343. "Report on Progress Toward Security and Stability in Afghanistan" (2012).

CHAPTER 4

Russia–Syria Internal Threat Alliance (2010–2016)

This chapter applies the book's framework onto the Russia–Syria internal threat alliance. It traces Russia's cooperation with the Bashar al-Assad regime in Syria to defeat anti-government rebels. It shows that the al-Assad administration sought Russian assistance in order to thwart anti-government rebels and remain in power, while Russia provided military capabilities to the embattled regime in order to safeguard its single military base outside the former Soviet Union, preserve access to oil and gas fields, and protect an array of other economic interests. Concerning bandwagoning, the chapter shows that some elements of Syria's military colluded (bandwagoned) with rebels, but the majority followed central orders and worked to defeat (balance) them. Finally, it demonstrates that the Russia–Syria alliance has been effective due to its accumulation of sufficient resources to weaken rebels as well as the al-Assad regime's ability to head off collusion by government actors with the belligerents.

Russia–Syria Internal Threat Alliance (2010–2016):
Historical Overview

The conflict in Syria initially began as relatively peaceful protests demonstrating against al-Assad's repressive regime but since then has transformed into a war that has drawn in regional and world powers. Fighting between the government and anti-regime rebels has continued almost

© The Author(s) 2017
P.W. Quirk, *Great Powers, Weak States, and Insurgency*,
DOI 10.1007/978-3-319-47419-9_4

unabated since 2011. At the time of this writing, the civil war remains one of the worst humanitarian crises in recent history—at least 500,000 have died and millions have been displaced. Nearly 50 percent of the population is internally displaced or living abroad as refugees.

In December 2010, what has become known as the "Arab Spring" began in Tunisia, where increasingly violent street protests eventually ousted President Zine El Abidine in January 2011. Similar anti-government demonstrations then spread to Egypt, where President Hosni Mubarak would eventually resign, and Libya, where protests and a UN-backed bombing campaign coupled with an internal revolt would depose President Muammar Gaddafi.[1] This revolutionary fervor reached Syria in March 2011, when thousands of anti-government protesters massed in cities across the country to protest against al-Assad's regime.

Initial protests in the Syrian town of Daraa were sparked by the government detaining and torturing 15 children for painting graffiti calling for Assad's government to end.[2] Outrage against the security forces' brutality, the larger Arab Spring sentiment, and other grievances such as disenchantment with corruption pushed aggrieved Syrians to mobilize in street protests. Demands for President al-Assad to resign spread throughout the country. Rather than engage or pacify protesters with reforms, however, al-Assad deployed security forces to crush the internal dissent with force.[3] By July 2011, clashes between security forces and protesters had increased in frequency and intensity. The opposition decided to take up arms to defend themselves against the state, battle the regime for control of cities, and eventually seek to overthrow the government. What had originated as small, peaceful demonstrations in a southern town quickly escalated into a full-blown insurgency. Citizens formed rebel brigades, such as the Free Syrian Army, with the broad aim of removing Assad from power.

As the conflict escalated, external powers aligned with the government or opposition in order to secure their respective interests. Russia came to al-Assad's aid. This began with Russia offering political support and funneling arms to Assad's government and then, in 2015, Russian President Vladimir Putin deploying military forces to Syria to thwart advances by the opposition. At least in part, recent events in Libya loomed in the background of Russia's decision to align with the embattled Syrian president. As a result of the NATO-led intervention in Libya, Russia lost an ally in Muammar Gaddafi as well as $4 billion in military contracts and agreements.[4] As the Syrian armed opposition gained in strength, therefore,

Russia decided to support its Syrian ally rather than stand by as other great powers sought to topple him.

Yet, Russia's relationship with and associated interests in Syria began long before the Arab Spring. Syrian President Bashar al-Assad's father, Hafez Assad, first turned to the Soviet Union for assistance in the 1970s. In the ensuing decades, Russia increased ties with Syria, most notably through financial and military aid. In 2005, Putin and Assad met in Moscow to discuss the emerging Syrian economic crisis. The leaders reached an agreement whereby Russia would write off the majority of Syria's debt ($9.8 billion of the total $13.4 billion) and sell arms to al-Assad in exchange for permission to establish permanent naval facilities in the Syrian port cities of Latakia and Tartus.[5] Bashar al-Assad's support for the Russian invasion of Georgia in 2008 drove his regime and Russia closer together. Where the international community largely condemned President Medvedev's recognition of South Ossetia and Abkhazia, al-Assad offered support: "we wish to once again express our support for the Russian position as regards the recent conflict and the general situation around Abkhazia and South Ossetia. We agree with the essence of the Russian position and understand the military reaction to the events that took place; we consider this to be a reaction to provocation by Georgia."[6] Al-Assad used the crisis as an opportunity to enhance Russian-Syrian relations. In the years that followed, Russia became one of the main providers of weapons and arms to the Syrian government. In the period spanning 2003–2010 alone, Russia's arms transfer agreements with Syria increased more than 120 percent, from $2.1 billion (2003–2006) to $4.7 billion (2007–2010).[7] During the same period, the Kremlin also agreed to accept Syria's exported crude oil in exchange for refined oil products. This was a deal the al-Assad administration desperately needed to stave off further economic decline and backstop military efforts.[8] The internal threat alliance formation began in this context. In the face of an increasingly robust insurgency, al-Assad and Russia aligned to secure their respective interests that the belligerents threatened. In order to ensure his regime's survival, Assad sought support from Russia, which provided munitions, weapons, airstrikes, and helicopters his regime used against the anti-government rebels.[9]

Characteristics of the Syrian State: Sectarian Tension, Fragmented Opposition, and Regional and World Powers

Before proceeding to examine the dynamics of this alliance, it is first necessary to explore the characteristics of the weaker state. As noted in Chap. 1, neoclassical realism holds that *states (in particular those outside of the West) are frequently* not *cohesive but, rather, fragmented and in some cases prone to instability* because they lack a monopoly on the legitimate use of force within their borders.[10] As such, the internal composition of these fragmented states—and the factors motivating actors therein—will influence their foreign policy decision-making.

In line with the characteristics of weak states involved in internal threat alliances, Syria lacked strong institutions, firm control over those agencies that exist, or a writ that extended throughout its complex topography. The al-Assad family has ruled the Syrian Arab Republic since 1971, with President Bashar al-Assad coming to power after his father's death in 2000. Hafez al-Assad led the country through the fall of the Soviet Union, the first Gulf war, and the Arab-Israeli peace process without any significant threats to his regime's stability.[11] Throughout this period state institutions remained weak and underdeveloped. Civil servant positions were predominantly given to loyal party members, which resulted in ministerial bureaucracies staffed with unqualified and ineffective staff: "the public sector remained huge, with grossly inefficient state-owned enterprises employing well over half of the workforce and another 23 percent of the labor force working directly for the government bureaucracy."[12] Refusing to adopt economic liberalization measures, Hafez pursued the Soviet model of a centrally planned economy with policies aimed at staving off rebellion and capturing the loyalty of key business elite and the Alawite.[13] The Alawite, Syria's largest non-Sunni minority, were openly privileged by the Assad regime.[14] Even though the country's institutions were relatively weak, Hafez designed his administration in such a way that he could control all aspects of government, including parliament, serving as the commander-in-chief of the Syrian Armed Forces and maintaining Executive authority of the intelligence services.[15] He also acted as the official head of the Ba'th Party. Together, these positions allowed him nearly absolute control of the state apparatus.[16] Despite rampant corruption, little foreign investment, and an undiversified portfolio, Hafez managed to survive several coup attempts and the fall of the Soviet Union.

As Hafez al-Assad's death was publicly announced, the Ba'th Party-controlled parliament acted in tandem with security forces to amend the constitution to lower the age requirement for presidential candidates (Bashar was 34, and the article set the minimum age at 40) and then close the airports and seal off the Lebanese border to ensure that no challengers would make a claim against Bashar.[17] By the following month, Bashar had won over 97 percent of the referendum vote and was inaugurated as president.[18] Similar to his father, Bashar assumed the roles of Secretary General of the Ba'th Party, commander-in-chief of the Syrian Armed Forces, and the head of state. The regime is comprised of the president, two vice presidents, a prime minster, and the Council of Ministers.[19] These were the primary actors who coordinated with Russian counterparts on security measures and alliance strategy. Also endowed with the power to appoint ministers, civil servants, and military personnel, al-Assad strategically placed Alawites in key military and security positions.[20] As such, the state operated as a neopatrimonial system that enabled Bashar to sustain his rule by maintaining robust networks of personal patronage.

After inheriting the presidency, al-Assad pursued policies that led to the creation of the *tabaqa jadida* ("new class"),[21] wherein members of his elite inner circle and patronage networks gained robust access to the Syrian economy. During the early years of Bashar's presidency, his rhetoric suggested plans to implement economic reforms by "removing bureaucratic obstacles to the flow of domestic and foreign investments, mobilizing public and private capital, and activating the private sector and giving it better business opportunities."[22] Despite numerous speeches and proposed legislation, al-Assad mostly avoided any serious economic liberalization and anti-corruption efforts. The limited degree of his policies is evidenced by numerous metrics: the World Bank's 2011 Ease of Doing Business Report ranked Syria at 144 of 183[23]; in 2011–2012 Global Competitive Index, Syria ranked 98 of 142[24]; and according to Transparency International's 2012 Corruption Perception Index, Syria ranked 144 of 178.[25] International and domestic optimism about Bashar's rule was short lived, and by 2010 it became evident that patronage would continue to trump reform. Individuals and families with close ties either to the Assad family or the military-security apparatus were able to corner large sectors of the Syrian economy. On the one hand, these networks further enmeshed patrons to the regime, but on the other they partially undermined Assad's ability to manage the economic and political sphere. For example, in 2005 when Assad did attempt to introduce some measure of economic reform, these networks successfully influenced the types of programs to be pursued and secured near monopolies over their respective segments of the economy.[26]

Even so, as protests turned to insurgency, al-Assad was able to activate and leverage these patronage networks to ensure that key military and state officials would remain loyal to the regime and fight for its survival. Bashar's continued survival throughout the conflict is perhaps less dependent upon the effectiveness of Syria's internal security forces (though this certainly played a role) and more reliant upon the military leadership's continued loyalty—and al-Assad's associated ability to prevent bandwagoning.[27]

Having provided an overview of the alliance period and characteristics of the Syrian state and regime state, the following sections apply the theoretical framework to the case. In so doing, they evidence the three main parts of the framework related to alliance formation, bandwagoning, and alliance effectiveness.

Alliance Formation

We support the Syrian government in confronting terrorist aggression. We have been providing and will continue to provide the necessary military and technical assistance to the Syrian government and urge other countries to join us.[28]

The purpose of this section is to evidence the theoretical framework's first core argument: that internal threat alliances will form in response to a threat that *is domestic in origin* and imperils the survival of a weak state's leadership regime. The weaker state's leadership will seek cooperation because it needs military or economic resources to thwart challenges to its existence, while the great power will become involved in order to safeguard interests linked to the regime's stability or survival.

To address each part of this argument, the section first demonstrates that Russia and Syria formed an alliance in response to a threat consisting of a high level of political violence generated by anti-regime insurgents. It then demonstrates that the core motivation underlying Russia/Syria alignment was to ensure the al-Assad regime's survival and the

Table 4.1 Russia–Syria Internal Threat Alliance Formation

	Theat / Motivation for Russia	Threat / Motivation for Syria	Type of Alliance
2010–2016 (SYRIA): al-Assad (RUSSIA): Putin	(Threat): Political violence from opposition (Motivation): Ensure Assad's regime survival to retain access to military base	(Threat): Political violence from opposition (Motivation): Preserving Bashar al-Assad's regime	Internal threat alliance

great power's interests associated with it. In so doing, the discussion below demonstrates that Russia and Assad formed an alliance based on a *common* threat from *within* the weaker state: the al-Assad administration needed military and economic capabilities to balance threats from insurgents and remain in power, while Russia aligned and provided such resources to preserve access to its naval facility and other economic interests. To safeguard these interests, it needed to make sure its ally regime did not fall. The table below provides a summary of these motivations (Table 4.1).

Profile of the Internal Threat: *Anti-regime Forces Threaten Russian Interests*

The threat that spurred Russia and al-Assad to bring their security policies into close cooperation and begin pooling resources consisted of political violence from armed opposition groups that threatened the regime's survival and the potentially devastating consequences that such volatility could have wreaked on Russia's strategic interests.

Evolution of the Internal Threat

The popular uprisings and demands for freedom that swept the Arab world shook Syria's autocracy to its core. What would eventually transform into one of the worst humanitarian crises in modern history began as small civil protests in the city of Daraa.[29] In late February 2011, 15 school boys were arrested for painting anti-regime graffiti on the walls of a school. The children had written "al-sha'b yurīd isqāt al-nizām" (the people want the fall of the system). In the context of the events unfolding in nearby Egypt,

Libya, and Tunisia, these acts drew a severe response from Syria's security forces.[30] The children were reportedly transferred to Damascus where they were detained, interrogated, and tortured.

Once news that the boys had been tortured spread, peaceful protests erupted in Daraa and Damascus. Despite mild rhetoric and no signs of violence, the security forces used lethal force to disperse large crowds. By April 2011, human rights groups had claimed that over 500 people had been killed.[31] Protests of varying scale continued throughout the country calling for al-Assad to step down. Unlike Tunisia and Egypt, however, the internal security forces and military continued to largely support and remain loyal to the regime.[32]

By June 2011 a range of anti-regime rebel brigades had taken up arms for self-protection, to take control of key cities from the state, and eventually to seek the overthrow of Assad's government. The Syrian army experienced its first encounter with armed rebels on June 4, when citizens in Jisr al-Shughour, a small northern town near the foothills of the Turkish border, raided a police station and killed members of the state's security forces.[33] Days after this incident, prominent Syrian Army Lieutenant Colonel Hussein Harmoush released a video announcing his defection from the military. Six other army officers defected soon thereafter.[34] The former military officers united with a large group of other armed resistance fighters to form the Free Syrian Army, one of most prominent anti-regime rebel groups. Other splinter groups developed thereafter, all of whom generated violence that imperiled the regime and associated Russian interests. Terrorist organizations, including a branch of Al-Qaeda and ISIL, took advantage of instability in Syria to establish operations and pose their own threat to the regime. Information on all of these actors is included in the section below.

Free Syrian Army
Though it is difficult to obtain definitive force numbers, most estimates suggest the Free Syrian Army consisted of 10,000 men by the end of 2011.[35] More recent reports for 2015 suggest that Free Syrian Army force numbers, despite internal rifts, were between 45,000 and 60,000.[36] The Free Syrian Army does not have authority over—or in some cases even affiliations with—many of the other armed rebel groups fighting against the regime. Reflecting the fractious nature of the armed opposition,

according to some reports in 2014, there were approximately 6,000 individual groups and military councils that loosely formed a shifting network of more than 1,000 distinct brigades, battalions, and armed groups.[37] In the early stages of the conflict, rebels launched several successful offensives and took control of large swathes of eastern Syria. This included seizing the provincial capital of al-Raqqa in March 2013.[38] Other key victories included the northern region in Jabal al-Zawiya, where the Harmoush Battalion significantly disrupted the regime's ability to move freely long its primary north-south line of communication.[39]

Islamic Front
In November 2013, seven of Syria's strongest rebel factions merged to create the Islamic Front. These groups included the Islamic Ahrar al-Sham Movement, the Suqour al-Sham Brigades, the Tawhid Brigade, the Haq Brigade, the Ansar al-Sham Battalions, the Islam Army, and the Kurdish Islamic Front.[40] The factions varied in ideology, with some identifying as Salafi, some as radical jihadists, and others as more moderate and secular.[41] At its peak, the Islamic Front boasted approximately 50,000 fighters spread across nearly all of Syria's subnational governorates,[42] which it used to capture key cities and provinces.[43]

Jabhat al-Nusra
As armed rebels factions sought to overthrow al-Assad, Al-Qaeda took advantage of the instability to establish a presence in Syria in the form of Jabhat al-Nusra.[44] In January 2012, Jabhat al-Nusra posted a video online announcing its formation and aim of deposing Assad. Despite its reportedly smaller force size relative to other groups, Jabhat al-Nusra managed to orchestrate several successful attacks against key regime targets, including the capture of the Taftanaz Air Base.[45] In 2013, Jabhat al-Nusra carried out approximately 600 total assassinations, suicide bombings, improvised explosive device attacks, and strikes on essential regime checkpoints and security forces infrastructure.[46]

ISIS/ISIL
Since it surfaced as an armed group in April 2013, the Islamic State in Iraq and al-Sham/Syria (ISIS) focused on controlling northern and east-

ern territories in Syria, especially in the provinces bordering Turkey and Iraq.[47] Though the group's size and effectiveness varied throughout the war, ISIS successfully seized some of Syria's state-owned oilfields[48] and established bases in Homs, Hama, and in Qalamoun and Eastern Ghouta of the Damascus countryside. While al-Assad officially declared his commitment to fighting ISIS, the majority of state-led attacks and military campaigns targeted anti-government armed groups, rather than ISIS strongholds.

The Syrian opposition's sustained attacks against the regime, its personnel, military equipment, and infrastructure—combined with similar attack from Jabhat al-Nusra and ISIS—threated the Assad regime's survival. As president during a struggling economy, Bashar al-Assad had military resources sufficient to deter the armed opposition but required additional resources to change the balance of power on the battlefield. In part as a result of this, Assad sought assistance from Russia for external support that would enable his regime to fight the rebels and remain in control of the Syrian state.

Why Russia and Syria Aligned: *To Safeguard the Regime and Russian Interests Associated With It*

Perceiving threats to their respective interests posed by the aforementioned armed groups, Russia and Syria agreed to align. For Assad's regime, the armed rebels threatened its survival and continued hold on power. Lacking the necessary capabilities to adequately respond to this threat, the embattled regime sought Russian support. For Russia, the armed rebels threatened their ally's survival and sowed instability that endangered various strategic interests. Since 2005, the Russian oil company Tatneft has had an agreement to explore and develop oil and natural gas in Syria. Other Russian companies have a commitment to perform construction on the Arab Gas Pipeline, which links Egypt to Turkey, making Syria a key transit region.[49] Russia also holds a large number of contracts for weapons sales to Syria—those already signed and new proposals in consideration are estimated to total around $5 billion.[50] Moscow also needed to retain access to its naval base in Tartus, which is Russia's only naval outpost on the Mediterranean. The port acts as a transport hub for newly acquired arms and a key route for damaged weapons, such as military helicopters, to return to Russia for repair.[51] The naval base is also connected to the mainland and can easily access a well-developed route of highways and roads. Russia's ability to secure the aforementioned economic, security, and political interests therefore hinged on Bashar Assad's survival and his regime's triumph over the rebels. For these reasons, Russia had an interest in providing economic and military resources sufficient to weaken the rebels and ensure Assad's regime survive. In this case, the tactical goal of suppressing the opposition was mutual and drove Syria and Russia to form an internal threat alliance. The ensuing sections explore these motivations further.

Vladimir Putin and Bashar al-Assad: *Regime Survival to Serve Geopolitical Interests*
Statements by Russian President Putin, his foreign policy team, and other senior officials demonstrate that the core factor motivating the great power to align was to balance perceived threats stemming from instability in Syria that could imperil Russian access to the naval base and other economic and material interests. After Putin replaced Medvedev as Russia's president, for example, he expressed clear and unwavering intention to support Assad and his regime:

> We took the decision upon your request to provide effective aid to the Syrian people in fighting the international terrorists who have unleashed a genuine war against Syria. Syria is Russia's friend and we are ready to make our contribution...to the military operations and the fight against terrorism.[52]

Since then, Russia has offered instrumental diplomatic assistance to Assad. This included employing its veto power within the United Nations Security Council to prevent the adoption of any resolution calling for intervention or military support to the opposition.[53] Putin, in other contexts, noted why it was important to provide continued support to the Assad regime: "We support the Syrian government in confronting terrorist aggression. We have been providing and will continue to provide the necessary military and technical assistance to the Syrian government and urge other countries to join us."[54] President Putin routinely characterized Assad as a key ally in the fight against religious extremism. Similarly, Russian Foreign Minister Sergey Lavrov remarked that "the Syrian president is the commander-in-chief of probably the most capable ground force fighting terrorism, to give up such an opportunity, ignore the capabilities of the Syrian army as a partner and ally in the fight against the Islamic State means to sacrifice the entire region's security to some geopolitical moods and calculations."[55]

Various statements by the Assad regime demonstrate that it aligned in order to obtain capabilities needed to thwart attacks from insurgents and remain in power. In an interview with Agence France-Presse (AFP), for example, Assad noted how crucial Russian efforts have been in sustaining his regime: "[r]eality has shown that Russian…support has been important and has contributed to Syria's steadfastness. Without this support, things probably would have been much more difficult."[56] Additionally, two months before the formal request for Russian airstrikes, al-Assad delivered a speech on July 26, 2015, where he acknowledged that Syria's military forces had been affected by defections, desertions, and deaths.[57] In his televised address, Assad tried to defend his decision to give up certain territories: "it was necessary to specify critical areas for our armed forces to hang on to. Concern for our soldiers forces us to let go of some areas…There is a lack of human resources… Everything is available [for the army], but there is a shortfall in human capacity."[58] In that same speech, Assad noted the importance of its Russian ally and that "[they] have constituted a safety valve that prevented the transformation of the Security Council into a tool for threatening peoples and a platform for aggression on states, particularly Syria."[59]

Vladimir Putin and Bashar al-Assad: *Regime Survival and Commercial Interests*

Russia has a substantial economic stake in Syria and therefore the stability of al-Assad's regime. According to one estimate, the value of Russian investments totaled $19 billion.[60] The two most important markets in this regard are arms sales and the energy sector. According to Assad, arms deals between the two states have remained in effect since the conflict started: "[t]here are contracts that had been sealed before the crisis started and were carried out during the crisis. There are other agreements on arms supplies and cooperation that were signed during the crisis and are being carried out now."[61] Further estimates suggest that Russia currently has over $5 billion worth of new military equipment sales which is in the process of fulfilling.[62]

Russia's commercial interests extend beyond arms sales. Many state-owned oil companies are also significantly invested in Syria's energy market.

Tatneft, Stroytransgaz, Soyuzneftegaz, and Gazprom all have numerous contracts and tenders with Syria for oil and gas exploration, extraction, and production.[63] Two years after the start of the conflict, Assad's government agreed to a 25-year contract with Soyuzneftegaz which allows the Russian oil giant to conduct gas drilling and exploration off the Syrian coast.[64] If Bashar al-Assad were to be ousted from office, it is likely that Russia would have lost hundreds of millions (if not billions) in investments. Russia's economic interests were best served by protecting Assad and providing him with the necessary resources to defeat the opposition.

Vladimir Putin and Bashar al-Assad: *Regime Survival and Strategic Military Interests*

Russia also assisted Assad's regime to safeguard strategic military interests. The Tartus naval base, on Syria's Western coast, is an important tactical asset for Russia as the only remaining naval base outside the former USSR.[65] Since the beginning of the conflict in Syria, Russia has used the base continuously. During the conflict, Russia used the port at Tartus to launch its biggest naval exercise since the end of the Cold War by assembling all four of its naval fleets in the eastern Mediterranean.[66] Reflecting how important the base is to Russian interests, Vice Admiral Viktor Chirkov, the Russian Navy's commander-in-chief, said, "this base is essential to us" and that the naval facility will play a key role in Russia's future.[67] Furthermore, the base is the only port to which Russia has access beyond the Bosporus, which is controlled by NATO-member Turkey. NATO's top commander, General Philip believes Tartus is part of a larger effort by Russia to establish an anti-access/area denial (A2/AD) bubble over Syria, which would prevent NATO forces from being able to take offensive action against Russia and its key allies in the region.[68] In an interview with state-owned news agencies Sputnik International and RIA Novosti, President al-Assad confirmed that Russia will have continued access to its military bases within Syria:

> I'm talking about Russia. There are no other states, because our relations with Russia are more than six decades old, and they are based on trust and clarity. Moreover, it is the case because Russia bases its policies on principles, and we base our policies on principles. That's why when there are Russian military bases in Syria, they do not constitute an occupation. On the contrary, they strengthen our relations and our friendship, and they strengthen security and safety, and this is what we want.[69]

All of these factors coalesced to impel Putin to align with Assad and provide the military assistance necessary to keep the leader in power. This included carrying out airstrikes against opposition targets. Following an official request from al-Assad, Russia's upper parliamentary house, the Federation Council, unanimously approved Putin's request to send in a military force beginning in September 2015.[70] In the public announcement of this decision, Federation Council Speaker Valentina Matviyenko stated: "in this situation, we could not refuse Syrian President Bashar Assad and continue watching how people die, how women and children die, how historical and cultural sites are being destroyed."[71] Russia's commitment to preserving the Assad regime remained stalwart. Estimates suggest that Russia launched up to 80 sorties per day from the time it began the airstrikes through the time of this writing.[72] In 2016, according to the state-run news agency, TASS, over 300 combat sorties were made during the first 10 days, targeting over 1,000 ISIS targets. Russia has deployed its Su-24 "Fencer" long-range ground attack aircraft, Su-30SM "Flanker" multirole fighters, Su-25 "Frogfoot" ground attack and close-air-support aircraft, Mi-24 "Hind" attack helicopters, as well as its Ka-52 "Alligator" attack helicopters in support of Assad.[73] The driving motivation behind Assad's decision to seek alignment was his need to obtain economic and military capabilities which would allow him to effectively combat the threat the rebels posed to his regime, since he was incapable of producing sufficient resources on his own.

BANDWAGONING

It is clear that Russia and Syria were engaged in an internal threat alliance. But, how did elements of the Syrian regime act after the alliance formed? Did all of these actors simply comply with the alliance strategy and work to balance the rebels, or did some elements of the Syrian state collude (bandwagon) with the anti-government rebel forces? Through examining these questions, this subsection evidences the portion of the theory which argues that balancing (resisting the target threat) and "bandwagoning" (appeasing the target threat) will occur *simultaneously* during internal threat alliances. Actors within the weak state will bandwagon to survive, end up on the winning side, or advance patron-client relationships. The discussion below will demonstrate that bandwagoning did indeed occur but mainly in the early stages of the conflict when Syrian military officers defected and joined the armed resistance. Thereafter, the strong patron-client ties of key officials and the armed forces to the Assad regime pushed these actors to remain loyal to their president rather than collude with the anti-government rebels seeking to overthrow his regime.

Bandwagoning to Survive: *Defections for Self-Preservation*

As part of their repertoire of action aimed at toppling the Assad regime, insurgents threatened civilian and security sector (e.g., military officers) regime actors to the point where they agreed to collude with the insurgents in order to survive. Rebel groups threatened, kidnapped, and killed civilian government workers and supporters with the goal of forcing them to support the armed opposition. Such attacks were mainly targeted toward Syria's minority groups—such as the Alawites, Druzes, Kurds, Christians—and other actors the rebels perceived to be loyal to the government (e.g., civilian employees). This strategy seems to have been more prevalent in the subnational areas of Jaramana, Sayyidah Zaynab, Akrama, al-Nazha, and al-Zahra, all of which had high concentrations of religious minorities.[74] Other sources estimate that between 2,000 and 3,000 politically motivated abductions took place during the early stages of the war. Victims tended to be civilian members of the regime, their family members, or those perceived to be Assad sympathizers.[75] Though not always, in some cases regime actors targeted by these techniques actors decided to collude with the opposition groups threatening them in order to save their own lives or those of their families. Facing threats of execution by the armed opposition, regime actors defected out of fear for their own survival.[76] Rebels also extorted government civilian employees by compelling them to relinquish alliance assets such as money, ammunitions, and weapons, in exchange for a kidnapped family member or permission to continue residing in a rebel-held region.[77] Hamza Fatahallah, a defector from the Syrian Arab Army who joined the Free Syrian Army, described this transaction: "We have caught many army prisoners [and] send them back home for a small amount of money on the condition they do not return to the regime. We use the money to buy weapons."[78] Other rebel commanders reportedly purchased Kalashnikov ammunitions and rifles, rocket-propelled grenade launchers, rockets, and machine guns at highly inflated costs from insider regime actors.[79]

Armed opposition groups not only threatened and forced Syrian government workers to surrender alliance resources to survive but also targeted businesses working for (or benefiting from strong ties to) the regime. Opposition fighters needing financial resources, for example, threatened business owners with property destruction, kidnapping, and death, if they refused to pay monthly protection fees that ranged from $4,000 to $5,000, on top of a "down payment" which some estimates put at upwards of $100,000.[80] Regime actors colluded with anti-government opposition groups by diverting alliance resources to rebels who would then use the illicitly obtained monies to fund attacks against the Assad regime.

Bandwagoning for Profit: *Switching to the "Winning" Side to Share in Spoils of Victory*

Regime actors and those supporting the regime also bandwagoned "for profit" by defecting to—or siding with—the armed opposition in order to side with the group perceived as most likely to win. The first form of collusion motivated by a desire to align with the winning side included Syrian business elite with strong links to the Assad administration either defecting to the rebel groups, by providing financial support to them, or playing both sides by supporting the regime during one stage and the rebel forces during another. Demonstrating how actors linked to the regime do what is best for their interests—vice always side with the central government—Syrian business elites hedged their bets during the conflict by oscillating between supporting the rebels and the government, depending on what was most expedient based on the reality in their specific section of the country.[81] The Assad regime exerted pressure on these actors to continue to remain loyal by insisting that they would only be able to enjoy economic, social, and political privileges if Assad and his associates retained power.[82] As a result of their connections to the regime, these elite benefited from state-led development projects as well as the procurement system the government later established, enhancing private-sector developments in key sectors of the market.[83]

Not all members of this elite group were considered equal, however; some enjoyed record profits under Assad's rule—such as Rami Makhlouf (Bashar al-Assad's cousin who is rumored to control over 60 percent of the Syrian economy) and his family members—while others had their enterprises seized by the state or lost out on valuable opportunities.

During the early stages of the conflict, it seems that this economic marginalization at least partially contributed to some business elites supporting the opposition rather than remaining steadfastly loyal to the regime. In June 2011, for example, leaders from opposition groups across the country organized a three-day Syrian Conference for Change with the goal of establishing dialogue among the various opposition groups in order to consolidate their position and develop a transition council. The conference resulted in a final declaration calling for Assad to step down. Three Syrian business elites bankrolled the conference.[84] These and other traditionally pro-government businessmen aligned with anti-regime actors in hopes of, it seems, benefiting economically should the opposition prevail. Others partook in this type of bandwagoning in an attempt to hedge their bets; should the rebels defeat the regime, they wanted to ensure continued access to their desired sectors of the economy.[85] Editor-in-chief of *The Syria Report*, Jihad Yazigi, commented on this dynamic: "I know of businessmen who have supported both the rebels and the government at the same time, for many months."[86] Despite current ties to the regime, these elite business families provided various opposition groups with material and public support, without completely severing ties to Assad.

Bandwagoning for Patron: *Defections to Protect Fellow Sunnis; Regime Actors Funnel Arms for Their Own Financial Gain*

I announced my resignation as Syrian ambassador to Iraq as I also declare my defection from the Syrian Baath party. I urge all honest members of this party to follow my path because the regime has turned it [the party] to an instrument to kill people and their aspiration to freedom. —Nawaf Fares, Syrian Ambassador to Iraq[87]

Distinct to internal threat alliances, fear for survival or a share in the spoils of victory cannot account for all instances of regime actors colluding with the enemy during this period. Indeed, central and subnational regime elements also colluded with the anti-regime rebels due to fealties linked to religious sect (to protect fellow Sunnis) and to advance their own financial interests (to benefit by selling arms to the opposition).

The first form of bandwagoning based on patron-client ties involved Sunni members of Syria's Armed Forces defecting to the opposition in order to protect, or at minimum not be involved in killing, fellow Sunnis.

As Syria's largest minority group, the Alawites held most key political appointments and disproportionately filled the ranks of security chiefs and military commanders—some estimate that over 90 percent of the regime's military offices are held by Alawites.[88] Hafez Assad strategically placed trusted members of his family's inner circle in high-ranking political and military positions as a way to safeguard against coup d'états and defections. Alawite military officers were less likely to collude with anti-regime efforts because their fate and personal survival depended on the survival of the Assad regime.[89] As a result, when the anti-regime demonstrations first broke out in 2011, there were few high-ranking military officials that outwardly sympathized with or defected to the opposition.

By contrast, Sunni army conscripts were not nearly as loyal to the regime. When Assad's office ordered security forces to fire on unarmed demonstrators, many Sunni rank and file refused and instead chose to defect and support the mostly Sunni protesters.[90] According to journalist accounts based on interviews with several former Syrian Armed Forces members: "when asked about why they left the army, the men say they were forced to detain people and to shoot people. These were their brothers, they say; they couldn't stay in this army and do this to their brothers."[91] The interests of the military officers differed from those of the draftees; the predominately Alawite officers fought on behalf of the regime to defend their sectarian privileges, whereas the Sunni conscripts had neither personal interests nor financial incentives to support the regime. Rather, many Sunni members of the army defected to form or join the Free Syrian Army in order to protect their fellow Sunnis.[92]

Defections from the army to support the anti-Assad movement took place in large waves, especially toward the beginning of the conflict. What began with the video defection statement of Army Lieutenant Colonel Hussein Harmoush shaped the creation of the Free Syrian Army.[93] Dozens of other officers and more than 3,000 Sunni soldiers joined Harmoush in leaving the infantry and colluding with the armed rebels.[94] The following are illustrative statements from mid-ranking officers explaining why they were defecting to join the anti-government rebel forces:

> I am Engineer Abdo Hussameddin, Deputy Syrian Oil and Mineral Resources minister… I announce my defection from the regime and my resignation as Deputy Oil and Mineral Resources minister…and I am resigning from the Arab Baath party…I declare that I am joining the revolution of this nation, which did not and will not accept injustice, despite the brutality

of this regime and its supporters, to crush the people who are seeking their freedom and dignity.⁹⁵

I address you today at this grave hour where the country is living under the brunt of genocide and barbarian brutal killing against unarmed people who are simply demanding freedom and a dignified life. Today I declare... that I have defected from the terrorist, murderous regime and [am] joining the holy revolution. And I declare that from today I am a soldier of this holy revolution.⁹⁶

I, General Abdel Aziz Jassem al-Shallal, commander of Syrian military police, announce that I am defecting from the regime army, to join the people's revolution. The army has deviated from its essential mission, which is to protect the country, and it has morphed into murderous, destructive gangs. The destruction of cities and villages, and the commission of massacres against our people, defenseless civilians, who took to the streets calling for freedom.⁹⁷

Anti-Assad brigades started to form in provinces such as Aleppo, Idlib, Hama, Homs, and Daraa, the majority of which have a loose affiliation with the Free Syrian Army. As noted earlier, the majority of defections occurred at the beginning of the conflict. Though estimates vary, 88 senior/high-ranking military and security officials defected between June 2011 and December 2012.⁹⁸ Reflecting the Assad administration's ability to curb such collusion, however, only 15 high-ranking officials defected thereafter.⁹⁹

Regime actors also colluded with the armed opposition to advance their own immediate financial interests. The primary form of bandwagoning here involved regime actors (e.g., military officers) providing arms, fuel, or other support to the rebel groups in exchange for money or other assets. Syria's long history of trafficking in people, arms, drugs, and other illicit commodities had established large network of criminal entrepreneurs across the borders in Turkey, Lebanon, Jordan, and Iraq. Both rebels and regime actors alike seemed to have utilized these networks as transit routes for funding their activities and profiting from others.¹⁰⁰ State security forces working in border regions were especially well known for their participation in such smuggling networks, the majority of which were aimed at putting weapons into the hands of rebels.¹⁰¹ Reports indicate that military personnel could easily be bribed to provide resources such as weapons, ammunitions, and fuel and access to roads and facilities to armed opposition fights. As one individual who defected from Syria's air force to the opposition said: "We buy [weapons] from [regime] double agents, they need the money...They don't care about anything else. If you give them money they'll even sell you their own mother."[102] Bandwagoning motivated by this priority seems to have been the most widespread, resulting in the collusion between the armed opposition groups and the regime security forces throughout the country. One former officer recounted how he was able to utilize his position at a military airport fuel depot near to Damascus to sell fuel to rebels in Hama.[103]

According to another source, the rebel group Jaysh al-Islam, operating in East Ghouta, purchased two T-72 tanks from a corrupt Syrian army officer in 2014.[104] The Suqour al-Sham rebel group, which fought primarily in Jabal al-Zawiya, reported that they received approximately 40 percent of their weapons and ammunition from deals made with Syrian government actors; a member of the rebel group commented that "these officers sell to us not because they love the revolution, but because they love money."[105] In other provinces in the country, Syrian Army troops struck covert deals with local rebel commanders consisting of government artillery gunners firing heavily upon rebel-held structures but then overreporting the ammunition used to their superiors.[106] The agreement reached, according to a diplomatic source, was that "the soldiers would be over-resupplied with shells and they would sell the surplus to the rebels...the rebels then turned the shells into Improvised Explosive Devices (IEDs) on the condition that they would not use the bombs against the soldiers who sold them the shells in the first place."[107]

The above section demonstrated that elements of the Syrian state colluded with the alliance's primary threat rather than working to defeat these actors. The following section explains how this influenced the alliance's effectiveness.

Alliance Effectiveness

The result is an almost entire Alawite officer corps that is stubbornly loyal to the Assads, willing to use every weapon it can (from cluster bombs and ballistic missiles to helicopter gunships and, reportedly, ethical munitions), and annealed against repeated attempts to persuade key officials to defect.[108]

It is now clear that Russia and Syria were engaged in an internal threat alliance and components of the Syrian state actively colluded with the enemy, rather than implemented alliance strategy and seeking to defeat it.

But, did the alliance achieve its objectives? Why, or why not, were Russia and Assad's regime able to weaken the rebels? How did Bashar al-Assad's interests influence his regime's willingness to work with Russia and therefore alliance cohesion and effectiveness?

This subsection will provide a thorough examination of these questions and evidence the portion of the theory which argues that effectiveness of internal threat alliances will depend on whether allies have military resources sufficient to weaken their common enemy *and* are able to control subnational bandwagoning. The principal determinant of internal threat alliance effectiveness will be allies' ability to bring together capabilities sufficient to weaken or defeat the threat. And only when the great power and regime are able to agree on goals, strategy, and tactics and to coordinate activities directed toward those ends (enjoy high alliance cohesion) will they be able to collectively amass resources sufficient to weaken or defeat their common menace. However, alliances will not be effective if the weaker state's leadership is not willing and able to stop their bureaucratic actors from colluding with the enemy. Capabilities *and* curbing bandwagoning must be the recipe for success. To evidence this argument, the section cites examples from 2010 to 2016. It begins by examining some of the measures Assad implemented to promote unity within his ranks and then examines how Russian provided arms tipped the balance in Assad's favor.

Effective Efforts to Limit Bandwagoning: *Raising the Costs of Defection, Paying for Loyalty*

The Assad regime, over time, developed an elaborate system of incentives and costs to promote loyalty to the regime that enabled him to limit collusion by regime actors with rebels. To ensure government forces worked in unison to defeat the rebels—and seemingly to prevent bandwagoning—the regime distributed orders through a system of loyal clients with strong personal allegiance to the regime rooted in sectarian, familial, or business motives.[109] For example, Bashar al-Assad's cousin, Rami Makhlouf, privately funded the Tiger Forces (Qwaat al-Nimr) and placed it under the leadership of General Suheil al-Hassan, an Alawite intelligence officer; Bashar's brother Maher al-Assad acted as the de factor Division commander of the elite 4th Armored Division, and the Republican Guard was commanded by Talal Makhlouf, a first cousin of al-Assad's mother.[110] Like his father before him, Bashar al-Assad dedicated significant resources to convincing loyalist officers that their physical survival and privileged social status was inextricably linked to his regime's survival. Assad made it clear that the cost of defection for those in his inner circle would be high. Because of the formal structures (e.g., neopatrimonialism) by which Assad staffed the high-ranking positions, early rank-and-file defections were not critical to the military's overall performance.[111]

The Syrian Armed Forces officers were clients in a patronage network that linked most aspects of their personal and professional lives to the survival of the al-Assad regime. As a Syrian analyst noted: "the leaders of the Syrian army, most of whom are members of the Syrian president's family, tribe, or ethnic group, know that unlike Egypt, where the Egyptian defense minister took the reins of government from Mubarak and became the favorite son of Tahrir Square, in Syria the protesters also want the heads of the top brass of the army and security forces, so that if Bashar falls, they fall too."[112] While the sectarian affiliation of the officers influenced their continued allegiance, other factors such as financial benefit also influenced their decision to remain loyal to Assad.

Assad's provision of housing to the military seemed to promote unity within its ranks. This included the military housing complex, located in Dahiyat al-Assad, northeast of Damascus, which provided officers the opportunity to own property in the capital, social advancements unavailable anywhere else, and a place for their families to live amid the ongoing economic crisis.[113] In addition to providing military officers and their families with essential material goods, Dahia developed and reinforced a network of patronage that created a shared interest among people of various backgrounds to remain loyal to the regime and discourage defection. As one scholar who interviewed residents in the state-subsidized military complex writes:

> The benefits Dahia [the housing complex] provides come at a steep cost. With the move into military housing, officers effectively complete their buy-in, linking their personal and familial fortunes to the survival of the regime. All the trappings of an officer's life, and the social respectability it provides, are thus granted by and dependent on the regime.[114]

For many military officers and civilian workers, financial survival was inextricably linked to the Assad regime. In an attempt to buy their loyalty, the regime increased the salaries of the armed forces and security personnel three times since the uprisings began. First, in March 2011, a presidential decree instituted a one-time 1,500 Syrian-pound monthly raise for all public employees, a 30 percent salary increase for all military and civilian employees making less than 10,00 Syrian pounds per month, and a 20 percent increase for those earning above 10,000. The second set of salary increases, in June 2013, involved a presidential decree mandating that soldiers and civil servants receive a 40 percent raise on the first 10,000 Syrian pounds earned and a 20 percent increase on the second 10,000 pounds as well as an increase of the pensions of military personnel. The third and final raise was implemented in January 2015, when the Syrian government mandated that employees receive a one-time payment of 4,000 pounds added to their next salaries.[115] The military also instituted a bounty system whereby military officers received further salary increases and cash bonuses in exchange for information about potential deserters or soldiers that were collaborating with the rebels.[116] Another reason Alawi bandwagoning has been limited is because most families have a minimum of one member in either the security forces or the civilian ministries, and if the regime should fall, they would stand to lose their source of economic income. Overall, it seems that aligning with the regime brought economic incentives—and associated costs for non-compliance—that the rebel groups were unable to match. Economic incentives were clearly an important driver of armed forces unity. However, basic fear of retribution also seemed to play a role. Many reportedly feared the retributive punishment that the Sunnis would deliver should the rebels defeat the heavily Alawi regime.[117] The regime's willingness and ability to curtail bandwagoning contributed to alliance effectiveness.

While Assad employed several strategies to deter potential defectors and deserters, he also was willing to pay for loyalty. In addition to relying heavily on its elite military units, all of which were led by Alawi officers, the regime hired locally organized pro-regime militant groups known as *Shabbiha* groups.[118] These mercenaries performed a range of illicit services for the regime and were paid by the Assad government or private-sector defense companies owned by former high-security offices.[119] In the early stages of the conflict, the collective size of these fighters was roughly 20,000. Survivor accounts suggest that *Shabbiha* members were responsible for some of the most brutal attacks on peaceful protestors in Daraa, Homs, and Hama.[120] To augment the number of forces fiercely loyal to him, Assad also bolstered the ranks of the National Defense Force, a nationwide organization consisting of small, self-organized, pro-regime militants who operated in localized communities against armed opposition groups.[121] Membership in these units drastically increased in 2013, with one estimate placing overall membership at 60,000.[122]

Shifting the Balance of Power: *Russian Military Resources Increase Alliance Effectiveness*

Military resources are critical to internal threat alliance effectiveness. Though al-Assad was able to preserve unity within his elite military units, by 2015 he was struggling with financial and manpower shortages and facing mounting threats from anti-government rebels, Kurdish militia groups, and ISIL forces. Rebels had seized parts of Aleppo as well as portions of Hama, Idlib, and Daraa. ISIS had captured Palmyra.[123] The defection of Jihad Makdissi, the Syrian Foreign Ministry's Spokesman; Nawaf al-Fares, Syria's Ambassador to Iraq; Riyad Hijab, Syrian Prime Minister; and Brigadier General Manaf Tlass, a Republican Guard commander (and the highest-ranking military officer to defect) in 2012—combined with significant territory losses in 2013 and 2014—challenged al-Assad's ability to balance the increasing attacks against his regime.[124]

Facing a surge in threats from armed resistance fighters and Islamist groups, in September 2015, President al-Assad formally requested that Russia launch a military intervention in Syria. The first rounds of airstrikes were allegedly aimed at ISIL strongholds, but international observers have argued that the sorties largely targeted opposition groups, which is in line with the motivation for internal threat alliance formation.[125] An additional concern that seems to have further pushed Assad to seek Russian assistance was the need to recapture Aleppo, Syria's largest city and the site of one of the armed opposition's first real major offensives.[126] Located in the northern region of the country, Aleppo served as an important city for both opposition forces and terrorist groups because it contained one of the last two secure routes that offers access to Turkey.

Though Russian airstrikes did not liberate all desired territory from the armed groups, the five-month Russian bombing campaign did turn the tide of the war in Assad's favor. As observed by Lieutenant General Vincent R. Stewart, head of the US Defense Intelligence Agency: "the Russian reinforcement has changed the calculus completely."[127] Russian airstrikes decimated certain opposition strongholds and allowed the regime to recapture key swaths of territory in the northern and southern parts of the country. For example, Russian air raids and assistance were instrumental in Assad making decisive gains and retaking control of large parts of Aleppo. Russian warplanes coordinated with Assad's forces to complete the encirclement of the city as the first step to retaking it. Prior to Russian intervention, the city had served as a reliable opposition stronghold for over three years.[128] The regime campaign to recapture the city included targeted airstrikes in the northern countryside to draw out opposition forces as well as assassinations of key operation commanders, such as the Saudi-backed powerbroker Zahran Alloush in an attempt to weaken the rebels resolve as well as their fortitude. Though the regime had not yet fully retaken control of the city at the time of this writing, Assad was only able to make significant advances after Russian agreed to begin airstrikes.

Russian resources also enabled the regime to recapture the city of Palmyra. After weeks of coordinated attacks, the Syrian Army managed to push ISIS out and reclaim the city. In an interview in Damascus, Assad announced: "the liberation of the historic city of Tadmur (Palmyra) today is an important achievement and is evidence of the efficacy of the strategy adopted by the Syrian army and its allies in the war on terrorism."[129] The eviction of ISIS from Palmyra marked a turning point in the struggle. In January 2013, prior to Russia's military involvement, Assad delivered a televised speech in which he said, "these feelings of agony, sadness, challenge and intention are huge energy that will not get Syria out of its crisis unless it turns this energy into a comprehensive national move that saves the homeland from the unprecedented campaign hatched against it."[130] At that time, rebel gains had been substantial and the regime was struggling. Two years later, with the assistance of the Russian Federation, the emboldened president was markedly more confident. Speaking to parliament in 2016, al-Assad proclaimed: "As we liberated [Palmyra] and before it many areas, we will liberate every inch of Syria from their hands. Our only option is victory, otherwise Syria will not continue."[131] Reflecting the Assad regime's recognition that Russian assistance was critical to shifting the balance of power in his government's favor, Assad noted: "I wanted to express my huge gratitude to the whole leadership of the Russian federation for the help they are giving Syria. If it was not for your actions and your decisions, the terrorism which is spreading in the region would have swallowed up a much greater area and spread over an even greater area."[132] Russian intervention increased alliance effectiveness by enabling Assad to regain territorial control over strategic regions and thereby increase the chances of his survival.

Alliance Effectiveness Remains High as Conflict Enters Its Fifth Year
Beginning in 2011 and continuing in 2012, the armed resistance initially made significant gains throughout Syria. In January alone, for example, rebels had taken control of Zabadani and Douma (near Damascus).[133] Rebel groups even managed to control large areas in Homs as well as additional suburbs in Damascus. One of the most significant losses for the regime was the air base Menagh and the eastern portions of Syria's largest city and commercial urban center, Aleppo.[134] As the Syrian civil war reached its fifth year, though, alliance effectiveness was moderate to high. The percent of territory under permanent or substantial opposition presence decreased significantly: from 70 percent in 2012 to 20 percent in 2016.[135] After Russia began launching airstrikes in 2015, the percentage of population under rebel control went from 40 percent in 2014 to 25 percent in 2015. Though the opposition forces are not fully defeated, the alliance effectively removed the existential threat to the Assad regime's survival and, by extension, preserved Russia's strategic interests in the country.

Case Conclusions

In this chapter I used the Russia–Syria case to evidence the three main elements of the book's theoretical framework. The chapter traced Russia–Syria cooperation to defeat anti-regime insurgents and protected linked Russian interests. It showed that the Syrian government of President Bashar al-Assad sought Russia's assistance to thwart rising threats to his survival from rebel militants, while the Russia aligned in order to protect material and economic interests. Regarding bandwagoning, the chapter showed that while some elements of the Syrian Army actively cooperated with the anti-government rebels (bandwagoned), the majority of the regime actors strove to advance alliance strategies and fight against the opposition. Finally, the chapter demonstrated that the alliance was mostly effective due to Russia's economic and military capabilities and Assad's ability to prevent elements of his regime from colluding (bandwagoning) with the belligerents.

Notes

1. Jason Brownlee, Tarek Masoud, and Andrew Reynolds, *The Arab Spring: Pathways of Repression and Reform* (Oxford, UK: Oxford University Press, 2015). See also Marc Lynch, *The Arab Uprisings Explained* (Columbia, NY: Columbia University Press, 2014).
2. Human Rights Watch, "Syria: Crimes against humanity in Daraa," June 1, 2011
3. Lucy Rodgers, David Gritten, James Offer, and Patrick Asare, "Syria: the story of the conflict," *BBC*, March 11, 2016.
4. Alexei Anishchuk, "Gaddafi fall cost Russia tens of blns in arms deals" *Reuters*, November 2, 2011
5. Anna Borshchevskaya, "Russia in the Middle East," *Washington Institute for Near East Policy*, Vol. 142 (February 2016), 37.
6. Richard Weitz, "Syria's Assad Sees Georgia War as Opening Moscow Options," *World Politics Review*, September 3, 2008.
7. Richard F. Grimmet, "Conventional Arms Transfers to Developing Nations," *Congressional Research Service* (September 22, 2011), 43–44.
8. Thomas Grove, "Syria reaches oil deal with ally Russia," *Reuters*, August 3, 2012.
9. There are conflicting reports as to the precise level and type of assistance Russia provided to Syria. However, reports indicate this assistance included guns, helicopters, and a missile defense system. See, for example, Chris McGreal, "US says Russian-made weapons are killing Syrians on 'an hourly basis'," *The Guardian*, June 13, 2012. Syria also sought similar military assistance from China.
10. Steven David makes this point in (1991b) "Explaining Alignment in the Third World," 239. See also David (1992) "Why the Third World Still Matters."
11. Shmuel Bar, "Bashar's Syria: The Regime and its Strategic Worldview," *Comparative Strategy*, Vol. 25, No. 25 (2007), 353.
12. Leverett, *Inheriting Syria: Bashar's Trial by Fire* (2005), 31.
13. Ethan Kapstein and Amanda Mayoral, "Peace Economics: Why Syria must reign in unemployment, food prices, and corruption to ensure a stable future," *United States Institute of Peace*, December 6, 2013.

14. Kapstein and Mayoral, "Peace Economics: Why Syria must reign in unemployment, food prices, and corruption to ensure a stable future" (2013).
15. Bar, "Bashar's Syria: The Regime and its Strategic Worldview," 354.
16. Flynt Leverett, *Inheriting Syria: Bashar's Trial by Fire* (Washington, DC: The Brookings Institute, 2005), 24.
17. Joshua Stacher, "Reinterpreting Authoritarian Power: Syria's Hereditary Succession," *Middle East Journal*, Vol. 65, No. 2 (Spring 2011), 198.
18. Stacher, "Reinterpreting Authoritarian Power: Syria's Hereditary Succession" (Spring 2011), 198.
19. Department of State, "Background Notes Series: Syria," March 9, 2012.
20. Department of State, "Background Notes Series: Syria," March 9, 2012.
21. Department of State, "Background Notes Series: Syria," March 9, 2012.
22. Alan George, *Syria: Neither Bread nor Freedom* (New York: St. Martin's Press, 2003), 161.
23. World Bank, "Doing Business 2013 Report: Comparing Business Regulations for Domestic Firms in 185 Economies" (2013), 198.
24. World Economic Forum "Global Competitiveness Index 2011–2012," 3.
25. Alan George, "Patronage and Clientelism in Bashar's Social Market Economy," in *The Alawi's of Syria: War, Faith and Politics in the Levant* eds., Michael Kerr and Craig Larkin (London: C. Hurst & Co., 2015), 172.
26. Michael Kerr and Craig Larkin, *The Alawis of Syria: War, Faith and Politics in the Levant* (New York: Oxford University Press, 2015), 73.
27. Michael Kerr and Craig Larkin, *The Alawis of Syria: War, Faith and Politics in the Levant* (New York: Oxford University Press, 2015), 73.
28. "Syria Conflict: Russia 'to continue Assad military aid'," *BBC*
29. Joe Sterling, "Daraa: the spark that lit the Syrian flame," *CNN*, March 1, 2012.

30. Michael Provence, "Unraveling the Syrian revolution," *Regions & Cohesion* 2 (Winter 2012): 160.
31. Hafizullah Emadi, "Requiem for the Baath Party: Struggle for Change and Freedom," Mediterranean Quarterly 22 (Fall 2011), 74.
32. Emadi, "Requiem for the Baath Party: Struggle for Change and Freedom" (Fall 2011), 78.
33. Joseph Holliday, "Syria's Armed Opposition," *Middle East Security Report 3* (March 2012), 11.
34. Joseph Holliday, "Syria's Armed Opposition," *Middle East Security Report 3* (March 2012), 14.
35. Christopher Harress, "What Is The Free Syrian Army?" *IBTimes*, October 1, 2015.
36. Christopher Harress, "What Is The Free Syrian Army?" *IBTimes*, October 1, 2015.
37. "Syria Countrywide Conflict Report #4," *The Carter Center*, September 11, 2014.
38. Elizabeth O'Bagy, "The Free Syrian Army," *Middle East Security Report 9* (March 2013), 6.
39. Joseph Holliday, "Syria's Armed Opposition," *Middle East Security Report 3* (March 2012), 35.
40. Aron Lund, "The Politics of the Islamic Front Part 1: Structure and Support," *Carnegie Endowment for International Peace*, January 14, 2014.
41. Lund, "The Politics of the Islamic Front Part 1: Structure and Support," January 2014.
42. Charles Lister, "Dynamic Stalemate: Surveying Syria's Military Landscape," *Brookings Institution Doha Center* (May 2014), 2.
43. Tim Lister, "Islamic Front in Syria deals another blue to rebel alliance," *CNN*, December 12, 2013.
44. Charles Lister and William McCants, "The Syrian Civil War: Political and Military State of Play," *The Brookings Institution*, February 18, 2016.
45. Andrew J. Tabler, Jeffrey White, and Aaron Y. Zelin, "Fallout from the Fall of Taftanaz," The *Washington Institute*, January 14, 2013.
46. Tabler, White, Zelin, "Fallout from the Fall of Taftanaz," January 2013.

47. Lister, "Dynamic Stalemate: Surveying Syria's Military Landscape," 9.
48. Suleiman Al-Khalidi "Islamic State takes Syrian state's last oilfield," *Reuters*, September 7, 2015.
49. Roy Allison, "Russia and Syria: explaining alignment with a regime in crisis," *International Affairs*, Vol. 89, No. 4 (2013), 807.
50. Krishnadev Calamur, "Who Are Syria's Friends and Why Are They Supporting Assad?" *NPR*, August 28, 2013.
51. Ron Synovitz, "Why is Tartus so Important to Moscow?" *Radio Free Europe*, June 19, 2012.
52. "Meeting with President of Syria Bashar Assad," October 21, 2015.
53. Colum Lynch, "Why Putin Is So Committed to Keeping Assad in Power," *Foreign Policy*, October 7, 2015.
54. "Syria Conflict: Russia 'to continue Assad military aid'," *BBC*, September, 15 2015.
55. "No reasons to evade cooperating with Syrian leadership—Russia FM," *TASS*, September 17, 2015.
56. "Interview with President Bashar al-Assad," *Agence France-Presse*, January 20, 2014.
57. Sam Dagher and Thomas Grove, "Russia Seen Reassessing Support for Assad," *The Wall Street Journal*, July 27, 2015.
58. "Syria's Assad admits army struggling for manpower," *Al Jazeera*, July 26, 2015.
59. Bashar al-Assad, "Address to the Nation," July 27, 2015.
60. "An Economic Researcher: Russia's Investments in Syria Are About $19 Billion Dollars," *Syrian Economic Forum*, May 8, 2014.
61. Dmitry Gorenburg, "Why Russia Supports Repressive Regimes in Syria and the Middle East," *PONARS Eurasia Policy Memo*, No. 198 (June 2012), 2.
62. "Assad: Russia signed arms deals during Syria conflict," *Al Jazeera*, March 30, 2015.
63. Gorenburg, 2.
64. Salam Al-Saadi, "Russia's Long-Term Aims in Syria," *Carnegie Endowment for International Peace* (October 6, 2015) http://carnegieendowment.org/sada/?fa=61521
65. Edward Delman, "The Links Between Putin's Military Campaigns in Syria and Ukraine," *The Atlantic*, October 2, 2015.

66. Dmitri Trenin, "The Mythical Alliance: Russia's Syria Police," *The Carnegie Papers* (February 2013), 12.
67. Frank Gardner, "How vital is Syria's Tartus port to Russia?" *BBC*, June 27, 2012.
68. Delman, "The Links Between Putin's Military Campaigns in Syria and Ukraine," October 2, 2015.
69. RIA Novosti and Sputnik, "Interview with President Bashar al-Assad," March 30–31, 2016.
70. Bill Chappell, "Russia Begins Airstrikes in Syria at Assad's Request," *NPR*, September 30, 2015.
71. Bill Chappell, "Russia Begins Airstrikes in Syria at Assad's Request," *NPR*, September 30, 2015.
72. Paul Armstrong, "Hundreds of civilians killed in Russian airstrikes in Syria—Amnesty," *CNN*, December 23, 2015.
73. Daniel Wasserbly, "Russia begins airstrikes in Syria," *Janes Defense Weekly HIS*, September 9, 2015.
74. Human Rights Watch, "'He Didn't Have to Die' Indiscriminate Attacks by Opposition Groups in Syria," March 22, 2015.
75. Marah Mashi, "Kidnapping in Syria: An Economy of War," *alakhbar English*, September 28, 2012.
76. Marah Mashi, "Kidnapping in Syria: An Economy of War," *alakhbar English*, September 28, 2012.
77. Serene Assir, "Chaos turns Syria into paradise for kidnappers," *Agence France-Presse* (September 19, 2012).
78. Tracey Shelton, "Inside Syria: Who Arms the Rebels?" *GlobalPost*, June 7, 2012.
79. Tracey Shelton, "Inside Syria: Who Arms the Rebels?" *GlobalPost*, June 7, 2012.
80. Tracey Shelton, "Inside Syria: Who Arms the Rebels?" *GlobalPost*, June 7, 2012.
81. Samer Abboud, "Syria's Business Elite Between Political Alignment and Hedging Their Bets," *World Affairs Journal*, Vol. 22 (August 2013), 2.
82. Samer Abboud, "Syria's Business Elite Between Political Alignment and Hedging Their Bets," *World Affairs Journal*, Vol. 22 (August 2013), 2.
83. Samer Abboud, "Syria's Business Elite Between Political Alignment and Hedging Their Bets," *World Affairs Journal*, Vol. 22 (August 2013), 2.

84. Lauren Williams, "Syrian businessmen back opposition conference," *The Guardian*, May 30, 2011.
85. Abboud, "Syria's Business Elite Between Political Alignment and Hedging Their Bets" (August 2013), 2.
86. "Syria's Business Elite: Shifting Away From Assad," *News Deeply*, October 31, 2012.
87. "Syria defections raise pressure on Assad," *Al Jazeera*, July 12, 2012.
88. Sharon Erickson Nepstad, "Mutiny and nonviolence in the Arab Spring: Exploring military defections and loyalty in Egypt, Bahrain and Syria," *Journal of Peace and Research*, Vol. 50 (2013), 344.
89. Sharon Erickson Nepstad, "Mutiny and nonviolence in the Arab Spring: Exploring military defections and loyalty in Egypt, Bahrain and Syria," *Journal of Peace and Research*, Vol. 50 (2013), 344.
90. Sharon Erickson Nepstad, "Mutiny and nonviolence in the Arab Spring: Exploring military defections and loyalty in Egypt, Bahrain and Syria," *Journal of Peace and Research*, Vol. 50 (2013), 344.
91. Kelly McEvers, "Defectors Offer Insider's View of Syrian Army," *NPR*, April 9, 2012.
92. The Free Syrian Army, one of the first semi-organized rebel groups, was established after thousands of former regime armed forces members defected. The composition of the regime's army, much like the country itself, was largely Sunni.
93. Joseph Holliday, "Syria's Armed Opposition," *Middle East Security Report 3* (March 2012), 14.
94. Kheder Khaddour, "Strength in Weakness: The Syrian Army's Accidental Resilience," *Carnegie Endowment for International Peace* (March 16, 2016), http://carnegieendowment.org/2016/03/14/strength-in-weakness-syrian-army-s-accidental-resilience/iuy6
95. "Syria minister: defection statement," *BBC*, March 8, 2012.
96. "Syria Prime Minister Riyad Hijab," *BBC*, August 6, 2012.
97. "Syria military police chief defects to rebels," *Al Jazeera*, December 28, 2012.
98. Dorothy Ohl, Holger Albrecht, and Kevin Koehler, "For Money or Liberty? The Political Economy of Military Desertion and Rebel Recruitment in the Syrian Civil War," *Carnegie Endowment for International Peace*, November 24, 2015.

99. Basma Atassi "Interactive: Tracking Syria's defections," *Al Jazeera*, July 30, 2012.
100. Matt Herbert, "Partisans, Profiteers and Criminals: Syria's Illicit Economy," *The Fletcher Forum of World Affairs*, Vol. 38 (Winter, 2014), 75.
101. Herbert, "Partisans, Profiteers and Criminals: Syria's Illicit Economy" (Winter, 2014), 75.
102. "Syrian rebels buying weapons arms from the regime," *AFP* (October 30, 2012).
103. Ohl, Albrecht, and Koehler, "For Money or Liberty? The Political Economy of Military Desertion and Rebel Recruitment in the Syrian Civil War," November 24, 2015.
104. Scott Lucas, "Syria Feature: How the Rebels of Jaysh al-Islam Survive," *EA Worldview*, March 23, 2016.
105. Ohl, Albrecht, and Koehler, "For Money or Liberty? The Political Economy of Military Desertion and Rebel Recruitment in the Syrian Civil War," November 24, 2015.
106. Nicholas Blanford, "Profit trumps principle on Syria weapons black market," *CS Monitor*, February 4, 2014.
107. Blanford, "Profit trumps principle on Syria weapons black market," February 4, 2014.
108. Steven Heydemann, "Syria and the Future of Authoritarianism" *Journal of Democracy*, Vol. 24 (October 2013), 66.
109. Heydemann, "Syria and the Future of Authoritarianism" (October 2013), 66.
110. Joseph Holliday, "Syria's Armed Opposition," *Middle East Security Report 3* (March 2012), 44.
111. Heydemann, "Syria and the Future of Authoritarianism" (October 2013), 66.
112. Ian Black, "Six Syrians who helped Bashar al-Assad keep iron grip after father's death," *The Guardian*, April 28, 2011.
113. Kheder Khaddour, "Assad's Officer Ghetto: Why the Syrian Army Remains Loyal," *Carnegie Endowment for International Peace, Middle East Center*, November 4, 2015.
114. Khaddour, "Assad's Officer Ghetto: Why the Syrian Army Remains Loyal," November 4, 2015.
115. Ohl, Albrecht, and Koehler, "For Money or Liberty? The Political Economy of Military Desertion and Rebel Recruitment in the Syrian Civil War," November 24, 2015.

116. Ohl, Albrecht, and Koehler, "For Money or Liberty? The Political Economy of Military Desertion and Rebel Recruitment in the Syrian Civil War," November 24, 2015.
117. Ohl, Albrecht, and Koehler, November 24, 2015.
118. Droz-Vincent, 39.
119. Droz-Vincent, 39.
120. "The Use of Mercenaries in Syria's Crackdown," *Stratfor*, January 12, 2012.
121. "Syria: Pro-Government Paramilitary Forces," *The Carter Center*, November 2013, 3.
122. "Syria: Pro-Government Paramilitary Forces," *The Carter Center*, November 2013, 4.
123. Kareem Shaheen, Shaun Walker, and Ian Black, "Bashar al-Assad thanks Putin for Syria strikes as Russia announces US talks," *The Guardian*, October 21, 2015.
124. David Arnold, "Syria High-level Defections Reveal Assad Weakness" (July 16, 2012); Aron Lund, "Is Assad Losing the War in Syria?" (May 13, 2015).
125. Ben Quinn, "Russia's military action in Syria—timeline," *The Guardian*, March 14, 2016.
126. Kathy Gilsinan, "What Happens if Aleppo Falls?" *The Atlantic*, February 11, 2016.
127. Josh Cohen, "Why—and how—Russia won in Syria," *Reuters*, March 15, 2016.
128. Nick Paton Walsh, "You thought Syria couldn't get any worse. Think again," *CNN*, February 5, 2016.
129. Kareem Shaheen, "Assad hails Syrian regime's capture of Palmyra from ISIS," *The Guardian*, March 27, 2016.
130. President Bashar al-Assad, "Speech at Damascus Opera House," January 6, 2013.
131. "Defiant Assad vows to liberate every inch of Syria," *Al Jazeera*, June 7, 2016.
132. Shaheen, Walker, and Black, October 2015.
133. Jonathan Spyer, "Fragmented Syria: The Balance of Forces as of Late 2013," *Middle East Review of International Affairs*, Vol. 17 (Fall 2013), 9.

134. Spyer, "Fragmented Syria: The Balance of Forces as of Late 2013" (Fall 2013), 9.
135. See Annex Three, which includes a table with data on threat levels during the conflict.

CHAPTER 5

Conclusions

In particular after the Berlin Wall's collapse, political violence and intra-state conflict (especially within weak states) have eclipsed their inter-state counterpart as the major form of mass organized violence in the international system.[1] Just as inter-state war endangers states across the globe, so too does intra-state violence in the form of rebellion and insurgency. Such insurrections can topple the leadership of weak states and imperil great power interests by challenging the survival of allies, creating instability that terrorist organizations exploit to orchestrate attacks, jeopardizing access to natural resource reserves, and causing mass migration of refugees, among others. To counter these threats, and much like their responses to external enemies, great powers and the rulers of weak states have formed internal threat alliances to secure their respective interests. However, the IR and policy-oriented literatures have yet to catch up and offer a theory to understand this emerging form of statecraft. To fill this policy-relevant gap in the literature, this book put forth a theoretical framework that explains the dynamics of state responses to these threats—that is, why great powers and weak states form such alliances and why some such alliances are more effective than others. To evidence the framework's core components and associated arguments, the book examined three contemporary and policy-relevant cases of internal threat alliances: US cooperation with the Colombian government to defeat leftist rebels and narco-traffickers, US collaboration with Afghanistan's political elite to quell threats from the

Taliban and Al-Qaeda, and cooperation between Russia and Syria's Assad regime to defeat anti-government rebels.

As we continue into an age where a core threat to states within the international system will likely be high levels of political violence (and its consequences) within weak states—rather than only state-on-state violence—the theory presented here, as well as insights from the three cases, will provide policy-makers and scholars a framework to understand the dynamics of state responses to these threats. This concluding chapter has three objectives: first, to summarize the book's main arguments and evidence from the cases that substantiates these points; second, to outline future areas of research; and finally, to discuss the book's relevance to policy. The chapter proceeds in three core sections—one each to address these three items.

SUMMARY OF THE ARGUMENT: INTERNAL THREAT ALLIANCES: A NEW CONCEPTUAL FRAMEWORK

This section summarizes the book's core arguments and evidence from the three examined cases to the new theoretical framework that explains why internal threat alliances form, why some are more cohesive than others, and why some are effective while others are not.

Alliance Formation

This part of the theory argues that internal threat alliances will form in response to a threat that *is domestic in origin* and imperils the survival of a weak state's leadership regime. The weaker state's leadership will seek cooperation because it needs military or economic resources to thwart challenges to its existence, while the great power will become involved in order to safeguard interests linked to the regime's stability or survival. This is different than traditional alliances, where the threat is *external in origin* (another state or group of states) and the involved states align in order to secure their national interest and territorial survival. Evidence from the three cases substantiate this core argument.

In Colombia, the regime aligned because it needed military and economic resources to secure its core interests as well as thwart challenges to its existence from guerrillas and narco-traffickers, while the USA got involved to safeguard interests linked to the regime's stability including curbing drug flows onto American streets, maintaining access to oil reserves, and preserving stability in its "backyard," among others. In Afghanistan, the Karzai regime aligned because it needed capabilities to safeguard its political and economic priorities as well as thwart challenges to its existence from insurgents. As for the USA, it needed to ensure terrorists could not again use Afghanistan as a base to plan and launch attacks (as Al-Qaeda did on September 11, 2001) and ensure access to natural resources in the region. And finally, in Syria, the Bashar al-Assad administration needed military and economic capabilities to balance threats from insurgents and remain in power, while Russia agreed to provide resources because it had an interest in maintaining access to its naval facility and preserving economic interests, both of which were tied to the al-Assad regime's survival.

Bandwagoning

The second part of the theory argued that balancing (resisting the target threat) and "bandwagoning" (appeasing the target threat) will occur *simultaneously* during internal threat alliances. This is in contrast to traditional military alliances, where countries will either balance or bandwagon when faced with an external enemy. Due to the weaker state's internal fragmentation and lower capacity, its central leadership is unable to control all of its component actors (e.g., subnational governors, the military, or police forces) each of whom will routinely pursue their own interests (e.g., financial gain, cementing patron-client ties) at the expense of alliance goals. As a result, the central leadership may work with the great power to implement alliance strategy and defeat (balance) the common threat, while elements of its police or military are colluding bandwagoning) with actors fomenting violence.

In all three cases, regime actors in the capital or subnational areas such as police, military, governors, or central regime actors contravened alliance strategy and colluded with insurgents or rebels in order to survive, "for profit" (share in the spoils of victory), or to maximize their power/influence (as rooted in patron-client relations). In the case of cooperation between the USA and Colombia, some elements of the Colombian Army fought against the anti-government FARC rebels, while others actively colluded with them; similarly, various Colombian governors resisted rebel incursions, while others actively cooperated with the worst of the terrorist organization's leaders. During the US–Afghanistan alliance, many Afghan police and soldiers fought against the Taliban; however, at the same time, subnational governors and other Afghan Army or Police units colluded with the Taliban by carrying out "green-on-blue" attacks and killing alliance personnel, accepting bribes or other financial incentives to aid the insurgents, and diverting alliance capabilities to the insurgents. Much the same occurred in Syria where, especially in the early portions of the conflict, soldiers in the Syrian Armed Forces defected to join the opposition either in order to survive or safeguard their fellow Sunni citizens. Others, such as the political elite, also colluded with the insurgents in order, it seems, to continue benefiting economically in the event of an opposition victory. Lack of access to first-hand accounts in Syria makes deciphering specific motives difficult; nonetheless, it is clear that bandwagoning and balancing occurred simultaneously.

Alliance Effectiveness

The third and final part of the theory holds that the effectiveness of internal threat alliances will depend on whether allies have military resources sufficient to weaken their common enemy *and* are able to control subnational bandwagoning. The principal determinant of internal threat alliance effectiveness will be allies' ability to bring together capabilities sufficient to weaken or defeat the threat. And only when the great power and regime are able to agree on goals, strategy, and tactics and to coordinate associated activities will they be able to collectively amass resources sufficient to weaken or defeat their common menace. However, alliances will not be effective if the weaker state's leadership is not willing and able to stop their bureaucratic actors from colluding with the enemy. This central leadership circle may have political priorities (or patron-client relationships) that alter its willingness to curb subnational bandwagoning. At precise junctures and in response to threats, then, the regime may decide that working to defeat specific actors or implement specific tactics (and collaborating with the great power to do so) is detrimental to regime political survival, power, and influence. And in turn, this can decrease alliance effectiveness. This is a distinct feature of internal alliances and not found in their traditional military counterpart examined in the IR literature where states engage in capital-to-capital communication and either do or do not work together to balance a common enemy.

All three cases demonstrate how level of resources and ability to curb bandwagoning directly influence alliance effectiveness. For the US–Colombia alliance, effectiveness increased during the Andrés Pastrana

(1998–2002) and Alvaro Uribe (2002–2010) administrations due in part to the alliance's ability—through *Plan* Colombia—to amass resources sufficient to begin militarily weakening the insurgents. The Colombian government's consistent efforts under Pastrana and Uribe to purge civilian and security agencies of actors' colluding with the narco-guerilla threat also contributed to increased effectiveness from the early 2000s through the end of Uribe's term. Much the same occurred in Syria, where Assad and Putin were able to amass resources sufficient—at the time of this writing—to ward off existential threats to the regime's survival. The Assad regime's ability to maintain unity within its armed forces—and prevent substantial collusion, in the form of mass defections—also contributed to relatively high alliance effectiveness. In Afghanistan, by contrast, Afghan President Karzai's insufficient efforts to curb bandwagoning hindered alliance effectiveness, as did the allies' inability to amass resources sufficient to substantially weaken or defeat the insurgents.

Future Areas of Research

Just as the academy enriched our understanding of the dynamics of alliances to defeat or deter external enemies, more can be done to understand what will likely be the more prominent form of alliance moving forward. As a first step, the academy would benefit from stand-alone studies on internal threat alliance formation, bandwagoning, and effectiveness. One question studies might examine is why great powers select alliances over other forms of statecraft. This could take the form of statistical analysis over a large number of cases or, like this book, in-depth case study analysis of other alliances.

Similarly, IR theorists could examine in greater detail the various aspects of subnational bandwagoning present in internal threat alliances. Among other areas, research could problematize whether (and if so how) great powers have sought to curtail this regime behavior (or simply allowed it to transpire). Though it would include a more comparative politics lens, theorists could construct a model including threat thresholds to determine at what level regime actors choose to bandwagon (for survival) rather than work with the alliance to balance it.

More can also be done to understand variation in cohesion of internal threat alliances. As a starting point, scholars might construct a framework for gauging degree of internal fragmentation of weaker states. After developing a scale that assigns value to these degrees, they might employ quantitative analysis to determine across a broader set of cases the strength of relationship between internal fragmentation and cohesion. This book would suggest that as fragmentation increases, cohesion should decline. Additionally, scholars might examine the influence of alliance duration on allies' ability to devise strategy and tactics. This variable is referenced—though under examined—within the traditional alliance literature yet could provide useful insights for theory and policy alike.

Whether and if so why allies achieve their goal is equally important to understanding why alliances form in the first place; however, effectiveness has not received attention comparable to that given to other alliance dynamics. IR theory could benefit from analysis of variables—other than capabilities—that determine alliance effectiveness. As this book demonstrated, the weaker ally's willingness and ability to promote unified balancing (to curb bandwagoning) influences whether the great power and regime are able to weaken the internal threat.

POLICY IMPLICATIONS

Future wars *between* states cannot be ruled out. The diffusion of power and accompanying "rise" of China and other "emerging" powers may point in the long term to greater competition over resources and interests. And as some analysis in the field of power transition suggests, a reigning hegemon (such as the USA now) may choose to engage in preventative war to curb the ascent of a rising challenger.[2] Just as states formed alliances to balance external threats before, they may do so again. This points to the continued policy relevance of the extant literature on traditional military alliances, such as the seminal works of Walt, Snyder, and Weitsman.

Even as inter-state war remains an ever-present possibility, states will continue to face threats—rebellion and insurgency—emanating from within weak states. Factors driving insurgencies and rebellion show no sign of abating. So too, then, will these menaces continue to pose core challenges to the interests of great powers and the rulers of these weaker polities as they seek to secure their interests and remain in power. Moving forward, then, the generalizable insights this book presented should help great power policy-makers as they navigate alliances with other weaker states. This includes policymakers trying to navigate alliances already formed and whether to form such partnerships anew.

This book has several potential insights that could be useful for policy-makers, of great powers or weak states, who are grappling with how to secure their interests in the face or insurgency and rebellion, whether to form an internal threat alliance, and how best to navigate one in which they are already engaged.

First and foremost, great power policy-makers entering into such an alliance should assume that all actors within the weaker ally will not necessarily follow alliance strategy, that is, balance in a unified manner. As a result, these policy-makers must carefully calibrate expectations about what their partners will and will not do. Simply because leaders in the capital agreed to align does not mean all of their bureaucratic actors (e.g., the police or military) or components therein will fall in line and proceed accordingly. Orders from the capital do not always trickle down to subnational districts and in some cases are never made from the center to begin with. In contrast to alliances formed to defeat other states, the major internal fragmentation of the weaker state and the clientelistic relationships that undergird power dynamics (financial and political) therein mean that the unified balancing commonplace with traditional alliances cannot be assumed. Instead, the great power should assume that some element within their weaker ally will endeavor to defeat the rebellion or insurgency, while others will actively collude with it. Simply because the USA and Afghan President Hamid Karzai agreed to a specific strategy, for example, did not mean Afghan actors at various subnational areas would play along—instead, they often pursued their own interests at the expense of alliance objectives.

Second, great powers engaging in this type of alliance should plan to manage relationships between cooperative central leaders on the one hand and (national and subnational) bureaucratic actors colluding with the enemy on the other. To account for this, policy-makers should carefully analyze the political, economic, and traditional relationships between key regime actors in order to identify leverage points great powers can exploit to push these actors toward complying with alliance strategy and away from colluding with the enemy. Policy-makers would be well suited to perform in-depth analysis and intelligence gathering on their potential regime ally's internal makeup—particularly, whether its core bureaucratic agencies have intra-fragmentation that could lead to factions colluding with the target threat rather than working to defeat it.

Third, in cases where the weaker state's internal fragmentation is so deep suggest no possible way to curb substantial collusion with the enemy, the great power should question the utility of forming such an alliance to begin with. Careful consideration should be given to the range of alternatives available (e.g., targeted special operations raids and counter-terrorism operations) to secure their interests. Long-term, resource heavy engagements are not always the answer.

Fourth, great powers should be wary of leaders in weak states inflating the severity of the internal threat. Before agreeing to align, independent estimations of threat level—to that regime and associated great power interests—should be made.

Finally, policy-makers in the developing world or capitals of Western great powers should understand that capabilities alone will not be sufficient to achieve alliance objectives. This is contrary to a core assumption underlying traditional military alliances that states will be victorious provided they amass sufficient resources to defeat their enemy. In other words, capabilities are the recipe for a highly effective traditional alliance. With internal threat alliances, this assumption does not necessarily hold. In the cases of Colombia, Afghanistan, and Syria, we see that the regime's actors may—or may not—apply alliances resources against the target threat. As a result, to be effective an internal threat alliance must couple sufficient military resources as well as a host government taking action to prevent collusion with the enemy. To address this issue, great power policy-makers would be well served to devote more attention to using diplomacy and associated incentives to push actors to balance (or to prevent collusion) in addition to making sure that the alliance has enough resources to guarantee military victory.

Final Thoughts

Alliance making has been a core tenet of statecraft for centuries. This book aimed to help understand what is likely to be the more common form of alliance moving forward. Rebellion, insurgency, and state responses to such threats are issues relevant to IR theory and human well-being more broadly. As we continue into an age where the principal threat to states will likely be political violence and consequences emanating from within weak states—rather than only state-on-state violence in the territories or sea lanes of the international system—this book should be useful to theorists and policymakers alike.

Notes

1. In this book "civil war," "intra-state war," and "internal war" are used interchangeably. Although many agree that civil wars have negative consequences, the definition for what actually constitutes a "civil war" is itself disputed. This debate essentially revolves around the number of battlefield deaths that must occur initially and for each year of the conflict thereafter. I use the essential elements of the CoW definition as set forth by Small and Singer, that a civil war comprises the following elements: (1) military action internal to borders of the state, (2) active military action taken by the national government, and (3) effective resistance from the national government and opposition group or groups. Melvin Small and David Singer, *Resort to Arms: International and Civil War, 1816–1980* (Beverly Hills, CA: Sage Publishing, 1982). I find the 1000 battlefield death threshold somewhat arbitrary and do not include it here; however, nor do I offer a different threshold.
2. Robert Gilpin, *War and Change in World Politics* (Cambridge: Cambridge University Press, 1981), 191.

Appendix 1: US–Colombia Internal Threat Alliance (1980–2010)

Tables: Threat Level Indicators, Alliance Resources

Table A1.1 Level of threat to Colombia and the USA: force size, number of attacks, and control of territory

Year	Force size—number troops		Fronts		Number of armed actions		Municipal capitals under opposition control	
	FARC	ELN	FARC	ELN	FARC	ELN	FARC	ELN
1980	980	70	11	3	–	–	–	–
1981	1200	80	11	3	–	–	–	–
1982	1300	100	15	4	–	–	–	–
1983	1570	150	25	5	–	–	–	–
1984	1640	350	27	4	–	–	–	–
1985	2590	700	30	7	95	56	7	6
1986	3650	1000	32	11	152	162	–	–
1987	4280	1200	39	14	237	197	1	1
1988	4700	1700	40	16	209	357	5	5
1989	4750	2000	45	20	150	314	–	–
1990	4800	2200	46	23	280	385	12	9
1991	4900	2300	49	25	668	316	18	8
1992	5300	2400	50	27	423	426	22	10
1993	5900	2500	55	29	350	327	5	3
1994	6200	2700	58	30	389	310	18	3
1995	6400	3000	60	32	521	425	12	1

(*continued*)

Table A1.1 (continued)

Year	Force size—number troops		Fronts		Number of armed actions		Municipal capitals under opposition control	
	FARC	ELN	FARC	ELN	FARC	ELN	FARC	ELN
1996	6500(7000)	3300 (3000)	62	32	609	462	34	4
1997	6600 (7000)	4000 (3000)	63	33	706	460	33	6
1998	6700(8–12,000)	4500 (3–5000)	63	33	597	347	54	13
1999	10–12,000 (8–12,000)	4400–4500 (3–6000)	–	40	684	369	49	8
2000	Est. 10,000 (9–12,000)	Est. 5000 (3–6000)	–	40	888	579	39	8
2001	17,000 (9–12,000)	Est. 5000 (3–5000)	–	–	1032	540	15	–
2002	17,000 (9–12,000)	Est. 3500 (3–5000)	64	–	1873	420	14	3
2003	Up to 18,000 (9–12,000)	Est. 3500 (3000)	–	–	780	230–240	4	–
2004	18,000 (9–12,000)	Est. 3500 (3000)	–	–	720–760	140	1	1
2005	18,000 (15,000)	4000(3000)	60 (crisis)	–	440–460	~100	6	–
2006	12,000+ (15,000)	3000(3000)	–	–	520	~100	1	–
2007	12,000+ (9–12,000)	3000(3000)	–	75	640–660	~90	3	–
2008	12,000+ (9–12,000)	3000(2000)	64	–	400	60–80	2	–
2009	10–11,000 (9–12,000)	(2000)	–	–	280	40	9	2
2010	8000 (8–9000)	3000(2000)	61	–	220–230	20		

Table A1.1 provides data that reflects the level of threat to the allies—both intensity and proximity. For specific years and as reflected by '-' data were not available for specific years. Due to the political nature of the conflict and associated reporting on these indicators—in particular the number of FARC and ELN troops and 'fronts'—where possible, data from multiple sources are included. "Est." reflects those years for which numbers for specific measures vary and therefore the author was required to derive an estimate. The sources used for the measure are as follows. **Numbers of FARC and ELN troops and Fronts** (1980–1998) provided by: (1980–1998) Velez Maria Alejandra. "FARC-ELN Evolución y Expansión

Territorial. *Revista de Desarrollo y Sociedad.* No.47. March 2001. http://economia.uniandes.edu.co/investigaciones_y_publicaciones/CEDE/Publicaciones/Revista_Desarrollo_y_Sociedad/Ediciones/revista_desarrollo_y_sociedad_no_47/farc_eln_evolucion_y_expansion_territorial; (1999–2010) International Institute for Strategic Studies. *The Military Balance.* Vols. 1999/2000–2010. (1996–2010) Dept. of State. International Narcotics and Law Enforcement Affairs Reports 1996–2012. Numbers from State Dept. in parenthesis. All Fronts after 1998 found in annual reports on Colombia by the International Crisis Group: http://www.crisisgroup.org/en/regions/latin-america-caribbean/andes/colombia.aspx; **Number of Armed Actions for FARC and ELN troops**: (1985–2002) Lopez, Mauricio Uribe. *El Conflicto, Callejon con Salida. Informe Nacional de Desarollo Humano Colombia 2003: Capitulo 2.* United Nations Development Program: Bogota, Colombia. Sept. 2003. http://pnud.org.co/indh2003(2003–2010) Centro de Investigacion y Educacion Popular.*Conflicto Armada en Colombia Durante 2011.* June 2012. http://issuu.com/cinepppp/docs/informe_especial_cinep_ppp_junio_2012. Accessed January 2, 2012. Number of attacks are based on numbers from the former Observatorio de Derechos Humanos (now known as the programa presidencial de los Derechos Humanas y Derecho International de la Vicepresidencia de la Republica) which includes attacks on the population, attacks on military installations, infrastructure, etc.; **Number of Municipal Capitals Under FARC and ELN Control:** Arcanos. "2008: En Qué Está La Guerra. *Corporación de Nuevo Arco Iris.* Vol. 11, Issue 14. December 2008. http://www.arcoiris.com.co/wp-content/uploads/2011/arcanos/revista_ARCANOS_14.pdf

Table A1.2 Totals for military and economic capabilities aggregated by USA due to alliance with Colombia for use to balance internal threat

Totals for military and economic capabilities aggregated by the USA to alliance with Colombia for use to balance internal threat ($US Dollars)

Year	Total military capabilities aggregated	Total economic capabilities aggregated
1980	610,000	50,015,948
1981	530,000	9,515,296
1982	20,830,000	6,112,298
1983	1,150,000	7,590,975
1984	46,980,000	15,253,348
1985	1,390,000	20,329,524
1986	1,760,000	20,325,531
1987	2,350,000	20,572,770
1988	7,000,000	17,106,059
1989	96,720,000	17,704,140
1990	140,360,000	32,558,192
1991	81,170,000	31,187,718
1992	84,530,000	35,246,128
1993	43,320,000	72,130,824
1994	12,020,000	30,258,387
1995	14,400,000	23,786,621
1996	5,830,000	22,677,899
1997	90,990,000	46,331,466
1998	88,740,000	61,186,479
1999	140,450,000	287,662,921
2000	164,690,000	1,298,176,792
2001	237,460,000	82,258,130
2002	144,750,000	470,555,985
2003	231,580,000	569,539,041
2004	324,796,176	545,732,793
2005	291,534,799	624,870,938
2006	254,425,513	1,196,315,027
2007	231,002,592	288,209,154
2008	179,032,143	727,179,899
2009	190,256,208	712,022,247
2010	190,778,031	672,269,751

Table A1.2 lists the total military and economic capabilities the USA aggregated as part of its alliance with Colombia for the period 1980–2010. Data obtained from following sources: US Agency for International Development (USAID). *U.S. Overseas Loans and Grants: Obligations and Loan Authorizations, July 1, 1945–September 30, 2010.* Washington D.C. http://gbk.eads.usaidallnet.gov/query/do (accessed December 10, 2012)

Table A1.3 Military capabilities aggregated by Colombia to alliance with USA for use to balance internal threat

Year	Military expenditure total ($US)	Military expenditure (% of GDP)	Size of active military (army, navy, air force)	Number of police	Number of aircraft	Number of helicopters	Number of vehicles
1980	921,160,000	–	67,500	50,000	158	51	–
1981	877,980,000	–	70,000	50,000	154	57	57
1982	741,250,000	–	67,800	50,000	132	31	59
1983	754,370,000	–	69,700	50,000	–	–	–
1984	854,860,000	–	70,000	50,000	215	116	313
1985	965,210,000	–	66,200	50,000	209	87	348
1986	947,560,000	–	66,200	50,000	317	111	323
1987	1,038,780,000	–	66,200	55,000	187	110	323
1988	2,177,000,000	1.5	76,000	55,000	193	96	323
1989	2,439,000,000	1.6	86,300	55,000	233	136	323
1990	2,505,000,000	1.6	130,400	80,000	273	200	278
1991	2,480,000,000	1.6	134,000	80,000	261	159	278
1992	2,832,000,000	1.8	139,000	85,000	277	160	292
1993	3,648,000,000	2.2	140,000	85,000	305	174	292
1994	3,811,000,000	2.1	146,400	79,000	212	148	292
1995	4,449,000,000	2.4	146,000	87,000	213	154	300
1996	6,897,000,000	3.7	146,300	87,000	214	152	300
1997	4,434,000,000	2.3	146,300	87,000	226	176	304
1998	5,297,000,000	2.9	146,300	87,000	232	191	304
1999	5,636,000,000	3.2	155,000	87,000	–	–	–
2000	5,720,000,000	3	144,000	87,000	146	129	122
2001	6,291,000,000	3.3	153,000	95,000	134	124	357
2002	6,606,000,000	3.4	158,000	104,600	111	194	351
2003	6,939,000,000	3.5	158,000	104,600	113	202	371
2004	7,406,000,000	3.5	207,000	121,000	117	209	363
2005	7,541,000,000	3.4	207,000	121,000	152	183	437
2006	7,973,000,000	3.3	207,000	121,000	250	254	437
2007	8,458,000,000	3.3	208,600	121,000	263	271	538
2008	9,997,000,000	3.7	254,259	136,097	342	259	421
2009	10,503,000,000	3.8	267,231	136,097	346	243	362
2010	10,422,000,000	3.6	285,220	136,097	305	234	411

Table A1.3 summarizes those capabilities aggregated by Colombia to the alliance with the USA for use to balance the common internal threat. All military expenditure figures are in constant US 2010 dollars, calculated using BLS inflation calculator (http://www.bls.gov/data/inflation_calculator.htm). Sources for data are as follows: (1980–1987) U.S World Expenditures and Arms Transfers Report. http://www.state.gov/documents/organization/185658.pdf); (1988–2010) Stockholm International Peace Research Institute. *Military Expenditures and Percentage of GDP for Colombia 1988–2010.* (http://milexdata.sipri.org/result.php4). Figures tracked by the World Bank with the first recording in 1988. Armed Forces numbers and equipment: International Institute for Strategic Studies. *The Military Balance.* Vols. 1979/80–2010. World Bank Indicators of Governance as calculated by a surveying number of worldwide indicators and estimates. Earliest estimates go back only to 1996. Range from −2.5 indicating weak governance to 2.5 indicating strong governance. World Bank. *The Worldwide Governance Indicator Project.* Updated 2012. http://info.worldbank.org/governance/wgi/index.asp. Accessed December 30, 2012. Approval of the Presidents' Handling of Corruption 1995–2009; survey conducted only in urban centers (Bogota, Medellin, Cali, and Baranquilla). Gallup. "Opinion Briefing: Mexico's War on Drug Traffickers." Feb., 18, 2009. http://www.gallup.com/poll/115210/opinion-briefing-mexico-war-drug-traffickers.aspx (accessed January 4, 2013). Military Expenditures from 1980–1988 may understate the actual amount spent by the Colombian government. As detailed in the Department of State's 1996 World Military Expenditures and Arms Transfer Report, reporting standards changed in the mid- 1980s to encompass not only *actual expenditures,* but also for budgeted and planned expenditures. http://www.state.gov/documents/organization/185650.pdf

APPENDIX 1

Table A1.4 Breakdown of military capabilities aggregated by the USA to alliance with Colombia for use to balance internal threat

Breakdown of military capabilities aggregated by the USA to alliance with Colombia – 1980–2010 ($US)

Year	MAP grants	International military education and training	Foreign military financing program	Transfer from excess stock	Foreign military financing direct loan program account	NADR	Drug interdiction and counter-drug activities defense (non development activities)	Total
1980	0	610,000	0	0	0	0	0	610,000
1981	0	530,000	0	0	0	0	0	530,000
1982	0	690,000	0	0	20,140,000	0	0	20,830,000
1983	0	1,150,000	0	0	0	0	0	1,150,000
1984	0	1,400,000	0	0	45,580,000	0	0	46,980,000
1985	0	1,390,000	0	0	0	0	0	1,390,000
1986	0	1,760,000	0	0	0	0	0	1,760,000
1987	0	2,350,000	0	0	0	0	0	2,350,000
1988	5,060,000	1,940,000	0	0	0	0	0	7,000,000
1989	94,320,000	2,400,000	0	0	0	0	0	96,720,000
1990	27,280,000	2,380,000	110,700,000	0	0	0	0	140,360,000
1991	7,170,000	4,110,000	40,230,000	0	29,660,000	0	0	81,170,000
1992	13,070,000	3,350,000	68,110,000	0	0	0	0	84,530,000
1993	1,300,000	3,740,000	38,280,000	0	0	0	0	43,320,000
1994	0	1,250,000	10,690,000	80,000	0	0	0	12,020,000
1995	0	800,000	13,600,000	0	0	0	0	14,400,000
1996	5,120,000	130,000	0	580,000	0	0	0	5,830,000

(continued)

Table A1.4 (continued)

Breakdown of military capabilities aggregated by the USA to alliance with Colombia – 1980–2010 ($US)

Year	MAP grants	International military education and training	Foreign military financing program	Transfer from excess stock	Foreign military financing direct loan program account	NADR	Drug interdiction and counter-drug activities defense (non development activities)	Total
1997	33,520,000	0	0	120,000	0	0	57,350,000	90,990,000
1998	35,300,000	1,140,000	0	0	0	0	52,300,000	88,740,000
1999	56,030,000	1,170,000	0	30,000	0	0	83,220,000	140,450,000
2000	0	1,130,000	0	2,660,000	0	0	160,900,000	164,690,000
2001	0	1,270,000	0	3,590,000	0	0	232,600,000	237,460,000
2002	0	1,420,000	0	0	0	0	143,330,000	144,750,000
2003	0	1,370,000	20,150,000	4,000,000	0	0	206,060,000	231,580,000
2004	0	1,900,000	113,120,000	320,000	0	86,176	209,370,000	324,796,176
2005	0	1,890,000	110,380,000	0	0	5,694,799	173,570,000	291,534,799
2006	0	1,770,000	95,860,000	0	0	5,605,513	151,190,000	254,425,513
2007	0	1,670,000	89,300,000	520,000	0	4,362,592	135,150,000	231,002,592
2008	0	1,450,000	53,670,000	0	0	1,532,143	122,380,000	179,032,143
2009	0	1,410,000	55,900,000	400,000	0	3,706,208	128,840,000	190,256,208
2010	0	1,690,000	55,000,000	0	0	4,938,031	129,150,000	190,778,031

Table A1.4 lists the breakdown by funding category of military capabilities the USA aggregated as part of its alliance with Colombia for the period 1980–2010. Data obtained from following sources: U.S. Agency for International Development (USAID). *U.S. Overseas Loans and Grants: Obligations and Loan Authorizations, July 1, 1945–September 30, 2011*. Washington D.C. http://gbk.eads.usaidallnet.gov/query/do (accessed December 10, 2012). All numbers are reported by recipient countries.

Appendix 2: US–Afghanistan Internal Threat Alliance (2001–2012)

Tables: Threat Level Indicators, Alliance Resources

Table A2.1 Level of threat to Afghanistan and the USA: force size, number of attacks, and control of territory

Year	Number of insurgent forces	Number of armed actions	Insurgent revenue from opium (millions $USD)	Territory with permanent or substantial insurgent presence	Territory with percentage of Afghanistan under substantial Taliban presence
2000	–	–	–	–	–
2001	–	–	–	–	–
2002	(4000)	–	–	–	–
2003	1000 (7000/0)	–	–	–	–
2004	(9500)	7300	–	–	–
2005	2–3000(12,5000)	5475	$90–$160 m	–	–
2006	4000(17,000)	7665	$90–$160 m	–	–
2007	–	9125	$90–$160 m	54 %	38 %
2008	16,000	12,775	$100–$500 m	72 %	21 %
2009	25,000	31,025	$100–$150 m	80 %	7 %
2010	36,000	32,850	–	–	–

Table A2.1 provides data that reflects the level of threat to the allies—both intensity and proximity. For specific years and as reflected by '–' data were available for specific years. Due to the political nature of the conflict and associated reporting on these indicators—in particular the number of insurgent troops and attacks—where possible, data from multiple sources are included. The sources used for the measure are as follows: **Number of Insurgent Forces**: The figures provided are drawn from the following sources and refer mainly to the Taliban yet also include other insurgent forces. Antonio Giustozzi, *Koran, Kalashnikov, and Laptop: The Neo-Taliban Insurgency in Afghanistan*. Columbia University Press: New York. 2008. Parentheses indicate estimates by author. In addition to the Taliban, the two other insurgency groups in Afghanistan that are commonly cited by experts are Hezb-i-Islami and the Haqqani Network. Regarding Hezb-i-Islami the numbers are listed as "unknown" by the START program at the University of Maryland. (National Consortium for the Study of Terrorism and Responses to Terrorism. "Data: Hizb-I-Islam." University of Maryland. (Accessed March 20, 2013); The Washington post lists both Hezb-i-Islami and the Haqqani Network as approximately containing 1000 members each. (Tyson, Ann Scott. "A Sober Assessment of Afghanistan." The Washington Post. June 15, 2008. However, Reuters lists their numbers as closer to 4000. (Ferris, Rotman, Amie. "Haqqani Network Behind Afghan Attacks: U.S. Envoy." Reuters. April 19, 2012. **Number of Armed Actions:** These data reflect the annual number of "enemy-initiated" attacks against Afghan- or non-Afghan forces including direct and indirect fire, IED attacks, kidnapping, and any other such attacks. Data for this factor varies widely depending on the source. The annual totals listed reflect the middle point between the range of total number of attacks provided by sources. United States Government Accountability Office. *Afghanistan Security: Afghan Army Growing, but Additional Trainers Needed; Long-term Costs Not Determined*. Washington. Government Printing Office. Jan. 2011 Characterized as "Enemy initiated attacks " without breakdown as to type (kidnapping, explosions, etc.); **Territory with Permanent or Substantial Insurgent Presence:** Permanent presence is defined as areas that have had an average of at least one insurgent attack a week- this include both lethal and non-lethal; Substantial presence is defined as areas that have had an average of at least one insurgent attack a month- also both lethal and non-lethal. Sources for this data include: International Council on Security and Development: "ICOS Maps" (accessed January 28, 2013). Presence data determined based on public reports of level of daily insurgent activity/attacks. Gaps in the data exist between 2001 and 2006. This may be attributable to many things, including perceptions of resurgence within the USA. According to the Government Accountability Office: "Security and stability in Afghanistan have deteriorated in the past 3 years. In the first several years of the war, Afghanistan was relatively stable and secure and attacks by Taliban insurgency on US soldiers were rare. However, since 2006, the insurgency has reasserted itself, resulting in an escalation of violence, especially against U.S. and coalition forces." (Government Accountability Office. *Iraq and Afghanistan: Security, Economic, and Governance Challenges to Rebuilding Efforts Should be Addressed in U.S. Strategies."* (Washington, D.C. March 25, 2009), 11. According to Jane's Defense and Security: "While initially offering only low-level opposition to the new government of President Hamid Karzai, since 2006 there has been a significant escalation in Taliban operations, with the group carrying out an intensifying asymmetric insurgency." (Jane's Defense and Security. "World Insurgency and Terrorism: Taliban" Accessed March 21, 2013.

Table A2.2 Totals for military and economic capabilities aggregated by the USA to alliance with Afghanistan for use to balance internal threat

Totals for military and economic capabilities aggregated by the USA to alliance with Afghanistan for use to balance internal threat ($US Dollars)

Year	Total military capabilities aggregated	Total economic capabilities aggregated	Total capabilities
2001	3,420,000	25,360,000	28,780,000
2002	70,310,000	3,964,428,000	4,034,738,000
2003	417,920,000	618,750,000	1,036,670,000
2004	627,260,000	1,512,233,000	2,139,493,000
2005	823,840,000	1,569,780,000	2,393,620,000
2006	2,050,720,000	1,838,330,000	3,889,050,000
2007	4,082,703,000	1,838,980,000	5,921,683,000
2008	6,375,880,000	2,409,610,000	8,785,490,000
2009	6,113,560,000	2,673,950,000	8,787,510,000
2010	6,868,130,000	4,253,160,000	11,121,290,000
Total	27,433,743,000	20,704,581,000	48,138,324,000

Table A2.2 lists the total military and economic capabilities the USA aggregated as part of its alliance with Afghanistan for the period 2001 2010. Data obtained from following sources: (1) Military: Total amounts obtained from U.S. Agency for International Development (USAID). *U.S. Overseas Loans and Grants: Obligations and Loan Authorizations, July 1, 1945–September 30, 2010: Custom Report Afghanistan 2000–2010.* Washington D.C. http://gbk.eads.usaidallnet.gov/query/do (accessed January 29, 2013); (2) Non-military: U.S. Agency for International Development (USAID). *U.S. Overseas Loans and Grants: Obligations and Loan Authorizations, July 1, 1945–September 30, 2010: Custom Report Afghanistan 2001–2010.* Washington D.C. http://gbk.eads.usaidallnet.gov/(accessed January 29, 2013). All numbers are reported by recipient countries. Civilian forces deployed by US Government to Afghanistan: Livingston, Ian S. and Michael O'Hanlon. *Afghanistan Index.* Brookings Institute. May 16, 2012.

Table A2.3 Military capabilities aggregated by Afghanistan to alliance for use to balance internal threat

Size of Afghanistan's security forces and annual expenditures

Year	Military expenditure	AFG spending as percent of GDP	Min. of defense forces	Min. of interior forces	Total forces
			Army and support staff	All police forces and support staff	
2001					–
2002					–
2003	186,000,000	2.1 %	6000	0	6000
2004	191,000,000	2.2 %	24,000	33,000	57,000
2005	173,000,000	1.8 %	26,000	40,000	66,000
2006	188,000,000	1.8 %	36,000	49,700	85,700
2007	275,000,000	2.4 %	50,000	75,000	125,000
2008	242,000,000	2.2 %	57,800	79,910	137,710
2009	305,000,000	2 %	100,131	94,958	195,089
2010	576,000,000	3.8 %	149,533	116,856	266,389

Table A2.3 lists expenditures by government of Afghanistan on its military as well as the force size of its army and police over the course of the alliance. Data on military expenditures obtained from the following sources: (1) Military Expenditures, Percent of GDP: Stockholm International Peace Research Institute. *Military Expenditures and Percentage of GDP for Afghanistan 2001–2010.* (http://milex-data.sipri.org/result.php4). Figures tracked by the World Bank. (1) Afghan security force numbers (as of November/December of given year), Ian S. Livingston and Michael O'Hanlon, *Afghanistan Index.* Brookings Institute. May 16, 2012. Two notes: (1) *Ministry of Defense Forces*: refers to all forces under the control of this Ministry, which oversees the readiness and capabilities of the Afghanistan National Army. The operational arm of the ANA is divided into 5 corps, which is then further divided into several brigades. This arm comprises about seventy percent of ANA personnel and holds responsibility for different regions of Afghanistan. In support of these endeavors there are many institutions that sustain and support the Ministry of Defense including in the fields of logistics, communications support, regional military intelligence offices, training and recruitment, and Headquarters Support and Security Brigade. The figure provided seeks to capture all of these forces. (2) *Ministry of Interior Forces*: refers to all forces under the control of this Ministry, which oversees the protection of Afghan internal borders and enforces the rule of law. These forces include several police units all of which to some extent combat internal threats: Afghan Uniformed Police, assigned to police districts, provinces and regions, Afghan Border Police, providing law enforcement capabilities at international borders and entry points, Afghan National Civil Order Police, responsible with providing counter civil unrest and lawlessness, Criminal Investigative Division, leads investigations of national interest such as white collar crime, Counter-narcotics Police of Afghanistan, charged with reducing production and distribution of narcotics, and Counter Terrorism Police, charged with leading efforts to defeat terrorism and insurgency.

Table A2.4 Breakdown of military capabilities aggregated by the USA to alliance with Afghanistan

Breakdown of military capabilities aggregated by the USA to alliance with Afghanistan—2001–2010 ($US)

Year	Antiterrorism and related (NADR)	Foreign military financing	International military education and training	Military assistance (MAP) grants	Peacekeeping operations	Drug interdiction	Transfer from excess stock	Afghan security forces fund	Total military capabilities	US forces in Afghanistan
2001	3,420,000								3,420,000	
2002	8,420,000	60,150,000		1,490,000	–	250,000			70,310,000	2500
2003	13,320,000	225,090,000	460,000	171,470,000	–	270,000	7,310,000		417,920,000	9700
2004	9,580,000	475,780,000	430,000	51,710,000		85,100,000	4,660,000		627,260,000	13,100
2005	36,680,000	441,520,000	1,050,000		17,250,000	243,540,000		83,800,000	823,840,000	16,700
2006	24,030,000		1,050,000			82,560,000		1,943,080,000	2,050,720,000	17,800
2007	28,100,000		1,193,000			250,760,000		3,802,650,000	4,082,703,000	22,100
2008	29,500,000		1,680,000			208,410,000		6,136,290,000	6,375,880,000	24,700
2009	34,740,000		1,410,000			264,530,000		5,812,880,000	6,113,560,000	31,800
2010	69,600,000		1,760,000			325,340,000	30,000	6,471,400,000	6,868,130,000	67,400

Table A2.4 lists the breakdown by funding category of military capabilities the USA aggregated as part of its alliance with Afghanistan for the period 2001–2012. Data obtained from following sources: Total amounts obtained from U.S. Agency for International Development (USAID). *U.S. Overseas Loans and Grants: Obligations and Loan Authorizations, July 1, 1945–September 30, 2010: Custom Report Afghanistan 2000–2010.* Washington D.C. http://gbk.eads.usaidallnet.gov/query/do (accessed January 29, 2013). All numbers are reported by recipient countries. The following are brief explanations of the purpose of each specific funding source. Nonproliferation, Antiterrorism, Demining and Related (NADR): Funding used to support a broad range of security-related programs to reduce threats by targeting four arrears: nonproliferation, antiterrorism, regional stability and humanitarian assistance; Foreign Military Financing (FMF) Programs: Program provides grants to recipient countries for the purposes of funding the transfer of US defense equipment and services and trainings. Though the program primarily funds arms transfers, it does include a significant amount of military training; International Military Education and Training: US program to provide training and education on grant basis to military students at US military training institutions. Military Assistance Programs (MAP) Grants: Refer to the former system of grant aid distribution that allocated funds to country to allow them to obtain defense articles and services in support of US National Security Policy without requiring repayment to the USA. Around FY 1982 these grant funds and programs and funds became part of the Foreign Military Financing program; Peacekeeping Operations: Funding to provide support for international peacekeeping operations and to promote increased involvement of regional organizations in conflict resolution; Drug-Interdiction: Refers to all Counter-narcotics initiatives with a non-development component. It funds training of military and law enforcement to support drug interdiction operations; Transfer from Excess Stock: Refers to the sale of US defense articles no longer needed by US forces; Afghan Security Forces Fund: an account under DOD appropriations, funds are to enhance to the ability of the Afghan National Security Forces (ANSF) to combat terror and support US operations in Afghanistan. Assistance given under this account includes equipment procurement, training, supplies and services. Other sources are as follows: (1) Number of Students Trained: Department of State and Department of Defense. *Foreign Military Training: Joint Report to Congress, Fiscal Year 2010 and 2011; Executive Summary* (accessed January 26, 2013). The Foreign Military Training Reports, is a Joint Report by the Department of State and Department of Defense as required by the Foreign Assistance Act of 1961 as amended, and the Foreign Operations, Export Financing, and Related Programs Appropriations Act; as started in 2000. (2) US Forces in Afghanistan: Ian S. Livingston and Michael O'Hanlon. *Afghanistan Index*. Brookings Institute. May 16, 2012. (3) Number of troops as of January of each year; deployment numbers fluctuate throughout the year.

Appendix 3: Russia–Syria Internal Threat Alliance (2009–2016)

Tables: Threat Level Indicators, Alliance Resources

Table A3.1 Level of threat to Syria and Russia: force size, number of attacks, and control of territory

Year	Number of armed opposition forces	Territory with permanent or substantial insurgent presence	Percentage of population under substantial opposition control
2011	10,000	55 %	
2012	6140	70 %	
2013	85,680	65 %	20 %
2014			40 %
2015	30,000	45 %	25 %
2016	45,000–60,000	20 %	

TableA3.1 provides data that reflects the level of threat to Russia and Syria. Due to the recent nature of the conflict and associated reporting on these indicators it is difficult to obtain and verify the indicators. The sources used for the measure are as follows: **Number of Insurgent Forces**: The figures provided are drawn from the following sources and refer mainly to the Free Syrian Army yet also include other insurgent forces. Osama al-Koshak. "Mapping Southern Syria's Armed Opposition." *Al Jazeera Centre for Studies*. October 13, 2015. Christopher Harress. "What is the Free Syrian Army? Russia Targets CIA-Trained Rebels Opposed to Assad Regime." *IBTimes*. October 1, 2015. Aaron Lund. "The Political Geography of Syria's War: An interview with Fabrice Balance." *Carnegie Endowment for International Peace*. January 30, 2015. *Syria Countrywide Conflict Report #2*. The Carter Center. November 20, 2013. **Territory with Permanent or Substantial Insurgent Presence:** Sources for this data include: Salman Shaikh. "Losing Syria (and how to avoid it) Foreign Policy Briefing" The Brookings

Institution. October 2012. Alia Brahimi. "Half-light in Syria." *Al Jazeera*. September 19, 2012. Aaron Lund. "The Political Geography of Syria's War: An interview with Fabrice Balance." *Carnegie Endowment for International Peace*. January 30, 2015. **Percentage of Population under Substantial Opposition Control:** Aaron Lund. "The Political Geography of Syria's War: An interview with Fabrice Balance." *Carnegie Endowment for International Peace*. January 30, 2015. Salman Shaikh. "Losing Syria (and how to avoid it) Foreign Policy Briefing" The Brookings Institution. October 2012. Alia Brahimi. "Half-light in Syria." *Al Jazeera*. September 19, 2012. Aron Lund. "Syria's Phony Election: False Numbers and Real Victory." *Carnegie Endowment for International Peace*. June 9, 2014.

Table A3.2 Size of Syria's security forces and annual expenditures

Year	Military expenditure	Syria spending as percent of GDP	Min. of national armed forces and support staff	Total forces
2009	2,020,000,000	4.00 %	310,000	310,000
2010	2,060,000,000	4.10 %	310,000	310,000
2011	2,530,000,000	3.80 %	310,000	310,000
2012	2,410,000,000	5.89 %	290,000	290,000
2013			110,000	110,000
2014			125,000	125,000
2015			130,500	130,500
2016				

Table A3.2 lists expenditures by government of Syria on its military as well as the force size of its army and police over the course of the conflict. Data on military expenditures obtained from the following sources: (1) Military Expenditures, Percent of GDP: Stockholm International Peace Research Institute. *Military Expenditures and Percentage of GDP for Syria 2009–2015*. (https://www.sipri.org/databases/milex); (2) The Military Balance 2010–2016, International Institute for Strategic Studies.

BIBLIOGRAPHY

9-11 Commission. (2004). *The 9/11 commission report: Final report of the national commission on terrorist attacks upon the United States – Authorized edition.* New York: W.W. Norton & Company.

Abboud, S. (2013, August 22). Syria's business elite between political alignment and hedging their bets. *World Affairs Journal.*

Abdulkader, H. S. (2008). *Organizations at war in Afghanistan and beyond.* Ithaca: Cornell University Press.

Abrahimkhil, S. (2010, December 4). Report reveals political deals behind governors appointments. *Tolo News.*

Agence France-Presse. (2000, January 15). US aid depends on Colombia's approach to human rights. *Agence France-Press.*

Agence France-Presse. (2001, November 9). Colombian president plays down rebel ultimatum.

Agence France-Presse. (2012, October 30). Syrian rebels buying weapons arms from the regime. *Agence France Presse.*

Agence France-Presse. (2014, January 20). Interview with President Bashar al-Assad. *Agence France Presse.*

Agencia EFE. (2003, February 20). Presupuesto Defensa de Colombia de Este Año Será de 3.600 Millones de Dólares. Agencia EFE news (Spain).

Al Jazeera. (2012a, July 12). Syria defections raise pressure on Assad. *Al-Jazeera.*

Al Jazeera. (2012b, December 28). Syria military police chief defects to rebels. *Al Jazeera.*

Al Jazeera. (2014, May 8). An economic researcher: Russia's investments in Syria are about $19 billion dollars. *Syrian Economic Forum.*

Al Jazeera. (2015a, March 30). Assad: Russia signed arms deals during Syria conflict. *Al Jazeera.*

Al Jazeera. (2015b, July 26). Syria's Assad admits army struggling for manpower. *Al Jazeera*.
Al Jazeera. (2016, June 7). Defiant Assad vows to liberate every inch of Syria. *Al Jazeera*.
Al Jazeera Media. (2015). Interactive: Tracking Syria's defections. *Al-Jazeera*. http://www.aljazeera.com/indepth/interactive/syriadefections
Al-Khalidi, S. (2015, September 7). Islamic State takes Syrian state's last oilfield. *Reuters*.
Allen testimony. (2012, March 12). U.S. Senate Armed Services Committee.
Allison, G. T. (1999). *Essence of decision: Explaining the Cuban missile crisis*. New York: Little, Brown.
Allison, R. (2013). Russia and Syria: Explaining alignment with a regime in crisis. *International Affairs, 89*(4), 795–823.
Allison, G. T., & Halperin, M. H. (1972). Bureaucratic politics: A paradigm and some policy implications. *World Politics, 24*, 40–79.
Allison, G. T., & Szanton, P. (1976). *Remaking foreign policy: The organizational connection*. New York: Basic Books.
Almario, J. (1998, May 8). The FARC attacks, the government negotiates, and Colombia disintegrates. *EIR News Service*.
Almond, G., & Genco, S. (1977). Clouds, clocks and the study of politics. *World Politics, 29*(4), 489–522.
Al-Saadi, S. (2015, October 6). Russia'slong-term aims in Syria. *Carnegie Endowment for International Peace*.
Ambassador Ann Patterson. (2001, November 4). Las nuevas relaciones entre Estados Unidos y Colombia. *La Revista de El Espectador*.
Ambassador Karl W. Eikenberry. (2009, December 8). Testimony before the Senate Committee on Armed Services, p. 2.
Anishchuk, A. (2011, November 2). Gaddafi fall cost Russia tens of blns in arms deals. *Reuters*.
Arbeleaz, A. (2012, June 12). Deputy Minister of Defense for President Alvaro Uribe. Interview with author. Washington, DC.
Armstrong, P. (2015, December 23). Hundreds of civilians killed in Russian airstrikes in Syria—Amnesty. *CNN*.
Arnold, D. (2012, July 16). Syria high-level defections reveal Assad weakness.
Arrieta, C. G., Orjela, L. J., Sarmiento, E., & Tokatlian, J. G. (1990). *Narcotráfico en Colombia*. Santafé de Bogotá: Ediciones Uniandes/Tercer Mundo Editores.
Asare, P., Gritten, D., Offer, J., & Rodgers, L. (2016, March 11). Syria: The story of the conflict. *BBC*.
Associated Press. (2002, July 22). Karzai fires bodyguards, calls in U.S. Soldiers for protection. *Associated Press*.
Associated Press. (2005, August 4). Bush: U.S. won't be deterred by al-Qaida threat.

Associated Press. (2011, January 1). Wikileaks: US officials pressured Karzai to remove former warlord Ismail Khan for "corruption and ineffectiveness. *Associated Press.*

Atassi, B. (2012, July 30). Interactive: Tracking Syria's defections. *Al Jazeera.*

Atmar, M. H. (Minister of Interior). (2009, February 25). Speech delivered at the Brookings Institution. Washington, DC.

Aviles, W. (2007). *Global capitalism, democracy, and civil-military relations in Colombia.* Albany: State University of New York Press.

Bagley, B. (2001, February 7). Drugtrafficking, political violence and U.S. policy in Colombia in the 1990s. Working paper. Miami, FL: School of International Studies, University of Miami.

Bagley, B., & Tokatlian, J. (1985). Colombian foreign policy in the 1980s: The search for the leverage. *Journal of Inter-American Studies and World Affairs,* 27(3), 27–62.

Bagley, B., & Walker III, W. (1994). *Drug trafficking in the Americas.* New Brunswick: Transaction Publishing.

Baltimore Sun. (2004, September 12). Afghan governor removed from power. *Baltimore Sun.*

Bar, S. (2007). Bashar's Syria: The regime and its strategic worldview. *Comparative Strategy,* 353–445.

Barfield, T. (2010). *Afghanistan – A cultural and political history.* Princeton: Princeton University Press.

Bargent, J. (2012, December 4). Ex-Colombian intelligence head gets 13 years prison for drug ties. *InSight Crime.*

Barma, N. H. (2012). Peacebuilding and the predatory political economy of insecurity: Evidence from Cambodia, East Timor and Afghanistan. *Conflict, Security & Development,* 12(3), 273–298.

Barnett, M. N., & Levy, J. S. (1991). Domestic sources of alliances and alignments: The case of Egypt, 1962–1973. *International Organization,* 45(3), 370.

Basa, A., et al. (2007). *Ungoverned territories: Understanding and reducing terrorism risks.* Santa Monica: RAND Corporation.

BBC News. (2002, June 13). Karzai elected Afghan leader. *BBC News.*

BBC News. (2005a, October 20). Colombia re-election ban lifted. *BBC News.*

BBC News. (2005b, November 17). French violence 'back to normal'. *BBC News.*

BBC News. (2008a, September 23). Colombia seizes 'key Farc Data'. *BBC News.*

BBC News. (2008b, March 1). Top Farc leader killed by troops. *BBC News.*

BBC News. (2011, September 20). Afghan peace council head Rabbani killed in attack. *BBC News.*

BBC News. (2012a, March 8). Syria Minister: Defection statement. *BBC.*

BBC News. (2012b, August 6). Syria Prime Minister Riad Hijab. *BBC.*

BBC News. (2012c, March 23). Q&A: Syria sanctions. *BBC.*

BBC News. (2013, April 10). Profile: Syria's al-Nusra front. *BBC*.
BBC News. (2014, September 11). Syria countrywide conflict report #4. *The Carter Center*.
BBC News. (2015a, September 15). Syria conflict: Russia 'to continue Assad military aid'. *BBC*.
BBC News. (2015b, September). Syria conflict: Russia 'to continue Assad military aid'. *BBC*.
Beers, R. (2001, March 1). Assistant Secretary for International Narcotics and Law Enforcement Affairs. Testimony before the Western Hemisphere, Peace Corps, and Narcotics; Subcommittee of the Senate Foreign Relations Committee. Washington, DC.
Bejarano, A. M. (2011). *Precarious democracies – Understanding regime stability and change in Colombia and Venezuela*. Notre Dame: University of Notre Dame Press.
Bejarano, A. M., & Pizarro, E. (2004). Colombia: The partial collapse of the state and the emergence of aspiring state-makers. In P. Kingston & I. Spears (Eds.), *States within states – Incipient political entities in the post-cold war era*. New York: Palgrave MacMillan.
Belasco, A. (2011). *The cost of Iraq, Afghanistan, and other global war on terror operations since 9/11*. Washington, DC: Congressional Research Services.
Bennett, A., & Elman, C. (2006). Qualitative research: Recent developments in case study methods. *Annual Review of Political Science, 9*(1), 455–476.
Berman, S. (2010). From the Sun King to Karzai. *Foreign Affairs, 89*(2), 2–9.
Bibes, P. (2001). Transnational organized crime and terrorism: Colombia, a case study. *Journal of Contemporary Criminal Justice, 17*(3), 243–258.
Black, I. (2011, April 28). Six Syrians who helped Bashar al-Assad keep iron grip after father's death. *The Guardian*.
Blanford, N. (2014, February 4). Profit trumps principle on Syria weapons black market. *CS Monitor*.
Blattman, C., & Miguel, E. (2010). Civil war. *Journal of Economic Literature, 48*(1), 3–57.
Boadle, A. (1999, October 6). US closer to boosting military aid to Colombia. *Reuters*.
Bonner, R. (1997, May 2). France linked to defense of Mobutu. *New York Times*.
Bonnett Locarno, M. J. (1997, December). *Estrategia General De Las Esfuerzas Militares Por La Seguridad de la poblacion y sus recursos*.
Boone, C. (2003). *Political topographies of the African state: Territorial authority and institutional choice*. Cambridge: Cambridge University Press.
Borda, S. (2009). *The internationalization of domestic conflicts: A comparative study of Colombia, El Salvador, and Guatemala*. Dissertation, University of Minnesota.

Borshchevskaya, A. (2016, February). *Russia in the Middle East* (p. 142). Washington, DC: Washington Institute for Near East Policy.

Boulding, K. (1962). *Conflict and defense: A general theory*. New York: Harper and Row.

Bowden, M. (2001). *Killing Pablo—The hunt for the world's greatest outlaw*. New York: Penguin Books.

Boyatt, T. (U.S. Ambassador to Colombia). Interview with Author. Washington, DC.

Boyd, G. M. (1989, January 3). Reagan accuses Soviet Union, Cuba of aiding Latin terrorists. *Times-News*.

Brady, H., & David, C. (Eds.). (2000). *Rethinking social inquiry: Diverse tools, shared standards*. Lanham: Rowman Littlefield.

Bratton, M., & van de Walle, N. (1994). Neopatrimonial regimes and political transitions in Africa. *World Politics, 46*(4), 453–489.

Brittain, J. (2005). The FARC-EP in Colombia: A revolutionary exception in an age of imperialist expansion. *Monthly Review, 57*, 20.

Brooke, J. (1988, February 23). Gabon keeps strong links with France. *New York Times*.

Brooks, L. (1998, August 8). Colombian President inaugurated. *Washington Post*.

Brown, M. E., et al. (Eds.). (1995). *The perils of anarchy: Contemporary realism and international security*. Cambridge: MIT Press.

Brownlee, J., Masoud, T., & Reynolds, A. (2015). *The Arab spring: Pathways of repression and reform*. Oxford: Oxford University Press.

Buffalo News. (1999, May 6). Colombia'santi-drug chief fired in corruption case. *Buffalo News*.

Buitrago, A. L. (1989). *Estado y Politica en Colombia*. Bogota: Siglo Veintiuno de Colombia.

Calamur, K. (2013, August 28). Who are Syria's friends and why are they supporting Assad? *NPR*.

Calvocoressi, P. (1966). Europe's alliance blues. *Political Quarterly, 37*, 357–365.

Campbell, J. H., & Shapiro, J. (2009, January 21). Afghan index – 2009 – Tracking variables of reconstruction & security in post-9/11 Afghanistan. Washington, DC: Brookings Institution.

Campbell, J. H., & Shapiro, J. (2013, July 15). Afghan index – July 15, 2013. Washington, DC: Brookings Institution.

Carter, S., & Cox, A. (2011, September 8). One 9/11 Tally: $3.3 Trillion. *The New York Times*.

CBC News. (2004, October 29). Bin Laden claims responsibility for 9/11.

CBS News. (2009, November 2). Karzai Re-elected Amid Turmoil. *CBS News*.

Centeno, M. A. (2002). *Blood and debt: War and the nation-state in Latin America*. University Park: University of Pennsylvania Press.

Cepeda Ulloa, F. (2012, October). Interview with author. Bogota.

Chandrasekaran, R. (2009a, May 6). Administration is keeping Ally at Arm's length. *The Washington Post.*
Chandrasekaran, R. (2009b, May 6). Obama, Karzai: Not so chummy. *Washington Post.*
Chandrasekaran, R. (2012). *The war within the war for Afghanistan.* New York: Alfred Knopf Publishing.
Chayes, S. (2007). *The punishment of virtue: Inside Afghanistan after the Taliban.* London: Penguin Books.
Chepusiuk, R. (2003). *The bullet or the Bribe: Taking down Colombia's Cali drug Cartel.* New York: Praeger.
Chernick, M. (2009). The FARC at the negotiating table. In V. M. Bouvier (Ed.), *Colombia: Building peace in a time of war.* Washington, DC: United States Institute of Peace.
Chowdhury, A., & Krebs, R. R. (2010). The Afghan challenge is far tougher. *Foreign Affairs, 89*(4), 169–171.
Christensen, T. J., & Snyder, J. (1990). Chain gangs and passed bucks: Predicting alliance patterns in multipolarity. *International Organization, 44*(2), 138–168.
CNN News. (2001, September 21). Transcript of President Bush's address – September 20, 2011. *CNN News.*
Cogan, C. G. (1993). Partners in time: The CIA and Afghanistan since 1979. *World Policy Journal, 10*(2), 73.
Cohen, J. (2016, March 15). Why – and how—Russia won in Syria. *Reuters.*
Collier, D., & Elman, C. (2008). Qualitative and multimethod research: Organizations, publication, and reflections on integration. In J. M. Box-Steffensmeier, H. E. Brady, & D. Collier (Eds.), *The Oxford handbook of political methodology.* Oxford, UK: Oxford University Press.
Colombia May Get U.S. Aid in Civil War. (1997, October 13). *Washington Times.*
Colombian Ministry of Defense. (2009, February). Logros de la Política de Consolidacíon de la Seguridad Democratica. Report.
Colombian Ministry of Defense. (Vice Minister of Strategy and Planning, Sectorial Studies). Public forces operational results – Violence and criminality – terrorism. www.mindefensa.gov.co
Cook, J. L. (2012). *Afghanistan: The perfect failure – a war doomed by the coalition's strategies, policies, and political correctness.* New York: Xlibris Publishing.
Correlates of War (COW) project. *Inter-State War Data Set (4.0) and Intra-State War Data Set (4.0)* http://www.correlatesofwar.org/COW2%20Data/WarData_NEW/WarList_NEW.html#Intra-State War Data
Craig, G. A. (1965). The World War I alliance of the Central Powers in retrospect: The military cohesion of the alliance. *The Journal of Modern History, 37,* 336–344.
Crandall, R. (2002). *Driven by drugs: U.S. policy toward Colombia.* Boulder: Lynne Rienner.

Dagher, S., & Grove, T. (2015, July 27). Russia seen reassessing support for Assad. *The Wall Street Journal*.
Danspeckgruber, W., & Finn, R. (2007). The Afghan economy. In W. Danspeckgruber & R. Finn (Eds.), *Building state and security in Afghanistan*. Princeton: Liechtenstein Institute on Self-Determination at Princeton University.
David, S. R. (1979). Realignment in the horn: The soviet advantage. *International Security, 4*, 69–90.
David, S. R. (1980, November). Wielding alignments: Adjusting to the reality of the Third World. *American Spectator*, pp. 18–22.
David, S. R. (1982a). Coup and anti-coup. *The Washington Quarterly, 5*, 189–201.
David, S. R. (1982b). The superpower competition for influence in the Third World. In S. P. Huntington (Ed.), *The strategic imperative* (pp. 229–252). Cambridge, MA: Ballinger.
David, S. R. (1984, May–June). "Third world interventions," problems of communism (review essay), pp. 65–71.
David, S. R. (1985). *Defending Third World regimes from coups d'Etat I*. Cambridge: Center for International Affairs, Harvard University/University Press of America.
David, S. R. (1986). Soviet involvement in Third World coups. *International Security, 11*, 3–36, updated version selected for publication in Alberto, C. (Ed.) (1990). *Secret warfare and international order*. Washington, D.C: The United States Institute of Peace.
David, S. R. (1987). *Third World coups d'Etat and international security*. Baltimore: The Johns Hopkins University Press.
David, S. R. (1991a). *Choosing sides: Alignment and realignment in the Third World*. Baltimore: Johns Hopkins University Press.
David, S. R. (1991b). Explaining alignment in the Third World. *World Politics, 43*, 233–256.
David, S. R. (1992). Why the Third World still matters. *International Security, 17*(3), 127–159.
David, S. R. (1995). The necessity for American military intervention in the post-cold war world. In *The United States and the use of force in the post-cold war era* (pp. 29–70). Queenstown: The Aspen Institute.
David, S. R. (1997a). Internal war: Causes and cures. *World Politics, 49*, 552–576. (review essay).
David, S. R. (1997b). The primacy of internal war. In S. Neuman (Ed.), *International relations theory and the Third World*. New York: St. Martin's Press.
David, S. R. (2007, March/April). On Civil War. *The American Interest*.
David, S. R. (2008). *Catastrophic consequences: Civil wars and American interests*. Baltimore: Johns Hopkins University Press.

De Young, K. (2011, July 24). US trucking funds reach Taliban, military-led investigation concludes. *Washington Post*.

De Young, K., & Duque, C. J. (2011, August 20). U.S. aid implicated in abuses of power in Colombia. *Washington Post*.

Delman, E. (2015, October 2). The links between Putin's military campaigns in Syria and Ukraine. *The Atlantic*.

Department of State. (2012, March 9). Background notes series: Syria.

Deudney, D. (2007). *Bounding power: Republican security theory from the Polis to the global village*. Princeton: Princeton University Press.

Diamond, J. (1999, September 23). Capitol Hill divided over Colombian aid appeal. *Chicago Tribune*.

Dietl, G. (2004). War, peace and the warlords: The case of Ismail Khan of Herat in Afghanistan. *Alternatives – Turkish Journal of International Relations*, 3(283), 41–65.

Dinerstein, H. S. (1965). The transformation of alliance systems. *American Political Science Review*, LIX, 599.

Discursos sobre la paz. (1998, August 11). De la retórica de la paz a los hechos de paz.

Dix, R. H. (1986). *The politics of Colombia*. New York: Praeger Publishers.

Downes, R. (1999). *Conference report – landpower and ambiguous warfare: The challenge of Colombia in the 21st century*. Washington, DC: Strategic Studies Institute.

Duchacek, I. D. (1966). *Nations and men: International politics today*. New York: Holt.

Dudley, S. (2004). *Walking ghosts: Murder and Guerrilla politics in Colombia*. New York: Routledge.

Duffield, J. (2007). What are international institutions? *International Studies Review*, 9(1), 1–22.

Dugas, J. C. (2003). The emergence of neopopulism in Colombia? The case of Alvaro Uribe. *Third World Quarterly*, 24(6), 1117–1136.

Eaton, K. (2006). The downside of decentralization: Armed clientelism in Colombia. *Security Studies*, 15(4), 533–562.

Eckstein, H. (1975). Case study and theory in political science. In F. Greenstein & N. Polsby (Eds.), *Handbook of political science*. New York: Addison Weslet Publishing.

Edmond, R. (2012, December 14). Former Colombia police general sentenced to 13 years in U.S. prison. *Colombia Reports*.

Eide, K. (2012). *Power struggle in Afghanistan – An inside look at what went wrong – and what we can do to repair the damage*. New York: Skyhorse Publishing.

Eisenstadt, M. & White, J. (2006, May/June). Assessing Iraq's Sunni-Arab insurgency. *Military Review*.

"El Embrujo Autoritario: Primer Ano de Gobierno de Alvaro Uribe Velez," *Plataforma Colombiana de Derechos Humanos, Democracia y Desarollo.* Bogota, Colombia: 2003.

El Espectador. (2009, October 21). Recursos para seguridad y defensa superarán por primera vez los de educación," *El Espectador* (Colombia).

El Gammal, M. M. (2011). Fighting corruption, lessons learned from international experiences: Colombia. *World Academy of Science, Engineering and Technology, 56*, 330–334.

El Norte. (1996, April 23). ¿Narcopolítoicos?: Colombia del circo a la política. *El Norte.*

El Tiempo. (2003, March 21). Para Pedir Solidaridad Debemos Ser Solidarios. *El Tiempo.*

Emadi, H. (2011). Requiem for the Baath Party: Struggle for change and freedom. *Mediterranean Quarterly, 22,* 62–79.

Eronen, O. (2008). PRT models in Afghanistan: Approaches to civil-military integration. *CMC Finland Civilian Crisis Management Studies, 1*(5), 7.

Farah, D. (1998a, April 10). Colombian rebels seen winning War; U.S. study finds army inept, Ill-Equipped. *Washington Post.*

Farah, D. (1998b. December 27). US aid to Colombian military: Drug-dealing rebels take toll on army. *Washington Post.*

Farah, D. (1999a, February 18). Colombian army fighting legacy of abuses. *The Washington Post.*

Farah, D. (1999b, October 9). Pact near on aid to Colombia. *Washington Post.*

Fedder, E. H. (1968). The concept of alliance. *International Studies Quarterly, 12,* 65–86.

Filkins, D. (2009, October 24). The great American arm-twist in Afghanistan. *The New York Times.*

Filkins, D. (2010, June 6). Convoy guards in Afghanistan face an inquiry. *New York Times.*

Finn, R. (2012, September 20). U.S. Ambassador to Afghanistan, Interview with author.

Fishtein, P., & Wilder, A. (2012). *Winning hearts and minds? Examining the relationships between aid and security in Afghanistan.* Boston: Feinstein International Center, Tufts University.

Flyvbjerg, B. (2006). Five misunderstandings about case study research. *Qualitative Inquiry, 12*(2), 219–245.

Forero, J. (2008, October 30). Colombia fires 27 from army over killings. *Washington Post.*

Fox News. (2008, November 4). Report says Afghan police chief, Governor aided insurgents attack. *FoxNews.*

Franco, G. H. (2000). Their darkest hour: Colombia's government and the narco-insurgency. *Parameters, 30,* 83–94.

Frechette, M. Former U.S. Ambassador to Colombia, Interview with author. Washington, DC.

Freedberg Jr., S. (2015, September 28). Russians in Syria building A2/AD 'Bubble' over region: Breedlove. *Breaking Defense*.

Friedman, J. R. (1970). Introduction: Alliance in international relations. In *Alliance in international relations*. Boston: Allyn and Bacon Publishers.

Fundación Pais Libre (FPL). *Estadisticas Secuestro*, 1996–2006.

Gall, C. (2004a, September 12). Afghan government removes a powerful regional leader. *The New York Times*.

Gall, C. (2004b, June 8). Karzai shows he'll cast lot with a corps of warlords. *The New York Times*.

Gamarra Vergara, J. R. (2006, November). *Agenda Anticorrupcion en Colombia: Reformas, Logros y Recommendaciones*. Cartegena: Banco de la Republica/Centro de Estudios Economicos Regionales (CEER).

Gamini, G. (1996, September 3). Colombia fights back as Guerrilla launch fiercest raids in decades. *Time*.

Gannon, K. (2004, May/June). Afghanistan unbound. *Foreign Affairs*.

Garamone, J. (2002, January 16). U.S. forces to help Philippines fight terrorists. *American Forces Press Service*.

Garcia, M. (2003, January 21). In a torn Afghanistan, leader's hold still shaky – Turmoil festers in Afghanistan. *Philadelphia Inquirer*.

Gardner, F. (2012, June 27). How vital is Syria's Tartus port to Russia? *BBC*.

Geddes, B. (1994). *Politician's dilemma: Building state capacity in Latin America*. Berkeley: University of California Press.

Gelbard, R. (1996, March 7). Testimony before the U.S. house of representatives, international relations committee, subcommittee on the Western Hemisphere. Certification for Drug Producing Countries in Latin America. http://www.justice.gov/dea/pubs/cngrtest/ct960307.htm

George, A. L. (1979). Case studies and theory development: The method of structured, focused comparison. In P. G. Lauren (Ed.), *Diplomacy: New approaches in history, theory and policy* (trans. Lauren, P. G.). New York: Free Press.

George, A. (2003). *Syria: Neither bread nor freedom*. New York: St. Martin's Press.

George, A. (2015). Patronage and clientelism in Bashar's social market economy. In M. Kerr & C. Larkin (Eds.), *The Alawi's of Syria: War, faith and politics in the Levant*. London: C. Hurst & Co..

George, A. L., & Bennett, A. (2005). *Case studies and theory development in the social sciences*. Cambridge, MA: MIT Press.

George, A. L., & McKeown, T. J. (1985). Case studies and theories of organizational decision-making. In R. F. Coulam & R. A. Smith (Eds.), *Advances in information processing in organizations* (Vol. 2). Greenwich: JAI Press.

Gerring, J. (2004). What is a case study and what is it good for. *American Political Science Review, 98*(2), 341–354.

Gerring, J. (2007a). *Case study research: Principles and practices*. Cambridge: Cambridge University Press.
Gerring, J. (2007b). Review article: The mechanismic worldview – Thinking inside the box. *British Journal of Political Science, 38*(1), 161–179.
Ghafour, H. (2004, January 5). Afghans agree to new charter. *Los Angeles Times*.
Ghani, A. (2010, Jan/Feb). Karzai and 22,000 villages. *The National Interest*.
Gilbert, M. (2004). *The Second World War: A complete history*. New York: Holt.
Gilsinan, K. (2016, February 11). What happens if Aleppo falls? *The Atlantic*.
Ginsberg, T. (2002, December 1). Latin battleground – The U.S. is joining its anti-terror fight with the war on drugs in Colombia. It could be a success, or a mess. *Philadelphia Inquirer*, Sunday.
Ginty, R. M. (2010). Warlords and the liberal peace: Statebuilding in Afghanistan. *Conflict, Security & Development, 10*(4), 573–595.
Giustozzi, A. (2000). *War, politics and society in Afghanistan, 1978–1992*. Washington, DC: Georgetown University Press.
Giustozzi, A. (2012). *Empires of mud: Wars and warlords in Afghanistan*. New York: Columbia University Press.
Giustozzi, A., & Ullah, N. (2007). The inverted cycle: Kabul and the strongmen's competition for control over Kandahar, 2001–2006. *Central Asian Survey, 26*(2), 167–184.
Giustozzia, A., & Orsini, D. (2009). Centre–periphery relations in Afghanistan: Badakhshan between patrimonialism and institution-building. *Central Asian Survey, 28*(1), 1–16.
Glasser, S. B. (2002, August 4). Among threats to Karzai's control is country's own secret service. *The Washington Post*.
Gobierno de Colombia. (2010, February 26). Programa Presidencial de lucha contra la corrupcion.
Goldgeier, J. M., & McFaul, M. (1992). A tale of two worlds: Core and periphery in the post-Cold War era. *International Organization, 46*, 467–491.
Gopal, A. (2010). *The battle for Afghanistan*. Washington, DC: New America Foundation.
Gorenburg, D. (2012, June). Why Russia supports repressive regimes in Syria and the Middle East. *PONARS Eurasia Policy Memo*, no. 198.
Government of Colombia. (2011). Programa de Atencion Humanitaria al Desmovilisado. www.mindefensa.gov.com. Accessed 31 Oct 2011.
Grimmet, R. F. (2011, September 22). *Conventional arms transfers to developing nations*. Washington, DC: Congressional Research Service.
Gross, J. G. (1970). Some theoretic characteristics of economic and political coalitions. In *Alliance in international relations*. Boston: Allyn and Bacon Publishers.
Grove, T. (2012, August 3). Syria reaches oil deal with ally Russia. *Reuters*.

Guetzkow, H. (1957). Isolation and collaboration: A partial theory of international relations. *Journal of Conflict Resolution, 1*, 158.
Haas, E. B. (1969). *Tangle of hope –American commitments and world order.* Englewood Cliffs: Prentice Hall.
Haas, E. B., & Whiting, A. S. (1956). *Dynamics of international politics.* New York: McGraw-Hill.
Harknett, R. J., & VanDenBerg, J. A. (1997). Alignment theory and interrelated threats: Jordan and the Persian Gulf crisis. *Security Studies, 6*(3), 112–153.
Harnden, T. (2009, October 17). Joe Biden: The worrying rise of Barack Obama's Mr Wrong. *The Telegraph.*
Harress, C. (2015, October 1). What is the free Syrian army? *IBTimes.*
Herbert, M. (2014). Partisans, profiteers and criminals: Syria's illicit economy. *The Fletcher Forum of World Affairs, 38,* 69–86.
Herbst, J. (2000). *States and power in Africa.* Princeton: Princeton University Press.
Hess, S. (2010). Coming to terms with neopatrimonialism: Soviet and American nation-building projects in Afghanistan. *Central Asian Survey, 29*(2), 171–187.
Heydemann, S. (2013). Syria and the future of authoritarianism. *Journal of Democracy, 24,* 59–73.
Hironaka, A. (2005). *Never-ending wars: The international community, weak states, and the perpetuation of Civil War.* Cambridge, MA: Harvard University Press.
Hoggard, S. (2004). Preventing corruption in Colombia: The need for an enhanced state-level approach. *Arizona Journal of International & Comparative Law, 21*(2), 577–619.
Holliday, J. (2012, March). Syria's armed opposition. *Middle East Security Report 3.*
Holloway, J. (2012). *Superiority and subordination in US-Latin American relations: A discourse analysis of Plan Colombia.* Ph.D. dissertation, American University, School of International Service.
Holmes, J. S. (2005). Drugs, terrorism, and congressional politics: The Colombia challenge. In R. G. Carter (Ed.), *Contemporary cases in U.S. foreign policy.* Washington, DC: CQ Press.
Holsti, K. J. (1967). *International politics: A framework for analysis.* Englewood Cliffs: Prentice Hall Publishers.
Holsti, K. J. (1970). Diplomatic coalitions and military alliances. In J. R. Friedman, C. Bladen, & S. Rosen (Eds.), *Alliance in international politics.* Boston: Alyn and Bacon Inc.
Holsti, O. R., Hopmann, P. T., & Sullivan, J. D. (1973). *Unity and disintegration in international alliances: Comparative studies.* New York: Wiley.
Human Rights Watch. (2000, February). *The ties that bind: Colombia and military-paramilitary links.* Washington, DC: Human Rights Watch.

Human Rights Watch. (2011, June 1). *Syria: Crimes against humanity in Daraa.* Human Rights Watch.
Human Rights Watch. (2015, March 22). *'He didn't have to die' indiscriminate attacks by opposition groups in Syria.* New York: Human Rights Watch.
Human Security Report Project. (2011). *Human security report 2009/2010: The causes of peace and the shrinking costs of war.* New York: Oxford University Press.
Hynds, J. (2002, September 20). Colombia: President Alvaro Uribe implements new restrictions under state of unrest. *NotiSur.*
Ikenberry, G. J., & Walt, S. M. (2007). Offshore balancing or international institutions? The way forward to U.S. foreign policy. *Brown Journal of World Affairs, XIV*(1), 13–23.
International Crisis Group. (2006, November 2). *Countering Afghanistan's insurgency: No quick fixes.* Crisis Group Asia report no 123. Brussels/Kabul: International Crisis Group.
International Crisis Group. (2008, December 18). *Policing in Afghanistan: Still searching for a strategy.* Crisis Group Asia briefing no 85. Brussels/Kabul: International Crisis Group.
International Crisis Group. (2010a, November 28). *Afghanistan: Exit vs. engagement.* Crisis Group Asia briefing no 115. Brussels/Kabul: International Crisis Group.
International Crisis Group. (2010b, May 12). *A force in fragments: Reconstituting the Afghan National Army.* Crisis Group Asia report no 190. Brussels/Kabul: International Crisis Group.
International Crisis Group. (2011, June). The insurgency in Afghanistan's heartland. *International Crisis Group.* Brussels, Belgium.
International Crisis Group. (2012, October 8). *Afghanistan: The long, hard road to the 2014 transition.* Crisis Group Asia report no 236. Brussels/Kabul: International Crisis Group.
Isacson, A. & Poe, A. (2009, December). After plan Colombia: Evaluating integrated action – The next phase of U.S. assistance. *Center for International Policy.*
ISAF Briefing. (2009, December 22). State of the insurgency: Trends, intentions and objectives. Unclassified version.
Isby, D. (2010). *Afghanistan – Graveyard of empires: A new history of the Boderlands.* New York: Pegasus Books.
Isikoff, M. (2001, December 16). Bush decides military can take law agency role. *Austin American-Statesman.*
Jervis, R. (1976). *Perception and misperception in international politics.* Princeton: Princeton University Press.

Jervis, R., & Snyder, J. (Eds.). (1991). *Dominoes and bandwagons: Strategic beliefs and great power competition in the Eurasian rimland.* New York: Oxford University Press.

Jones, S. G. (2008). The rise of Afghanistan's insurgency state failure and Jihad. *International Security, 32*(4), 7–40.

Jones, S. G. (2009, April 2). *U.S. strategy in Afghanistan.* Testimony before the committee on foreign affairs subcommittee on Middle East and South Asia. United States House of Representatives.

Jones, S. G. (2010). *In the graveyard of empires: America's war in Afghanistan.* New York: W Norton.

Kaplan, E. (2009, December 17). Congress launches investigation into Taliban Payola. *The Nation.*

Kapstein, E. & Mayoral, A. (2013, December 6). *Peace economics: Why Syria must reign in unemployment, food prices, and corruption to ensure a stable future.* United States Institute of Peace.

Karzai, H. (2005, May 15). Interview: Voice of America. Voice of America. http://www.globalsecurity.org/military/library/news/2005/05/mil-050515-2c7d9c7d.htm

Katz, M. N. (2015, September 30). The threat of islamist extremism in Russia: Who is Putin really protecting Assad from? Presented to *The House Committee on Foreign Affairs, Subcommittee on Europe, Eurasia, and Emerging Threats.*

Katzman, K. (2011). *Afghanistan: Post-Taliban governance, security, and U.S. policy.* Washington, DC: Congressional Research Services.

Kaufman, R. R. (1974). The patron-client concept and macro-politics: Prospects and problems. *Comparative Studies in Society and History, 16*(3), 284–308.

Kaufman, R. G. (1992). To balance or to bandwagon? Alignment decisions in 1930s Europe. *Security Studies, 1*(3), 417–447.

Kennedy, P. M. (1987). *The rise and fall of the great powers: Economic change and military conflict from 1500 to 2000* (1st ed.). New York: Random House.

Khaddour, K. (2015, November 4). Assad's officer ghetto: Why the Syrian Army Remains Loyal. *Carnegie Endowment for International Peace Middle East Center.*

Khaddour, K. (2016, March 16). Strength in weakness: The Syrian Army's accidental resilience. *Carnegie Endowment for International Peace.*

Khalizad, Z. (2003, October 23). Testimony before U.S. Senate Committee on Foreign Relations on U.S. Senate Committee on Foreign Relations.

Khan, R. A. (1993). Pakistan in 1992: Waiting for change. *Asian Survey, 33*(2), 129–140.

Kilcullen, D. (2004). Counter-insurgency Redux. *Survival, 48*(4), 111–130.

King, G., Keohane, R., & Verba, S. (1994). *Designing social inquiry.* Princeton: Princeton University Press.

Kissinger, H. (1965). *The troubled partnership*. New York: McGraw Hill.
Klare, M. (2000). Detras del petroleo colombiano: intenciones ocultas. *Agencia Latinoamericana de Informacion*.
Kline, H. F. (1995). *Colombia: Democracy under assault*. New York: Westview Press.
Kline, H. F. (1999). *Statebuilding and conflict resolution in Colombia, 1986–1994*. Tuscaloosa: University of Alabama Press.
Kline, H. F. (2007). *Chronicle of a failure foretold: The peace process of Colombian President Andrés Pastrana*. Tuscaloosa: University of Alabama Press.
Lacey, M. (2008, November 1). In Mexico drug war, sorting good guys from bad. *The New York Times*.
Ladron de Guevara, F. D., & Buitrago, A. L. (2010). *Clientelismo: el sistema político y su expresión regional*. Bogota: Universidad de Los Andes Press.
Landay, J. S., & Bernton, H. (2009, October 16). While U.S. debates Afghanistan policy, Taliban beefs up. *McClatchy Newspapers Report*.
Langer, W. L. (1967). *The Franco-Russian alliance, 1890–1894*. New York: Octagon Books.
Lebow, G. N. (2000). What's so different about a counterfactual? *World Politics*, 52(4), 550–585.
Leverett, F. (2005). *Inheriting Syria: Bashar's trial by fire*. Washington, DC: The Brookings Institute.
Levy, J. S., & Barnett, M. N. (1992). Alliance formation, domestic political economy, and third world security. *Jerusalem Journal of International Relations*, 14(4), 19–40.
Lieven, A. (2009). The war in Afghanistan: Its background and future prospects. *Conflict, Security and Development*, 9(3), 333–359.
Lijphart, A. (1971). Comparative politics and the comparative method. *The American Political Science Review*, 65(3), 682–693.
Liska, G. (1968a). *Alliances and the third world* (p. 40). Baltimore: Johns Hopkins University Press.
Liska, G. (1968b). *Nations in alliance – The limits of interdependence*. Baltimore: Johns Hopkins University Press.
Lister, T. (2013, December 12). Islamic front in Syria deals another blue to rebel alliance. *CNN*.
Lister, C. (2014, May). Dynamic stalemate: Surveying Syria's military landscape. *Brookings Institution Doha Center*, p. 2.
Lister, C. & McCants, W. (2016, February 18). The Syrian civil war: Political and military state of play. *The Brookings Institution*.
Livingston, I. S., & O'Hanlon, M. (2009, January 21). *Afghan index – March 2012*. Washington, DC: Brookings Institution.

Livingstone, G. (2004). *Inside Colombia: Drugs, democracy and war.* New Brunswick: Rutgers University Press.

Lobell, S. E. (2006). The international realm, framing effects, and security strategies: Britain in peace and war. *International Interactions, 32*(1), 27–48.

Lobell, S. E. (2009). Threat assessment, the state, and foreign policy: A neoclassical realist model. In N. M. Ripsman & J. W. Taliaferro (Eds.), *Neoclassical realism, the state, and foreign policy.* Cambridge, UK: Cambridge University Press.

Lobell, S. E. (2012). Power disparities and strategic trade: Domestic consequences of U.S.-Jordan trade concessions. In K. P. Williams, S. E. Lobell, & N. G. Jesse (Eds.), *Beyond great powers: Why secondary states support, follow, or challenge.* Stanford: Stanford University Press.

Lobell, S. E., Ripsman, N. M., & Taliaferro, J. W. (2009). *Neoclassical realism, the state, and foreign policy.* Cambridge, UK: Cambridge University Press.

Long, W. R. (1990, August 8). Colombia's new leader says he'll pacify nation: Gaviria takes office with a tough position against the Medellin drug cartel. *Los Angeles Times.*

Long, T. (2013). *Convincing the Colossus: Latin American leaders face the United States.* Ph.D. dissertation, American University School of International Service, Washington, DC.

Los Angeles Times. (2008, December 23). Karzai faults coalition, says it is using 'thugs' – "Interview with Hamid Karzai". *Los Angeles Times.*

Lowry, R. (2008). *The gulf war chronicles: A military history of the first war with Iraq.* New York: iUniverse.

Loyd, A. (2007, November 24). Corruption, bribes, and trafficking: A cancer that is engulfing Afghanistan. *Times.*

Lucas, S. (2016, March 23). Syria feature: How the rebels of Jaish al-Islam survive. *EA Worldview.*

Lund, A. (2014, January 14). The politics of the Islamic front part 1: Structure and support. *Carnegie Endowment for International Peace.*

Lynch, M. (2014). *The Arab uprisings explained.* Columbia: Columbia University Press.

Lynch, C. (2015, October 7). Why Putin is so committed to keeping Assad in power. *Foreign Policy.*

MacAskill, E. (2009, May 11). Obama replaces top general in Afghanistan. *The Guardian.*

Malik, H. (2008). *U.S. relations with Afghanistan and Pakistan.* Oxford, UK: Oxford University Press.

Manwaring, M. G. (2002). Non-state actors in Colombia: Threats to the state and to the Hemisphere. *Small Wars & Insurgencies, 13*(2), 68–80.

Marcella, G., & Schulz, D. (1999). *Colombia's three wars: US strategy at the crossroads.* Washington, DC: Strategic Studies Institute.

Marcy, W. L. (2010). *The politics of cocaine: How US foreign policy has created a thriving drug industry in Central and South America*. Chicago: Lawrence Hill Books.
Martz, J. D. (1997). *The politics of clientelism – Democracy and the state in Colombia*. London: Transaction Publishers.
Mashi, M. (2012, September 28). Kidnapping in Syria: An economy of war. *alakhbar English*.
Masters, R. D. (1961). A multi-bloc model of the international system. *American Political Science Review*, 55, 780–798.
Matinuddin, K. (1999). *The Taliban phenomenon, Afghanistan 1994–1997*. Oxford: Oxford University Press.
Mauceri, P. (2004). State, elites, and the response to insurgency. In J.-M. Burt & P. Mauceri (Eds.), *Politics in the Andes – identity, conflict, reform*. Pittsburgh: University of Pittsburgh Press.
McChrystal, S. (2009, August 30). *Commander's initial assessment*. Kabul: United States Army.
McGirk, T. (2002, March 4). Lonely at the top: An interview with Hamid Karzai. *Time*.
McGreal, C. (2012, June 13). US says Russian-made weapons are killing Syrians on 'an hourly basis'. *The Guardian*.
Menzel, S. H. (1997). *Cocaine quagmire: Implementing the US anti-drug policy in the North Andes*. Boston: University Press of America.
Micolta, P. (2004, April 15). Illicit interest groups and their influence in U.S. – Colombian relations: A two level game analysis of the issue of extradition. *Paper presented at the annual meeting of the The Midwest Political Science Association*, Palmer House Hilton, Chicago, Illinois. http://www.allacademic.com/meta/p84490_index.html
Miller, W. L. (1959). The American ethos and the alliance system. In A. Wolfers (Ed.), *Alliance policy in the cold war*. Baltimore: Johns Hopkins University Press.
Miller, T. (2004, December 30). Christian. "US troops answered oil firm pleas. *Los Angeles Times*.
Mills, N. B. (2007). *Karzai – The failing American intervention and the struggle for Afghanistan*. Hoboken: Wiley.
Moreno, L. A. (2002, May 3). Op-Ed: Aiding Colombia's war on terrorism. *New York Times*.
Morgenthau, H. J. (1959). Alliances in theory and practice. In A. Wolfers (Ed.), *Alliance policy in the cold war*. Baltimore: Johns Hopkins University Press.
Morgenthau, H., & Thompson, K. (1985). *Politics among nations* (6th ed.). New York: Knopf.
Munck, G. L. (2005). "Symposium I: The quantitative/qualitative distinction," *Newsletter of the American Political Science Association – Organized Section on Qualitative Methods*.

Murillo, M. A. (2004). *Colombia and the United States – War, unrest and destabilization*. New York: Seven Stories Press.

Myrhe, D. (2003). *Colombia: Civil conflict, state weakness, and (In)security*. Princeton: Princeton University Press.

National Security Decision Directive 221. Narcotics and national security. Issued 1982. Federation of American Scientists, Intelligence Resource Program. https://www.fas.org/irp/offdocs/nsdd/nsdd-221.pdf. Accessed Mar 2013.

National Security Decision Directive 71. U.S. Policy Toward Latin America In the Wake of the Falklands Crisis. Issued November 30, 1982. Published on the Federation of American Scientists, Intelligence Resource Program Website. https://www.fas.org/irp/offdocs/nsdd/nsdd-71.pdf

National Security Directive 23. US relations with the Soviet Union. Issued September 22, 1989. Federation of American Scientists, Intelligence Resource Program. http://www.fas.org/irp/offdocs/nsd/nsd23.pdf

National Security Directive 18. Washington, D.C. George W. Bush Presidential Library. http://bushlibrary.tamu.edu/research/pdfs/nsd/nsd18.pdf. Accessed 18 Mar 2013.

NATO. (2006). *The Afghanistan compact*. London: NATO. http://www.nato.int/isaf/docu/epub/pdf/afghanistan_compact.pdf

Nepstad, S. E. (2013). Mutiny and nonviolence in the Arab Spring: Exploring military defections and loyalty in Egypt, Bahrain and Syria. *Journal of Peace and Research, 50*, 344.

Nesmeth, S. A. (2002, August 15). U.S. declares support for Colombia. *Associated Press*.

New Escalation in Repression. (2002, October/December). Colombia solidarity network.

New York Magazine. (2012, September). 9/11 by the numbers. *New York Magazine*.

Nitze, P. H. (1959). Coalition policy and the concept of world order. In A. Wolfers (Ed.), *Alliance policy in the cold war*. Baltimore: Johns Hopkins University Press.

North, R. C., Koch Jr., H. E., & Zinnes, D. A. (1970). The integrative functions of conflict. In *Alliance in international relations*. Boston: Allyn and Bacon Publishers.

Nuemann, R. (2012, July 2). U.S. Ambassador to Afghanistan, Interview with author.

O'Bagy, E. (2013, March). The free Syrian army. *Middle East Security Report 9*.

O'Donnell, L. (2010, January 18). Kabul on high alert after brazen Taliban strikes. *AFP*.

O'Hanlon, E. (2009, August 9). Karzai in his Labyrinth. *New York Times Magazine*.

O'Hanlon, M. E., & Sherjan, H. (2010). *Toughing it out in Afghanistan*. Washington, DC: Brookings Institution Press.
Obituary: The corrupt nepotist who ruled Gabon for 40 years. *The Independent (UK)*. June 9, 2009.
Ohl, D., Albrecht, H., & Koehler, K. (2015, November 24). For money or liberty? The political economy of military desertion and rebel recruitment in the Syrian civil war. *Carnegie Endowment for International Peace*.
Olson Jr., M., & Zeckhauser, R. (1970). An economic theory of alliances. In *Alliance in international relations*. Boston: Allyn and Bacon Publishers.
Oppel, Jr. R. (2009, August 8). Afghan leader courts the warlord vote, but others fear the cost. *New York Times*.
Oppel, R. A., & Bumler, E. (2009, December 8). Karzai says Afghan army will need U.S. until 2024. *The New York Times*.
Organski, A. F. K. (1968). *World politics*. New York: Alfred A. Knopf.
Osgood, R. E. (1968). *Alliances and American foreign policy*. Baltimore: Johns Hopkins University Press.
Ostrow, R. J. (1989, December 18). Ruling allows wider action By U.S. military. *Los Angeles Times*.
Otis, J. (1998, March 8). Colombian army suffers one of its worst defeats in fight with rebels. *Houston Chronicle*.
Otis, J. (2008, June 15). After dominating southern Colombia for years, numerous setbacks deal serious blows to FARC; Putting rebels on the run. *Houston Chronicle*, South America Bureau.
Otis, J. (2010, September 22). Colombia: The dark side of Alvaro Uribe. *The Global Post*.
Owen, J. M. (1997). *Liberal peace, liberal war: American politics and international security* (Vol. 37). Ithaca: Cornell University Press.
Oxford Analytica Daily Brief. (2012, January 26). Why Russia protects Assad. *CNN*. http://globalpublicsquare.blogs.cnn.com/2012/01/26/why-russia-protects-assad/
Pace, P. (2000). Advance questions for Lieutenant General Peter Pace. Defense reforms. United States Senate Committee on Armed Services. www.senate.gov
Pardo, R. (1987). La Politica Exterior de la Administracion Barco. *Análisis Político* N° 2 Agosto-Diciembre.
Passage, D. (2000). *The United States and Colombia: Untying the Gordian knot*. Washington, DC: Strategic Studies Institute.
Pastrana, A. (2006). *La Palabra Bajo Fuego*. Bogota: Planeta.
Patrick, S. (2006). Weakstates and global threats: Fact or fiction? *The Washington Quarterly*.
Patrick, S. (2011). *Weak links – Fragile states, global threats, and international security*. Oxford: Oxford University Press.
PBS. (1996, August). Bin Laden's fatwa. *PBS Newshour*.

Peters, G. (2010). *Seeds of terror: How drugs, thugs and crime are reshaping the Afghan war*. New York: Picador.

Pincus, W. (2006, March 1). Growing threat seen in Afghan insurgency: Defense intelligence agency chief cites surging violence in Homeland. *The Washington Post*.

Presidency of the Republic-Ministry of Defense. The effectiveness of the Colombian democratic security and defense policy. Republic of Colombia. www.mindefensa.gov

Presidential Decision Directive 14. Federation of American scientists, intelligence resource program. http://www.fas.org/irp/offdocs/pdd/pdd-14.pdf. Accessed Mar 2013.

PRI. (2010, January 18). Multiple Taliban attacks in Afghanistan. *PRI – The World*.

Provence, M. (2012). Unraveling the Syrian revolution. *Regions & Cohesion 2*.

Quinn, B. (2016, March 14). Russia's military action in Syria—timeline. *The Guardian*.

Rabasa, A., & Chalk, P. (2001). Colombian Labyrinth, the synergy of drugs and insurgency and its implications for regional stability. RAND Corporation Report.

Rafael Pardo. (former Minister of Defense of Colombia). (2012, October). Interview with author. Bogota, Colombia.

Ragin, C. (2000). Turning the tables: How case-oriented research challenges variable-oriented research. In H. Brady & C. David (Eds.), *Rethinking social inquiry: Diverse tools, shared standards*. Lanham: Rowman Littlefield.

Ramsey, R. D. (2009). *From El Billar to operations Fenix and Jaque: The Colombian security force experience, 1998–2008*. Fort Leavenworth, Kansas.

Randall, S. J. (1992). *Colombia and the United States – Hegemony and interdependence*. Athens: University of Georgia Press.

Rangel, C. (1989, August 24). Yes we can do something for Colombia. *The Washington Post*.

Rashid, A. (2001). *Taliban: Militant Islam, oil and fundamentalism in Central Asia*. New Haven: Yale University Press.

Rashid, A. (2009). *Descent into chaos – The U.S. and the disaster in Pakistan, Afghanistan, and Central Asia*. New York: Penguin Books.

Rashid, A. (2011, March/April). How Obama lost Karzai. *Foreign Policy*.

Regan, P. M. (2000). *Civil wars and foreign powers*. Ann Arbor: University of Michigan Press.

Reid, B. (2006). Bush and the Philippines after September: Hegemony, mutual opportunism, and democratic retreat. In M. Beeson (Ed.), *Bush and Asia*. New York: Routledge.

Reina, M. (1990). *Las Relaciones entre Colombia y Estados Unidos*. Bogotá: CEI.

Restrepo, J., & Vargas, J. F. (2004, July). The severity of the Colombian conflict: Cross-country datasets versus new micro data. *Seminar paper presented at the 8th ECAAR conference on economics and security*. Bristol, UK.

Reuters. (1999a, May 19). Rebels accuse Colombian army of highway robbery. *Reuters*.

Reuters. (1999b, May 21). US throws weight behind peace bid. *Reuters*.

Reuters. (2003, February 8). Colombia blames rebels for Bogota Club bomb. *Reuters*.

Reuters. (2015, October 22). Syria air strikes push Putin's rating to new high—Russian state pollster. *Reuters*.

Reynolds, A. (2007). Constitutional engineering and democratic stability: The debate surrounding the crafting of political institutions in Afghanistan. In W. Danspeckgruber & R. Finn (Eds.), *Building state and security in Afghanistan*. Princeton: Liechtenstein Institute on Self-Determination at Princeton University.

RIA Novosti and Sputnik. (2016, March 30–31). Interview with Pressident Bashar al-Assad.

Rich, N. (1973). *Hitler's war aims: Ideology, the Nazi state, and the course of expansion*. New York: Norton.

Richani, N. (2002). *Systems of violence: The political economy of war and peace in Colombia*. Albany: State University of New York Press.

Riker, W. H. (1962). *The theory of political coalitions*. New Haven: Yale University Press.

Ripsman, N. M., & Taliaferro, J. W. (2009). *Neoclassical realism, the state, and foreign policy*. Cambridge, UK: Cambridge University Press.

Rochlin, J. F. (2007). *Social forces and the revolution in military affairs*. New York: Palgrave MacMillan.

Roggio, B., & Lundquist, L. (2012, August 12). Green-on-blue attacks in Afghanistan: The data. *Longwar Journal*.

Rohter, L. (1999, December 5). Armed forces in Colombia hoping to get fighting fit. *New York Times*.

Rose, G. (1998). Neoclassical realism and theories of foreign policy. *World Politics, 51*(1), 144–172.

Rosen, S. (1970). A model of war and alliance. In Friedman, Blasen, & Rosen (Eds.), *Alliance in international relations*. Boston: Allyn and Bacon Publishers.

Rosenau, J. N. (Ed.). (1964). *International aspects of civil strife*. Princeton: Princeton University Press.

Rosencrance, R. (1986). *The rise of the trading state: Commerce and conquest in the modern world*. New York: Basic Books.

Roston, A. (2010. June 21). Congresisonal investigation confirms: US military funds Afghan warlords. *Nation*.

Rothstein, R. (1966). Alignment, non-alignment, and small powers. *International Organization, 20*(3).
Rothstein, R. (1968). *Alliances and small powers.* New York: Columbia University Press.
Rubin, B. (1995). *The fragmentation of Afghanistan.* New Haven: Yale University Press.
Rubin, B. (2004). Crafting a constitution for Afghanistan. *Journal of Democracy, 13*(3), 5–19.
Rubin, B. R. (2007, January–February). Saving Afghanistan. *Foreign Affairs.*
Rubin, B. (2013). *Afghanistan from the cold war through the war on terror.* Oxford: Oxford University Press.
Ruiz, B. (2001). *The Colombian civil war.* London: McFarly and Company Publishers.
Russett, B. M. (1963). *Community and contention: Britain and America in the twentieth century.* Cambridge, MA: MIT Press.
Russett, B., & O'neal, J. (2001a). Both democracy and economic interdependence reduce conflict. In *Triangulating peace: Democracy, interdependence and international organizations.* New York: Norton.
Russett, B., & O'neal, J. (2001b). From democratic peace to Kantian peace. In *Triangulating peace: Democracy, interdependence and international organizations.* New York: Norton.
Saideman, S. M. (2001). *The ties that divide: Ethnic politics, foreign policy, and international conflict.* New York: Columbia University Press.
Sarkees, M. R. (2000). The correlates of war data on war: An update to 1997. *Conflict Management and Peace Science, 18*(1), 123–144.
Schatz, E. (2004). *Modern clan politics: The power of 'blood' in Kazakhstan and beyond.* Seattle: University of Washington Press.
Schiewek, E. (2007). Keeping the peace without peacekeepers. In W. Danspeckgruber & R. Finn (Eds.), *Building state and security in Afghanistan.* Princeton: Liechtenstein Institute on Self-Determination at Princeton University.
Schweller, R. L. (1994). Bandwagoning for profit: Bringing the revisionist state back. *International Security, 19*(1), 72–107.
Schweller, R. (1997). New realist research on alliances: Refining, not refuting, Waltz's balancing proposition. *American Political Science Review, 91*(4), 927–930.
Schweller, R. L. (1998). *Deadly imbalances: Tripolarity and Hitler's strategy of world conquest.* New York: Columbia University Press.
Schweller, R. (2001). The problem of international order revisited: A review essay. *International Security, 26*(1), 161–186.
Schweller, R. (2002). Institutionalized disagreement. *International Security, 27*(1), 174–185.

Schweller, R. L. (2004). Unanswered threats: A neoclassical realist theory of underbalancing. *International Security, 29*(2), 159–201.

Schweller, R. L. (2006). *Unanswered threats: Unanswered threats: Political constraints on the balance of power.* Princeton: Princeton University Press.

Schweller, R. (2010). The logic and illogic of contemporary realism. *International Theory, 2*(3).

Schweller, R., & Wohlforth, W. (2000). Power test: Updating realism in response to the end of the cold war. *Security Studies, 9*(3), 60–108.

Sengupta, K. (2003, December 4). Afghan Warlord agrees to hand over his weapons to British team. *The Independent.*

Shaheen, K. (2016, March 27). Assad hails Syrian regime's capture of Palmyra from ISIS. *The Guardian.*

Shaheen, K., Walker, S., & Black, I. (2015, October 21). Bashar al-Assad thanks Putin for Syria strikes as Russia announces US talks. *The Guardian.*

Sharan, T. (2011). The dynamics of elite networks and patron-client networks in Afghanistan. *Europe-Asia Studies, 63*(6), 1109–1127.

Shelton, T. (2012, June 7). Insdie Syria: Who arms the rebels? *GlobalPost.*

Sherif, M., & Sherif, C. (1953). *Groups in harmony and tension.* New York: Harper Press.

Shinwari, S. (2012, April 25). Afghan water & energy minister accused of corruption. *Rawa News.*

Shultz, G. (1984, October 19). *A forward look at foreign policy.* Washington, DC: U.S. Department of State.

Siddique, A. (2009, November 12). US special inspector: Afghan corruption a 'Mix' of external, internal factors. *Radio Free Europe/Radio Liberty News Report.*

Simons, G. (2004). *Colombia: A brutal history.* London: Saqi Publishers.

Small, M., & Singer, D. (1982). *Resort to arms: International and civil war, 1816–1980.* Beverly Hills: Sage.

Snyder, G. H. (1997). *Alliance politics.* Ithaca: Cornell University Press.

Sobek, D., & Payne, C. (2010). A tale of two types: Rebel goals and the onset of civil wars. *International Studies Quarterly, 54*(1), 213–240.

Spencer, D. E., et al. (2011). *Colombia's road to recovery: Security and governance 1982–2010.* Washington, DC: Center for Hemispheric Defense Studies, National Defense University.

Spyer, J. (2013). Fragmented Syria: The balance of forces as of late 2013. *Middle East Review of International Affairs, 17,* 9–18.

St. Petersburg Times. (1989, October 5). Colombia purges 2,075 police officers for bribery. *St. Petersburg Times.*

Stacher, J. (2011). Reinterpreting authoritarian power: Syria's hereditary succession. *Middle East Journal, 65*(2), 197–212.

Stapleton, B. J. (2007). The failure to bridge the security gap: The PRT plan, 2002–2004. In W. Danspeckgruber & R. Finn (Eds.), *Building state and security in Afghanistan*. Princeton: Liechtenstein Institute on Self-Determination at Princeton University.

Sterling, J. (2012, March 1). Daraa: The spark that lit the Syrian flame. *CNN*.

Stevens, F. B. (1961). Why alliances fall apart. *U.S. News and World Report*.

Stevens, W. O., & Westcott, A. (1942). *A history of sea power*. New York: Doubleday.

Stojanovic, D. (2002, July 23). Karzai replaces guards with American troops. *Associated* Press.

Stokes, D. (2002). Debating plan Colombia. *Survival, 44*(2), 183–188.

Stokes, D. (2009). *America's other war – Terrorizing Colombia*. London: Zed Books.

Stubbs, J. (2016, April 25). Syria, Russia sign deal worth 850 million euros to restore Syrian infrastructure: RIA. *Reuters*.

Suarez, A. R. (2000). Parasites and predators: Guerrillas and the insurgent economy of Colombia. *Journal of International Affairs, 53*(2), 577–601.

Suhkre, A. (2007). Reconstruction as modernization: The post-conflict project in Afghanistan. *Third World Quarterly, 28*(7), 1291–1308.

Suhrke, A. (2011). *When more is less: The international project in Afghanistan*. New York: Columbia University Press.

Sweig, J. (2002). What kind of war for Colombia? *Foreign Affairs, 81*(5), 122–141.

Synovitz, R. (2012, June 19). Why is tartus so important to Moscow? *Radio Free Europe*.

Tabler, A. J., White, J., & Zelin, A. Y. (2013, January 14). Fallout from the fall of Taftanaz. *The Washington Institute*.

Taliaferro, J. W. (2004). *Balancing risks: Great power intervention in the periphery*. Ithaca: Cornell University Press.

TASS. (2015, September 17). No reasons to evade cooperating with Syrian leadership—Russia FM. *TASS*.

Tenet, C. (2007). *At the center of the storm*. London: Harper Collins.

Teune, H., & Synnestvedt, S. (1970). Measuring international alignment. In Friedman & R. Blasen (Eds.), *Alliance in international relations*. Boston: Allyn and Bacon Publishers.

The Carter Center. (2013, November). Syria: Pro-Government paramilitary forces. *The Carter Center*, p. 4.

The Guardian. (2010, December 10). US embassy cables: Corrupt governor in eastern Afghanistan. *The Guardian*.

The White House. (1991, August). New National Security Policy of the United States. Washington, DC: United States Government Printing Office.

The White House. (1998, October 28). President Clinton and Colombian President Pastrana; Joint press conference. Office of the Press Secretary.

The White House. (2001, October 7). George W. Bush. Address to the Nation. The White House.
The White House. (2002a, January 28). Karzai, Hamid Afghan Interim Authority Chairman. President meets with Afghan Interim Authority Chairman. Press release. Office of the White House.
The White House. (2002b). The National Security Strategy of the United States of America.
The White House. (2002c, January 28). President George W. Bush, "President Meets with Afghan Interim Authority Chairman," Press Release. Office of the White House.
The White House. (2002d). President George W. Bush, "The National Security Strategy of the United States – 2002," Office of The White House. Washington, DC.
The White House. (2002e, March 13). Vice President Dick Cheney. "Remarks to Multinational Force of Observers: South Camp—Sharm el-Shekh, Egypt," Wednesday.
The White House. (2005, May 23). Joint declaration of the United States-Afghanistan strategic partnership. Office of Press Secretary. http://georgewbush-whitehouse.archives.gov/news/releases/2005/05/20050523-2.html
The White House. (2007, August 6). The President's news conference with President Hamid Karzai of Afghanistan at Camp David, Maryland; Office of the Press Secretary.
The White House. (2008, December 15). President Bush participates in press availability with Afghanistan President Karzai in Afghanistan. The Presidential Palace, Kabul, Afghanistan. http://merln.ndu.edu/archivepdf/afghanistan/WH/20081215.pdf
The White House. (2009a, December 1). Barack Obama, Presidential Address on Afghanistan, West Point, NY.
The White House. (2009b, March 27). Remarks by the President on a new strategy for Afghanistan and Pakistan. Office of the White House. http://www.whitehouse.gov/the_press_office/Remarks-by-the-President-on-a-New-Strategy-for-Afghanistan-and-Pakistan/
The White House. (2010, May 12). Joint statement from the President and President Karzai of Afghanistan. Office of the Press Secretary.
The White House. Remarks by Vice President Cheney and President Karzai of Afghanistan in press availability. Gul Khana Palace, Kabul, Afghanistan. http://merln.ndu.edu/archivepdf/afghanistan/WH/20080320.pdf
Their, A. J. (2006/7). The making of a constitution in Afghanistan. *New York Law School Law Review, 51*, 558–579.
Their, J. A. (2007). A third branch? (Re)establishing the judicial system in Afghanistan. In W. Danspeckgruber & R. Finn (Eds.), *Building state and secu-*

rity in *Afghanistan*. Princeton: Liechtenstein Institute on Self-Determination at Princeton University.

Their, A., & Chopra, J. (2002). The road ahead: Political and institutional reconstruction in Afghanistan. *Third World Quarterly, 23*(5), 893–907.

Thoumi, F. E. (2003). *Illegal drugs, economy, and society in the Andes*. Washington, DC: Woodrow Wilson Center Press.

Tickner, A. (2001). Colombia: An ambiguous foreign policy. *Presentation to annual conference of the Latin American Studies Association*, LASA, Washington, DC.

Tickner, A. B. (2003, February). Colombia and the United States: From counternarcotics to counterterrorism. *Current History, 102*, 77–85.

Tokatlian, J. G. (1988). National security and drugs: Their impact on Colombian-- U.S. relations. *Journal of Interamerican Studies and World Affairs, 30*(1), 143.

Tokatlian, J. G. (1994, August 15). *The drug problem in U.S.-Colombian relations*. Washington, DC: CSIS Americas Program Report.

Tokatlian, J. (2000). Colombia at war: The search for a peace diplomacy. *International Journal of Politics, Culture, and Society, 14*, 333–362.

Tomsen, P. (2011). *The wars of Afghanistan: Messianic terrorism, tribal conflicts, and the failures of great powers*. New York: Public Affairs Books.

Trenin, D. (2013, Februrary). The mythical alliance: Russia's Syria police. *The Carnegie Papers*.

U. S. Government Accountability Office. (2008). Report number 09–71 (Plan Colombia) to Committee on foreign relations, U.S. Senate.

U.S. Agency for International Development. (2008, March 27). USAID assistance to Afghanistan 2002–2008. *Press Release*.

U.S. Agency for International Development DST Team member. (2012, June). Interview with author, via Skype from Kandahar, Afghanistan.

U.S. Army captain who served in Afghanistan. (2012, September). Interview with author via Skype.

U.S. Department of Defense. (2012, April). Report on progress toward security and stability in Afghanistan: United States plan for sustaining the Afghanistan National Security Forces. U.S. Office of Government Printing.

U.S. Department of State. (2006, April). Office of the coordinator for counterterrorism. *Country Reports on Terrorism 2005*. U.S. Dept. of State.

U.S. Department of State. (2010). *Merida initiative*. http://www.state.gov/p/inl/rls/122397.htm

U.S. Envoy to Afghanistan James Dobbins. (2012, July 10). Interview with author. Washington, DC.

U.S. Government Accountability Office. (2008). Report number 09–71 (Plan Colombia) to committee on foreign relations, U.S. Senate. Washington, D.C: U.S. Office of Government Printing.

U.S. Government Accountability Office. (2009). Afghanistan security: US programs to further reform ministry of interior and national police challenged by lack of military personnel and Afghan cooperation. Washington, DC: GAO.

U.S. Government Accountability Office. (2010). *Latin America and the Caribbean: Illicit drug trafficking and U.S. counterdrug programs*. Washington, DC: United States Office of Government Printing.

U.S. House of Representatives: Committee on Government Reform and Oversight. (1997, July 9). Hearings on counternarcotics efforts in Colombia.

U.S. House of Representatives. House of Representatives Resolution 358 (H.R. 358). U.S. Office of Government Printing. http://www.gpo.gov/fdsys/pkg/BILLS-107hres358eh/pdf/BILLS-107hres358eh.pdf

U.S. House of Representatives. House Bill S.2749. To update the Silk Road Strategy Act of 1999. Washington, D.C. Office of Government Printing. http://www.gpo.gov/fdsys/pkg/BILLS-109s2749is/pdf/BILLS-109s2749is.pdf

U.S. Library of Congress. Congressional Research Service. *Mexico's drug Cartels* by Colleen W. Cook. Washington, DC Office of Congressional Information and Publishing. Retrieved 02 Nov 2008.

U.S. Library of Congress. (2011, January 7). Congressional Research Service. *Mexico's Drug Trafficking Organizations: Source and Scope of the Rising Violence*, by June S. Beittel. http://fpc.state.gov/documents/organization/155587.pdf

U.S. Senate. (2011a, June 8). Evaluating U.S. foreign assistance to Afghanistan. A majority staff report. Washington, DC: Committee on Foreign Relations, U.S. Senate.

U.S. Senate. (2011b, June 8). U.S. foreign assistance to Afghanistan. A majority staff report. Washington, DC: Committee on Foreign Relations, U.S. Senate.

U.S. Senate Committee on Foreign Relations. (1996). Corruption and drugs in Colombia: Democracy at risk. Washington, D.C: Senate Committee on Foreign Relations, 104th Cong., 2nd session.

U.S. Trade Representative. (2013). *U.S. census bureau – Foreign trade – Colombia*. http://www.census.gov/foreign-trade/balance/c3010.html

Ulloa, F. C. (1997). *La Corrupcion en Colombia*. Bogota: TM Editores.

United Nations Department of Public Information. (2011, October 4). Security council fails to adopt draft resolution condemning Syria's crackdown on anti-government protestors, Owing to Veto by Russian Federation, China. *United Nations Security Council*.

United States Embassy Cable. (2006, January). Syria's corrupt classes.

Uppsala Confict Data Program. UCDP data. Upsala University. www.ucdp.uu.se/database

Uribe, E. D. (1986). *El clientelismo en Colombia: Un estudio exploratorio*. Bogota: Ancora Editores.

Uribe, A. (2007, September 30). 'Hay que mostrarle los dientes a los violentos': Uribe. *Presidencie de la Republica*. www.presidencia.gov.com

US Department of State. (1960, February 23). Preliminary report, Colombia survey team, Colonel landsdale. U.S. Dept. of State. www.icdc.com

Van Evera, S. (1990). Primed for peace: Europe after the cold war. *International Security, 15*(3), 7–57.

Van Evera, S. (1999). *Causes of war: Power and the roots of conflict*. Ithaca: Cornell University Press.

Vargas, R. (1999, June 7). The Revolutionary Armed Forces of Colombia (FARC) and the illicit drug. *The Transnational Institute*.

Veillette, C. (2006, January 11). Plan Colombia: A progress report. Washington, DC: Congressional Research Service.

Walsh, N. P. (2016, February 5). You thought Syria couldn't get any worse. Think again. *CNN*.

Walt, S. (1987). *The origins of alliances*. Ithaca: Cornell University Press.

Walt, S. M. (1988). Testing theories of alliance formation: The case of Southeast Asia. *International Organization, 42*(2), 275–316.

Walt, S. (2001a). Alliances. In J. Krieger (Ed.), *Oxford companion to the politics of the world* (2nd ed.). Oxford: Oxford University Press.

Walt, S. (2001b). NATO's future (In theory). In M. Bawley & P. Martin (Eds.), *Allied force or forced allies? NATO after kosovo*. New York: St. Martin's.

Walt, S. (2002a). Keeping the world off-balance: Self-restraint and U.S. foreign policy. In G. J. Ikenberry (Ed.), *America unrivaled: The future of the balance of power*. Ithaca: Cornell University Press.

Walt, S. (2002b, October/November). A policy failure? *Boston Review*.

Walt, S. (2005). The relationship between theory and policy in international relations. *Annual Review of Political Science, 8*, 23–48.

Waltz, K. (1954). *Man the state and war*. New York: Columbia University Press.

Waltz, K. N. (1967). *Foreign policy and democratic politics: The American and British experience*. Boston: Little, Brown and Company.

Waltz, K. N. (1979). *Theory of international politics*. New York: McGraw-Hill.

Waltz, K. N. (1986a). Anarchic orders and balances of power. In R. O. Keohane (Ed.), *Neorealism and its critics*. New York: Columbia University Press.

Waltz, K. N. (1986b). Political structures. In R. O. Keohane (Ed.), *Neorealism and its critics*. New York: Columbia University Press.

Wasserbly, D. (2015, September 9). Russia begins airstrikes in Syria. *Janes Defense Weekly HIS*.

Weitsman, P. A. (1997a). *Enforcing cooperation: Risky states and intergovernmental management of conflict*. New York: St. Martin's Press.

Weitsman, P. A. (1997b). The intimate enemies: The politics of peacetime alliances. *Security Studies, 7*(1), 156–193.

Weitsman, P. A. (2003). Alliance cohesion and coalition warfare: The central powers and triple entente. *Security Studies, 12*(3), 79–113.
Weitsman, P. A. (2004). *Dangerous alliances – proponents of peace, weapons of war.* Stanford: Stanford University Press.
Weitsman, P. A., & Schneider, G. (1997). Eliciting collaboration from 'Risky' states: The limits of conventional multilateralism in security affairs. *Global Society, 11*(1), 93–110.
Weitsman, P. A., & Shambaugh, G. (2002). International systems, domestic structures, and risk. *Journal of Peace Research, 39*(3), 289–312.
Weitz, R. (2008, September 3). Syria's Assad Sees Georgia War as Opening Moscow Options. *World Politics Review.*
Wengraf, T. (2001). *Qualitative research interviewing: Semi-structured, biographical and narrative methods.* New York: Sage.
Whitlock, C. (2009, September 27). Diverse sources fund insurgency in Afghanistan. *Washington Post.*
Wilder, A., & Listed, S. (2007). State-building at the subnational level in Afghanistan: A missed opportunity. In W. Danspeckgruber & R. Finn (Eds.), *Building state and security in Afghanistan.* Princeton: Liechtenstein Institute on Self-Determination at Princeton University.
Williams, L. (2011, May 30). Syrian businessmen back opposition conference. *The Guardian.*
Williams, B. G. (2012). *Afghanistan declassified: A guide to America's long war.* Philadelphia: University of Pennsylvania Press.
Wilson, S. (2009, April 5). Which way in Afghanistan? Ask Colombia for directions. *Washington Post.*
Wissing, D. (2010, January 19). It's a perfect war. Everybody makes money. *GlobalPost.*
Wissing, D. (2012). *Funding the enemy: How US taxpayers bankroll the Taliban.* New York: Prometheus Books.
Wohlforth, W. C. (1993). *The elusive balance: Power and perceptions during the cold war.* Ithaca: Cornell University Press.
Wolfers, A. (1959). Stresses and strains in 'going it with others'. In A. Wolfers (Ed.), *Alliance policy in the cold war.* Baltimore: Johns Hopkins University Press.
Wolfers, A. (1962). *Discord and collaboration – Essays on international politics.* Baltimore: Johns Hopkins University Press.
Wolfers, A. (1968). Alliances. In D. L. Sills (Ed.), *International encyclopedia of the social sciences.* New York: MacMillan and the Free Press.
Wolfowitz, P., & O'Hanlon, M. (2011, October 28). Plan Afghanistan – Why the Colombia model – even if it means drug war and armed rebellion – is the best chance for U.S. success in Central Asia. *Foreign Policy.*
Wood, J. (2008, August 7). Funding the Taliban. *Global Post.*

Wood, D. (2009, December 1). Allegation: Some contractors in Afghanistan paying protection money to the Taliban. *Politics Daily*.

Woodward, B. (2010). *Obama's wars*. New York: Simon and Schuster.

Woodward, B., & Loeb, V. (2001, September 14). CIA's covert war with Bin Laden. *The Washington Post*.

World Bank. (2013). Doing business 2013 report: Comparing business regulations for domestic firms in 185 economies.

World Economic Forum. (2012). Global competitiveness index 2011–2012.

Xinhua News Agency. (2004, January 11). Colombia issues new Anti-Corruption Law. *Xinhua News Agency CEIS*.

Youngers, C. A. (2004). Collateral damage: U.S. drug control efforts in the Andes. Washington Office on Latin America.

Youngers, C., & Rosin, E. (2004). *Drugs and democracy in Latin America: The impact of U.S. policy*. Boulder: Lynn Reiner.

Zakaria, F. (1998). *From wealth to power: The unusual origins of America's world role*. Princeton: Princeton University Press.

Zakhilwal, O. (2002, June 16). Op-Ed: Stifled in the Loya Jirga. *The Washington Post*.

Index

A

Afghanistan, 1, 44, 101–77, 215, 233–9
Afghanistan National Army (ANA), 104, 107, 112, 152, 236
Afghanistan National Police (ANP), 104, 112, 152, 159n80
Afghan Militia Forces (AMF), 133, 134
Afghan National Auxiliary Police, 133
Afghan National Security Forces (ANSF), 103, 239
Akhundzada, 135, 149, 168n221
al-Assad, Bashar, 1, 2, 12, 17, 24, 179, 181, 182, 185, 188–91, 194, 199, 200, 204, 208n56, 208n59, 209n69, 211n112, 212n123, 212n130, 217
Al-Assad, Hafez, 181–3, 196
Aleppo, Syria, 197, 202–4, 212n126
alliance cohesion, 19, 44, 64, 68, 73, 136, 137, 140–2, 199
alliance effectiveness, 5, 7–8, 16–20, 23, 24, 35n51, 36n53, 37, 41, 45, 50, 64–79, 110, 115, 136–52, 184, 198–204, 218–20
alliance formation, 6–8, 11–14, 35n51, 50–8, 115–17, 181, 184–92, 202, 216–17, 219
alliance Theory, 3, 8, 17, 25n1, 27n3, 29n15
Al-Qaeda, 2, 103–5, 107, 117–19, 129, 132, 148, 154n8, 161n105, 162n113, 175n315, 186, 187, 216, 217
al-Raqqa, Syria, 187
Andean Initiative, 40
Arab Spring, 180, 181, 210n88–90

B

balancing, 4, 7, 14, 16, 21, 22, 30n23, 38, 41, 45, 48, 57, 58, 61–3, 73, 75, 77, 78, 104, 113, 115, 124, 130–2, 134, 135, 140, 141, 143, 145, 151, 152, 192, 217, 218, 220, 221

Note: Page number followed by "n" refers to endnotes.

bandwagoning (offensive, defensive), 4, 5, 7, 8, 11, 14–20, 22–4, 29n19, 36n53, 38, 41, 48, 50, 58–64, 68–70, 72–6, 78, 101, 104, 108, 110, 113, 115, 123–36, 141–3, 145–9, 151, 153, 155n22, 160n99, 167n208, 172n283, 179, 184, 192–202, 204, 217–20
Barco, Virgilio, 40, 56, 57, 61, 62, 64, 66–8, 89n130, 90n156, 91n159, 93n180, 93n181, 93n189, 93n190, 95n206
Betancur, Belisario, 54, 56, 64–6
bin Laden, Osama, 103, 129, 154n8, 162n113, 162n114, 162n119
Bogota, 34n46, 36n54, 36n55, 40, 41, 48, 55, 61, 64, 69, 71, 77, 80n15, 81n24, 85n78, 89n130, 91n156, 91n158, 93n188, 94n197, 94n200, 227, 230
Bongo, Omar, 13
Bonn Agreement, 103, 111, 114
Bush, George H.W., 39, 56, 62, 64, 93n189, 95n204
Bush, George W., 19, 43, 64, 83n48, 89n126, 103, 120, 162n117, 162n118

C
Cali cartel, 70
Caqueta, 71
Cauca, 59
Cheney, Dick, 105, 121, 155n25, 163n124
civil war, 1–3, 12, 27n4, 28n9, 31n28, 31n33, 32n34, 38, 42, 51, 79n2, 82n38, 86n91, 92n176, 93n189, 95n201, 105, 180, 204, 210n98, 223n1
clientelism, 30n27, 48, 49, 85n78, 86n85, 113–15, 159n87

Clinton, William, 41–3, 45, 64, 82n33, 91n164
Cold War, 2, 13, 26n2, 29n13, 39, 67, 84n68, 102, 158n74, 191
Colombia, 2, 37–100, 215, 225–32
Colombia Ministry of Defense, 47, 52, 72, 84n61, 94n197, 96n220, 99n265, 99n266, 99n268, 99n275, 133, 236
Colombian National Police, 24, 37, 79
the Compact, 106, 107
comprehensive counterinsurgency (COIN), 2, 107–9, 141, 143, 144, 157n48
Counter-insurgency, 31n28

D
Damascus, Syria, 186, 188, 198, 200, 203, 204
Daraa, Syria, 180, 185, 186, 197, 201, 202
David, Steven, 26n2, 28n9, 30n24, 31n33, 32n34, 84n65, 158n69, 205n10
Democratic Security and Defense Policy (DSDP), 45, 99n275

E
Egypt, 180, 185–6, 188, 200, 210n88
ELN. *See* National Liberation Army (ELN)
Escobar, Pablo, 36n55, 41, 52, 59, 62, 69, 91n158, 95n203

F
FARC. *See* Revolutionary Armed Forces of Colombia (FARC)
Faryab, 124, 164n142

France, 3, 6, 13, 27n2, 32n39, 190
Free Syrian Army, 180, 186–7, 193, 196, 197, 210n92, 241

G
Gabon, 13
Gaddafi, Muammar, 180, 205n4
Gaviria, Cesar, 18, 40, 41, 61, 62, 64, 68, 69, 74, 89n130, 91n156, 91n159, 94n197, 94n200, 94n201, 95n205, 95n206
Ghazni, 134–6

H
Hama, Syria, 188, 197, 198, 201, 202
Haqqani network, 117, 161n105, 234
Harmoush, Hussein, 186, 187, 196
Helmand, 125, 128, 134, 135, 142, 149, 150, 166n171
Herat, 130, 145, 155n23, 166n191, 172n280
Hezb-i-Islami, 117, 135, 161n105, 175n315, 234
Homs, Syria, 188, 197, 201, 204

I
Idlib Province, Syria, 197, 202, 204
insurgency, 1–3, 8–15, 17, 20, 21, 31n28, 34n49, 34n50, 42, 44, 56, 59, 66, 74, 96n222, 105–7, 110, 118, 123, 127–9, 133, 141, 149, 150, 155n26, 156n35, 161n105, 180, 181, 184, 215, 220–2, 234, 237
Internal threat alliance, 1–177, 179–213, 215–19, 221, 222, 225–30, 233–9, 241–2
International Security Assistance Force (ISAF), 126, 128, 155n26, 156n32, 157n46, 157n48, 175n321
inter-state war, 1, 3, 215, 220
intra-state war, 2, 27n4, 223n1
Islamic Stat in Iraq and Syria/Levant (ISIS/ISIL), 186–8, 192, 202, 203

J
Jabhat al-Nusra, 187, 188
Jalalabad Province, Afghanistan, 124, 155n22
Joint Declaration of Strategic Partnership, 105, 139

K
Kabul province, Afghanistan, 128
Kandahar, 102, 125, 128, 134–6, 144, 145, 148, 150, 151, 155n23, 162n108, 166n171, 172n278, 173n301
Karzai, Hamid, 4, 12, 19, 21, 24, 101, 103–12, 114–18, 120–7, 130–2, 134–51, 153, 156n43, 158n59–61, 160n95, 163n124, 163n128, 163n132, 164n140, 171n274, 172n280, 173n296–8, 217, 219, 221, 234
Khan, Ismail, 130, 145, 148, 155n23, 172n280, 173n296, 173n297
Kunar province, 125, 150

L
Latin Security Operation (LASO), 38
La Violencia, 38, 51
Lavrov, Sergei, 189
Libya, 180, 186
Lobell, S. E., 9, 29n13, 30n22, 30n23

M

Macarena, 76
Makhlouf, Rami, 194, 199
Mazar-i-Sharif, 133, 155n22, 162n108
McCaffrey, Barry, 53
McNamara, Thomas, 63, 91n162
Medellin cartel, 57, 59, 61, 66–8
Medvedev, Dimitry, 181, 189
Meta, 83n54, 99n271
military alliances, 1, 2, 4–8, 15, 22, 28n10, 28n13, 131, 217, 220, 222
mujahedeen, 102, 161n105

N

Nangahar, 125
Nangahar province, Afghanistan, 128
narco-insurgents, 18, 41, 42, 44, 58
narco-traffickers, 2, 39, 41–3, 45, 50–5, 57–68, 70–5, 77, 146, 151, 215, 216
National Army of Colombia, 47, 85n71
National Consolidation Plan (NCP), 45, 84n61
National Liberation Army (ELN), 38, 51–4, 59, 67, 71, 76, 77, 95n203, 225–7
National Security Decision Directive 221 (NSDD), 55
NATO, 156n43, 157n46, 157n48, 159n76, 180, 191
Neoclassical Interntional Relations Theory, 3
neorealist International Relations theory, 9
9/11 Attacks, 44, 103, 117, 119

Norte del Valle, 52
Northern Alliance (NA), 103, 104, 114, 129, 160n95
NSDD 18, 57, 89n126
NSDD 71, 56

O

Obama, Barack H., 11, 13, 107, 109, 110, 116, 122, 123, 137, 141, 149, 151, 157n51, 158n59, 158n62, 161n103, 173n303
Omar, Mullah, 102, 148
Operation Enduring Freedom Afghanistan, 103

P

Pakistan, 32n43, 102–4, 118, 126, 129, 137, 148, 149, 153n7, 154n17, 158n62, 158n63, 161n103, 162n108, 163n135, 175n316
Paktia, 128, 134–6, 150, 168n220
Paktia Province, Afghanistan, 134, 168n220
Paktika, 125
Palmyra, Syria, 202, 203, 212n129
paramilitaries, 52, 212n121
Pastrana, Andrés, 12, 18, 24, 37, 42–4, 61, 64, 65, 72–9, 81n27, 81n31, 82n33, 84n60, 84n66, 97n235, 97n237, 218, 219
patron-client relationships, 5, 16, 58, 110, 124, 148, 192, 218
People's Democratic Party of Afghanistan (PDPA), 102
Plan Colombia, 19, 24, 37, 42–5, 73, 77, 79, 80n10, 84n61, 96n218, 99n263, 100n278, 219

Plan Colombia Consolidation Plan (PCCP), 45
Plan Patriota, 45, 78
Putin, Vladimir, 180, 181, 185, 189–92, 208n53, 208n65, 209n68, 212n123, 219
Putumayo, 83n54

R
Rangel, Charles, 40, 80n14
Reagan, Ronald, 39, 54–6, 61, 64, 66, 67, 80n17, 88n112, 93n183
rebellion, 1, 3, 8–15, 17, 20, 21, 31n28, 32n39, 33n44, 182, 215, 220–2
Revolutionary Armed Forces of Colombia (FARC), 4, 15, 38, 40, 41, 44, 45, 49, 51–4, 59–61, 66–72, 76, 77, 80n16, 87n105, 88n112, 89n132, 89n134, 94n193, 94n197, 95n203, 96n219, 99n269, 217, 225–7
Russia, 1–4, 6, 12, 13, 17, 24, 27n2, 32n42, 110, 179–81, 184–5, 188–91, 198, 199, 202–4, 205n9, 216, 217, 241

S
Samper, Ernesto, 41, 61–5, 70–2, 91n163, 96n216
Schweller, Randall, 7, 8, 28n13, 29n19
Seko, Sese Mobutu, 13
Shabbiha, 201
Soviet Union, 13, 24, 38, 39, 51, 54, 56, 57, 89n124, 93n183, 102, 179, 181–3
structured focused comparison, 25, 36n57

the surge, 75, 108
Syria, 1, 2, 4, 13, 16, 17, 22, 24, 31n30, 32n42, 36n53, 179–93, 195–200, 202–4, 205n9, 205n13, 206n14, 206n25, 207n42, 208n61, 210n88–90, 212n133, 216–19, 222, 241–3
Syrian Arab Republic, 182

T
Talabani, Jalal, 16
Taliban, 1, 2, 12, 13, 15, 16, 24, 101–7, 109, 114, 116–20, 122–32, 135, 142–4, 148–51, 153, 161n105, 168n215, 168n218, 168n221, 172n283, 173n301, 173n303, 175n315, 175n316, 175n321, 216–18, 233, 234
Tambs, Lewis, 53
Tartus, 4, 181, 188, 191, 209n67
Task Force 435, 126
Tunisia, 180, 186
Turbay, Cesar, 39, 54, 55, 64–6

U
United Nations Security Council (UNSC), 189
Uribe, Alvaro, 18, 24, 37, 43–5, 74–9, 83n52, 83n53, 91n163, 98n246, 98n251, 219
U.S. Presidential Directive 18, 45
U.S. Southern Command (SOUTHCOM), 45, 84n61, 94n201
U.S. Special Representative for Afghanistan and Pakistan, 126

W

Walt, Stephen, 7, 8, 29n16, 29n17, 29n19
warlords, 102–5, 117, 118, 129–32, 137, 142, 145, 148, 154n18, 155n22, 155n23, 160n99, 165n155, 172n280, 173n296, 173n297

Z

Zaire, 13

GPSR Compliance
The European Union's (EU) General Product Safety Regulation (GPSR) is a set of rules that requires consumer products to be safe and our obligations to ensure this.

If you have any concerns about our products, you can contact us on

ProductSafety@springernature.com

In case Publisher is established outside the EU, the EU authorized representative is:

Springer Nature Customer Service Center GmbH
Europaplatz 3
69115 Heidelberg, Germany

www.ingramcontent.com/pod-product-compliance
Lightning Source LLC
LaVergne TN
LVHW020342260326
834688LV00045B/1485